The Gravity of Love

Willow River Press is an imprint of Between the Lines Publishing. The Willow River Press name and logo are trademarks of Between the Lines Publishing.

Copyright © 2023 by Brian Duren

Cover design by Cherie Fox

Between the Lines Publishing
1769 Lexington Ave N., Ste 286
Roseville, MN 55113
btwnthelines.com

Published: August 2023

Original ISBN (Paperback) 978-1-958901-37-3

Original ISBN (eBook) 978-1-958901-38-0

Library of Congress Control Number: 2023940877

The Gravity of Love

Brian Duren

Also from Brian Duren

Whiteout

Black Ivory

Early praise for *The Gravity of Love*

"THE GRAVITY OF LOVE *is a magnificent haunting duet of grief, absence, and the unshakable bonds of family ... a profoundly moving, profoundly human novel...*" - **Junot Diaz, Pulitzer Prize winning author of** *The Brief Wondrous Life of Oscar Wao.*

The Gravity of Love is that rare book that tells a story for everyone. It's obsessed with family and memory, the equal dominion those two things share over our lives, and the grief we often find there. In lyrical, looping, loving prose, Brian Duren has worked toward Proust, that grand master of remembrance. This book is hypnotic and stylish and unforgettable. **–Peter Geye, author of THE SKI JUMPERS**

Some books are best read in the sun on a beach, some in silence in the dead of night, and some are best suited to a long train ride. I recommend reading Brian Duren's *The Gravity of Love* during a snowstorm. That's what I did, looking up from the book now and then to watch the fat clumps of snowflakes fall straight and inexorably down, then back into this richly imagined, meticulously researched, and elegantly written novel of family and love, of inevitability and transgression—then again at the snow, which will melt, but I'll be thinking about *The Gravity of Love* for a very long time. **–Pete Hautman, National Book Award-winning author of** *Godless.*

The Gravity of Love is a family saga that digs into what we will do for love and what happens without it. An intense, deep story with a lot of heart—and even more soul. A remarkable read. **– Mary Logue, author of THE STREEL and THE BIG SUGAR**

THE GRAVITY OF LOVE is an evocative tale of the familial bonds that can grow stronger even as they're torn apart. This mother and son's journey through the jagged landscape of resentment and loss is often tragic, yet ultimately liberating. An immersive read that will stay with me a long time. *–Brian Malloy, author of The Year of Ice and After Francesco.*

The Gravity of Love is a wonderfully open-hearted novel about passion, affection, grief, and regret. Brian Duren asks all the best and most unanswerable questions: what inspires romantic or familial love, and what causes it to die -- or persist? Why do love or resentment often outlast the people who bring them to life? This is a deeply felt, memorable book, rich with detail.— **Julie Schumacher, Thurber Prize-winning author of** *Dear Committee Members*

For Jane, Cathy, Neil, Michael, and Daniel

David

I stood in front of our bedroom window, buttoning my shirt, looking out at the slope of our backyard and the yellow-green lawn that ends where the tall grass of the woods begins. I was watching the mist rise in wisps among the trees and evaporate in the shafts of sunlight off to the side, feeling exhausted and listless after again waking up before dawn and staring at the ceiling in the dark. I'd returned a few days ago from a conference where I'd given a paper on a French writer—a paper that had to become an article someday—and I would give another one on another writer in the fall, at another conference, and on and on *ad infinitum*. I felt trapped, and the only way to escape that feeling was to get up, get dressed, and get to work, so I could stop thinking.

Barbara came between me and the window, turned her back toward me, and asked me to fasten the hook on her dress. "Look at those squirrels," she exclaimed. "They're putting on quite a show." Two squirrels were scrambling up and down one of the trees, looping left and right, switching from pursuit to counter-pursuit, all at whiplash speed. She leaned into me, and I pressed my face against her hair, breathed the faint fragrance of her body, grazed the back of her neck with my lips, and hummed. She turned around, grinned in response to my smile, kissed me and whispered, "Tonight."

We had breakfast and left. She pulled out of the driveway, turned onto the road in front of the farmhouse we were renting, and headed for the highway that would take her to Cedar Rapids and her job as an art director. I turned the

7

other way, heading for Iowa City and my job as a professor. After my second class, I'd have coffee as usual on Fridays with a few of my grad students, who would probably go on and on about Jesse Jackson taking the fight all the way to the convention, and then I'd stop off at Prairie Lights Books and browse the shelves and talk with the owner. And in the evening, Barbara and I would go see a student production of a play by Mamet. And in five weeks, the semester would end, we would move to Minneapolis, and Alan would come stay with us for part of the summer. The thought of him coming made me step on the gas, as if by driving faster I could move ahead in time. Approaching the top of a hill, I realized something I couldn't see might be on the other side. I hit the brake and slowed down just as I passed the crest and saw in front of me a tractor towing a manure spreader.

From my office desk, I looked up at the picture I'd taken of Alan the summer before—a close-up of his face, his big grin revealing his front teeth and two gaps where he'd lost his baby teeth. Not knowing how I could make it through nine months without him, except for a visit at Christmas, I'd had the picture blown up to poster size and hung it on the wall. Every day that I come to my office, I look at him, at his deep brown eyes—his mother's eyes—smiling back at me. Sometimes I feel again what I lost, what I destroyed, and have to look away.

I looked down at my notes on my survey course on the French novel. The students were undergraduates, likely to fall in love in the next few years, if they hadn't already, and they would have to live with the consequences. Maybe that was in the back of my mind when I'd made up a list of questions they had to answer for each character who fell in love. Questions like: What does one character see in the other? Does he or she actually see the other? Is there something that mediates the character's perception of the other? And more, so many more questions, for something that might seem obvious. As I opened Swann's Way to one of the passages describing Swann's obsession with Odette, the phone rang. "David?" A woman repeated my name, her voice tense. It was my sister, Patty.

"I called you at home several times, but you didn't answer."

"What is it? What's the matter?"

"Ken called last night. He's scared. Mom didn't come home from work.

He wanted to know if I'd talked to her. I told him she hadn't called. He said he would call Linda. When he didn't call me back, I called him. Linda didn't know anything, either. So, he contacted the police, and they came to the trailer and helped him file a missing person report." I could hear her crying as I gripped the phone. She took a deep breath. "He called again, around one this morning, to find out if I'd heard anything. I've been up most of the night. I called him and Linda this morning, but they don't know anything." She fell silent, her breath trembling, and added, "I'm scared."

"I am too. Why didn't you call me last night?"

"You're in Iowa. How could you've helped us? Besides, we've got enough people already who can't sleep. Oh, God! What if she's run away? What if she's been kidnapped?"

"What if, what if—don't do that to yourself." I took a deep breath, and another. "We've got to stay calm."

"What can I do?"

"I don't know." I tried to think. "Look, why don't you check again with Ken and Linda and anyone else Mom might've talked to and see if you can find out something. I've got a class to teach. When I'm done, I'll call. Okay?"

"I'm so scared."

"I'll call you."

We hung up. I looked at my watch—a couple minutes after nine. I took a few deep breaths and tried to focus on what I had to do. I went to class and lectured about Swann, the aesthete, falling in love with Odette, the courtesan, and his perception of her mediated by the image of a woman from one of Botticelli's paintings. I projected slides of *The Trials of Moses* in the Sistine Chapel, a fresco of scenes from the prophet's life, and close-ups of Zipporah, the woman who would become his wife, with her thick blond hair, big brown eyes, and lips parted as if she were catching her breath. And then I had the students look at Proust's text, in which Swann gazes at a reproduction of Zipporah and holds it close, imagining he's embracing Odette, his own living, breathing Botticelli. As the students focused on the text, the memory of the phone call surged. My mind became riveted to it, to the panic in Patty's voice, the fear that something might've happened to Mom, until the raised hand of a student distracted me. I called on him and tried to listen to his question.

9

"So, what you're saying is this guy, Swann, falls in love because of a painting, and . . ." He paused.

I nodded, wanting to encourage him to complete his question, but my mind drifted. The student disappeared, and I saw a photograph of Mom, her eyes dilated and circled with black rings, like she hadn't slept in days, or like some coke addict. She appeared to have been moving at the time the photo was taken, perhaps standing up from a sitting position and turning toward the person holding the camera. She looked terrified, as if she'd been ambushed, and emaciated, like a death-camp survivor—in a black sleeveless dress, with lipstick and brown curls.

The photo disappeared, and I found myself in the classroom, the student staring at me. What had happened? I looked at my notes. The words were an incomprehensible blur. I tried to concentrate. Where did I stop? I had to say something. As I focused on the notes, I remembered the student had started to ask a question. I looked up and said, "Do you have a question?"

He squinted at me in disbelief. The other students did too. They looked at one another and back at me, their mouths hanging open. He must've already asked the question. Blood throbbed through my head. I couldn't focus.

"Would you mind repeating your question?"

"Okay." He paused as he continued staring at me. "I just found it kind of weird—a rich guy falling in love with a prostitute, because of a painting. And I'm wondering, well, is that realistic? I mean, Proust is supposed to be a realist, right? And do other characters in Proust fall in love that way?"

"I think we need to, ah, go into this in some depth, and ah . . ." I glanced down at my watch and saw the class was due to end. "And we really don't have time to continue this discussion today, so, for Monday, I want you to read the pages indicated on your syllabus, and we'll start class with a discussion of mediated perception and Swann falling in love with Odette. Have a good weekend."

I grabbed my notes and book, headed for the door and down the hall, oblivious to everyone around me. I ducked into my office and collapsed at my desk. I picked up the receiver, noticed my hand trembling, and stared at it. I shook my head and dialed.

Patty answered after the first ring. "I haven't heard anything more from

Ken. And Linda's not answering. She's probably left for work."

"I'll drive up."

"What can we do?"

"Nothing. We can wait. I'll wait with you."

I called Barbara. She wanted to come, but we decided she should stay at work, and I'd get back to her as soon as I knew something.

Haunted by the picture of Mom, I flew down the highway, remembering a time long before Alan was born, when Chantal and I were graduate students at the University of Minnesota, and we'd gone to visit Mom and Ken in their trailer house in Roseville. Ken had set up his screen in the living room and his carousel slide projector on an end table. I knew we were in for another boring evening, sitting on the couch, staring at pictures of his brown pickup with a white camper, or of his aluminum fishing boat resting on a boat trailer, or of him holding up a string of walleye under his proud grin. Sometimes there'd be a shot of Mom, but it was like she was just filler. That evening, while we watched another slide show, the picture of Mom appeared. I stopped breathing. Chantal must've too, because she seized my hand so hard her nails dug into my skin. Mom's image seemed to remain on the screen for several minutes. No one said a word. A click, the image disappeared, and another took its place.

When Chantal and I were driving back from the suburb to our apartment in Minneapolis, she asked about the picture.

"I've never seen it before."

"Why does she look that way? What happened to her?"

"I don't know. I was gone. Drifting around Europe. Or working, trying to save up money to go back to the U. Or, maybe I was—I wasn't there. For two years, 1967 to '69, I was gone." I'd wandered off, like some picaresque character, gone when my mother was suffering and needed me.

Chantal rested her hand on my shoulder as I continued driving. She knew there was something I didn't want to talk about. She probably thought we would someday.

There was always something I couldn't, or just wouldn't talk about. A zone of silence, around which I detoured conversations, questions, introspection. And not always intentionally. Feelings I didn't understand, couldn't articulate, couldn't even think about. A cavern inside me, made entirely of something missing—an absence, an emptiness that left me feeling worthless and that hollowed out everything good in my life. Its presence was in the back of my mind, in the words I didn't say, in the emotions that didn't get verbalized, not even to the psychiatrist I saw after Dad's death. That missing thing transformed everything self-destructive into a temptation. So many times, as I drove drunk or stoned down Mississippi River Boulevard along the river's bluffs, and the headlights brought into view a curve ahead in the road, I'd feel tempted to go straight, and it would all be over. So easy. And I'd feel at peace as I headed for the curve, like a child lulled to sleep in his mother's arms.

Instead of driving over the edge, I found Chantal. Dad had been dead for over five years, Mom had married Ken, and I'd returned home from my wanderings in Europe, full of rage about the Vietnam War, chanting to myself, burn it down, burn it down, burn the whole fucking country down. After years of working shit jobs—like damp-proofing the foundations of buildings at construction sites with hot, stinking pitch—I started graduate school in French. The day I attended my first department meeting, I walked to Folwell Hall, looking up at its steep roof, tall chimneys, and gargoyles. I entered the building and followed faculty members and other TAs down the hall and into a classroom, where I sat down in the back row. As the chairman addressed us, I looked to my side and saw her seated in the row ahead of me, her sandy blond hair pulled back into a coil. She seemed to feel my eyes on her, and for a second her dark brown eyes met mine, and I saw warmth and compassion in them.

A few days later, I saw that warmth again when I went into the office that I shared with a dozen other TAs and dropped my things on my desk. She looked up from the textbook lying before her, and her gaze felt like the sun shining on the surface of a lake. I walked past the desks between hers and mine and introduced myself. She spoke with a strong accent, so I switched to French, but when she continued in English, I switched back. She took a drag of her cigarette, smiled, offered me one, and nodded toward the chair at the side of her desk.

I lit up and sat down. "What part of France are you from?"

12

"Paris. *En fait*, Sceaux, a suburb."

"Never heard of it."

"It's one of the inner suburbs. You know Paris?"

"Oh, yeah." I nodded and grinned. "I spent a year in Europe, most of that time in Paris, living in cheap hotels and staying with friends, hanging out at *Le Select* and *La Coupole*, hoping to run into Jean Genêt. I'd heard he hung out there."

"Genêt hung out at *La Coupole*?" She arched her brows.

"You didn't know?"

She shook her head and grinned.

"Oh, yeah. Everyone knew that. I also hung out in the cafés and bistros around *le Boul' Mich', Saint-Germain-des-Prés, et la rue Mouffetard.*"

I watched her eyes as they focused on me, interpreting her smile as amused appreciation of my attempt to impress her. I didn't tell her I was always hard up for money in Paris, would often move in with the women I was sleeping with, and begged once on the Boul' Mich' for money—*Avez-vous un franc?*

"So," she smirked, "were you hanging out on the *Boul' Mich'* in May of '68?"

"Nah, I missed the student revolution. Damn! Had to leave about two months before. How about you? You participate in it?"

"*Soyez réalistes, demandez l'impossible.*"

"Be realistic, demand the impossible."

"*Il est interdit d'interdire.*"

"It's forbidden to forbid."

"*Faites l'amour, pas la guerre.*"

"So, you were there."

She took one last drag, grinned at me, and arched her eyebrows. "*Eh, oui.*"

And that's what we did—made love, not war. It was all love. I picked her up at her apartment in that old house on University Avenue and took her to a meeting with a bunch of other TAs to talk about unionizing. Then I invited her over to my place for a glass of wine. I can't remember what we talked about, maybe nothing. Just remember us kissing on the couch, fondling and caressing and . . . and making love in bed, my eyes returning to the warmth in her gaze.

13

I already loved her.

I desired her more than any woman I'd ever met, and with every month that went by, I got a little more. My roommate ended up staying at his girlfriend's apartment for days, and then weeks, and as he disappeared, Chantal's presence increased, until he moved out at the end of the academic year, and she moved in. Three years later, we got married in that apartment— a dump of a row house a company had built in the early 1900s for its workers. The ceilings and floors sagged, and when it rained, water dripped down the electric wire to the naked light bulb in our bedroom. When Chantal's mother saw our home and learned we'd hired a justice of the peace to come to the house and marry us, she had someone drive her to a floral shop and bought enough roses and lilies to conceal the cracks in the walls and draw attention away from the shabby furniture in the living room, where the ceremony would be performed, and transform that space into something beautiful. Chantal wore a floor-length skirt of multiple colors, a pear-green blouse, dangling earrings, and a long bead necklace—but no bra, because this was our hippie wedding. I wore red jeans and a white cotton shirt with a Nehru collar. It had long sleeves with flowers embroidered in red, green, blue, and yellow on the collar and the wrists. As the old man read his script, pausing from time to time to clear his throat or lick his dry lips, I gazed at her loving eyes. When I put the ring on her finger, I was worried the four gold bands, which curved in such a way they'd fit together only when lined up perfectly, might come apart. While picking out the ring, we'd joked it could be a metaphor for our relationship, because everything would have to line up perfectly for it to work. And coming from such different worlds, it sometimes seemed unreal that everything had lined up. But it had, and with her parents, and Mom and Ken, and Patty and Linda, and their guys, and a few friends, we celebrated our marriage with champagne and pizza. Corks popped, glasses clinked, and laughter filled the apartment. Chantal and I posed, my arm around her back, one of her hands on my shoulder and the other on my chest, as she leaned into me for our wedding picture. The picture I still look at, I still see.

Then, the following year, I got the scholarship from the French Ministry of Education. We moved to France, where I began my doctorate in French literature at the University of Paris. Living in our apartment in Paris was such a gas. We could wander around visiting the museums, go to theaters, and show one another our old haunts. We renewed friendships and went to dinner parties, like the one at the home of the couple with whom I'd become friends years before. The party started off with toasts of whiskey, followed by wine with dinner, cigarettes throughout, and cognac following dessert. A couple of the ladies lit up cigars to go with their drinks, something I'd never seen before. We celebrated the resignation of Nixon, lamented the victory of Giscard d'Estaing and the Right, and wondered when the fucking Left would get its act together. And we talked about the books we were reading and the new films we'd seen, like *Nashville*, *India Song*, and *Dersu Uzala*. Throughout our conversations we joked and laughed, and the whole evening had a raucous feeling, punctuated by moments of silence, when Chantal would tighten her grip on my thigh, and I'd lay my hand on hers. And at midnight, we dashed to catch the last metro.

We joined her parents for dinner at their home in Sceaux and for weekend visits at their summer house outside Paris, near a little medieval town on the Seine. There we'd wake up in the morning to birds singing, open the French doors onto the backyard and the patio, and sit at a table in the sun drinking coffee and eating *tartines au beurre*—and perhaps a peach we could pluck from the tree a few feet away. Her mother would smile and warm up our coffee and ask us if we'd slept well and what we would like to do that day, and her father would ask me about the dissertation I was going to write on Proust and the course I'd take on Céline, while drawing on his pipe with a reflective gaze, nodding, smiling his approval.

And then, the following spring, Chantal's parents gave us that trip to Venice as an early anniversary present. We got to know the canals and the basilica, and the Piazza San Marco, from which we set out to explore the city, over a thousand years old. We went walking down a narrow street that got narrower and curved and turned and—just as we felt lost and started to panic—opened onto a sunlit plaza, where people sat at tables in front of a café, women hung clothes to dry on lines strung across balconies, and kids were kicking a soccer ball around. We left the plaza and continued into the labyrinth, hoping it would lead us back to the Piazza.

Oh, I loved exploring the labyrinthian spaces of old European cities and felt reluctant about moving back home to Minneapolis. But we did, and a year later, Chantal got pregnant. It felt like a miracle, because we'd tried for months in Paris, with no luck. We figured she might've conceived the day I finished the dissertation. We got a good laugh out of that. Who would've guessed the tension surrounding the writing of a dissertation could serve as a method of birth control? The level of tension might've had something to do with the fact I'd gotten permission from the University of Minnesota to use my French *thèse* to complete my American Ph.D., so I would get two doctorates with one dissertation *if* I could satisfy faculty from both universities. I did, and went on the market, applying only to universities on the Atlantic and Pacific coasts, so we could get out of the Midwest. An offer on the East Coast fell through, so I accepted the job at the University of Texas and used what leverage I had to negotiate a position for Chantal as an instructor. I drove our furniture and books down the interstate to Austin and moved our things into our new place—a townhouse, surrounded by live oaks. And then Chantal and Alan, a couple months old at the time, flew down.

We arranged for Alan to stay in that daycare just off campus, so we could visit him between classes, see him napping or hold him, and sometimes Chantal would sit off to the side in a rocking chair and nurse him. Later, as the months passed, we would run over, and he would greet us with a grin that lit up his face as he cried *Mama, Papa,* and he would toddle toward us, or pretend not to see us, because he was busy watching another toddler play.

I could see the pictures we took of him at the daycare; and at Barton Springs Pool the following spring, when he's walking into the shallow end on the flat limestone, excitedly splashing another toddler a few feet away; and at Mustang Island, in the Gulf, where we buried him in sand to his waist as he stood still, and he walks out like Colossus, laughing as the mountain of sand collapses at his feet; and one of the Blue Bonnet trails, where we picnicked in a field of the blue flowers that reach his chest; and at Big Bend Park, where he rides on my back in a carrier as we hike through the hills, scaring off herds of musk hogs; and along the Rio Grande to the edge of the dark narrow canyons.

These memories would fill the cavern inside me, and the emptiness that left me feeling worthless and that hollowed out my life would disappear, but never completely. There were always moments, and during those moments, memories of my life before Chantal might return, like those of the woman I'd lived with for a year. She and I made beer and wine in ceramic tubs, lived in the pungent smell of fermentation that permeated our duplex, and drank ourselves into oblivion every night. We would make love, and I would realize her body had gone limp, pull back, and see her closed eyes and mouth agape, and feel I was making love to a corpse and recoil in disgust. And fear, because I could see where we were headed. Drunk, we said anything, did anything, and tempers flared and glasses flew. Once I triggered so much rage in her that she came up from behind and bashed me over the head with a wine bottle and knocked me to the floor. The last night I walked out of her apartment, she clawed my face and tried to rip off my clothes, and I got out the door with blood streaming down my cheek and neck, a buttonless shirt, and a jacket with a pocket ripped and hanging like a rag. A few months later, I was heading toward Chantal's warm, loving gaze. It was like swimming up from the cold, dark bottom of a lake toward the light shimmering on the surface.

The cavern was like a black hole, and I might succeed in distancing myself, but sooner or later its gravitational force would pull me through a labyrinth to the empty space, the missing thing, and suck me in. That hole felt at times like it was home, or something about home. After just two years in Austin, the University of Tulsa offered me what I thought was a better position, so I took it, and Chantal and Alan and I moved north, 450 miles closer to home. I found it more difficult to focus on the articles and the book I needed to write to get tenure and have a job until I retire, because of what was going on inside me. The next summer, I got the grant to go to New York and work on a book on French cinema, but on the flight to the city, I thought instead of writing a novel about a filmmaker whose lead actress and muse leaves him. As he watches the first fully mounted version of the first film he's made since she left him—a film about a filmmaker's troubled life as a child and a young man—his mind wanders from the scenes in this movie to those in the movies he made with Anna Céline, his muse, and every scene makes him feel again what he has lost. I got up the next morning in the apartment I had sublet on the upper West Side and set my typewriter on the desk in the front room. I opened the windows that looked out onto the street five floors down and on kids shouting and boomboxes blasting the Talking Heads and felt my energy pulsing and started typing. By the end of the summer, I'd written over two hundred pages of elegiac prose about the filmmaker's loss of his father, who died young, and of Anna, and how both continue living inside him. He feels their presence, hears them speaking to him, and he speaks to them, and wonders, Who was my father? Why was he absent in my life? Why did my muse cease to love me? Why was I unworthy of their love? The filmmaker never finds the answers, but what enables him to go on living is his love for his son.

It was hard to let go of that novel when I returned home, and hard to hang onto it, because I had to succeed in academe to support my family. Chantal and Alan greeted me with hugs and kisses, and Alan, from whom I'd never been separated for more than a week, wanted my attention all the time. But the next day, he refused to talk to me, to look at me, and pouted and pulled away every time I tried to touch his arm or shoulder, until that evening, when I pretended to be on the verge of tears, and he told me he was angry I hadn't taken him to New York, and next time I went there, I had to take him. I played with him, read to him, tried to make up for my absence, for missing his fourth birthday, all the while preparing my classes, thinking about the paper I should be writing for the next conference I would attend, and trying not to think about the book I was supposed to have started writing. And then came that night, after Chantal had put Alan to bed. I was pacing back and forth in the living room, clenching my fists, pausing from time to time to look out the picture window of our rented house at the houses across the street, not really seeing anything. Chantal came up from behind, rested her hand on my shoulder and her head against my back, and whispered, "What's the matter?"

I moved away from her toward the window, placed my forearm on the pane, and leaned on it. "I can't continue doing this."

"Doing what?"

I turned and saw her brows furrowed. "I can't continue developing new courses, preparing classes, attending conferences, writing papers and articles and a book for tenure, and write this novel. I just want to write the novel. I don't want to write any more academic crap. I can't."

"You won't get tenure."

"I know."

"What's your plan B?"

18

I stared at her eyes fixed on me and shook my head. I didn't have one.

And since I didn't and didn't know how we could live while I tried to realize plan A, I continued doing the things I'd told Chantal I could no longer do—except for writing the book that would get me tenure. I felt trapped, angry, depressed, and tried to liberate myself with whiskey. I'd get drunk, feel I'd escaped, and when the high wore off, I would plummet and realize I was still trapped, and get more depressed. Missing the high that came with the whiskey, I'd drink again. I began to feel Chantal was somehow part of the trap, and a few months later I started sleeping with Barbara.

I walked into the house one morning, and Chantal came running out of the kitchen and stopped, panic in her eyes.

"Where have you been?"

"Out."

"What's going on?"

"I spent the night with a woman."

Chantal stared at me, shook her head, and rushed past me to Alan's room to get him up and ready for daycare. That night, she begged me to see a marriage counselor. I refused. I really believed the only problem in my life was her.

I married Barbara, continued drinking, drinking even more, and nothing got better. One day I stopped by Chantal's house to drop off some things for Alan. She opened the door, invited me in, and Alan heard my voice and came running into the living room, shouting, "Daddy, Daddy." He grabbed my hand and pulled me inside, and his big brown eyes, his mother's eyes, looked up and seized my heart, and he pleaded, "Come on, Daddy, Daddy, come on, I wanna show you . . ." I realized the mistake I'd made. Chantal had never been responsible for my misery. She loved me, she was close to me, and because she was close, she was a convenient target, easy to blame. She and Alan and I . . . we'll pay for years for what I did. For the mistakes I made.

Mistakes. A year later, I realized my decision to take the position at Tulsa was also a mistake. The department I was in had been completely rebuilt with new assistant professors, and in my second year, we got a new chairman, and half-way through my third, he informed us of his new requirements for tenure—two books, a handful of articles every year, and a national and an international reputation. We knew none of us could achieve that in the two to four years we had left before we came up for review in the first semester of our sixth year. I went to the provost's office, reminded him of what he'd said when he recruited us—one book, a handful of articles, and good teaching evaluations. His face flushed red, and he bellowed he'd given the chairman *carte blanche, carte blanche,* to do whatever he thought was necessary to . . . When his bluster blew off, I asked him if I could use a novel for one of the two books, and he said, "That's not why we hired you." My colleagues and I lined up new positions at other colleges and universities and started submitting our resignations the following year. I took a one-year position at the University of Iowa, and my friend, Serge, went to Dartmouth.

And Barbara and I moved another six hundred miles north and closer to home. I had to leave Alan in Tulsa with Chantal, but he would come and visit me during the vacations. And then, just a couple months ago, I saw an opening at the University of Minnesota, applied for it, and got it. We'll be moving again in the summer, and Alan will get to know Mom, the woman who loved and protected me when I was a child, and she'll get to know him. And Serge put together a conference for this fall at Dartmouth that will draw some of the biggest names from Paris. He arranged for me to be one of the speakers—an opportunity that'll help me relaunch my career, so I'll have an income and can provide a home for Alan. I can't lose him. I won't. I'll find some little college in Minnesota where I can get tenure with a few articles and continue writing fiction, writing what's inside me, and we'll all be secure and happy.

I smiled as I drove down the highway, thinking of the happiness that lay ahead for Alan, Barbara, and me. Everything would be okay. I would arrive at Patty's house in St. Paul and learn Mom was fine, she'd spent the night at a friend's house, or something, something totally logical that would explain why she hadn't come home last night. And Patty and I would roll our eyes and sigh and laugh at how upset we'd gotten. I felt so good, I turned on the CD player and heard Talking Heads performing "Heaven," that song about a place where nothing ever happens, and started singing with David Byrne. I sang one song after another with him as I passed fields emptied by the harvest of the previous fall, some of them recently plowed, others with broken corn stalks reaching up from the black dirt like shattered limbs. Farmers would start planting any day, and in a few weeks the land would fill with new growth. I remembered the previous summer driving on the narrow country highways outside Iowa City, when the wheat and corn were tall, and blackbirds would flit from one stalk to another, and the singing and chirping of birds would carry across the silent fields, and the warm summer air would drift in through the open window. Sometimes, feeling the flow of the hills and fields, I'd let myself go and continue driving without a destination, just to feel that flow, hear the singing and chirping and breathe the warm air. And I'd find myself a child again in my grandfather's truck, riding with him from the farm to town or back, going no more than thirty miles an hour down that narrow highway in Wisconsin, so we could ride with the windows open and look out at his neighbors' fields of corn and wheat.

The CD came to an end. I spotted a Super America up ahead, glanced down at my gas gauge, and saw it was close to empty. I took the exit, pulled to a stop in front of one of the pumps, filled up the tank, and headed for the restroom, noticing a pay phone on the wall near the door. While pissing, I imagined arriving at Patty's house in St. Paul, and her answering the door, shaking her head, sighing, and saying, Oh, if only I could've contacted you, I would've told you Mom has returned home and everything's fine.

I phoned when I left the restroom.

"She hasn't called." Patty's voice sounded hollow, and her words were echoes from a deep chasm.

By the time I arrived in St. Paul, rush hour had begun, and the interstate was packed like a parking lot. I crept along a few miles, took an exit near the center of the city onto a thoroughfare lined with bars, liquor stores, and pawn shops, turned at one intersection and another, and drove down Patty's street, past dilapidated houses to the last one on the dead-end, pulled to a stop, and got out. On the other side of the wire mesh fence that creates a border with Patty's yard, the four-lane highway hummed with traffic. I walked toward her home, amazed as always at how narrow it is, twelve or thirteen feet wide, typical I guess for a lot of nineteenth century houses, and with its sinking shingled roof and dull gray walls it looked its age. I stepped onto the porch, felt the weathered planks sag beneath my weight, and pressed the doorbell. Sparrows landed on the wire mesh, looked around, and fluttered off in all directions, frightened perhaps by the constant racket of the droning tires. I pressed the doorbell again, remembered it didn't work, and knocked. I was about to knock again, when Patty's face appeared in the oval window, her eyes staring at me, her mouth agape.

She opened, I stepped inside, and she collapsed in my arms. "I'm so happy you're here," she cried. She pulled back, looked up at me, and tried to smile, but couldn't. Her red eyes and ashen skin evoked her sleepless night. "Come on in."

I followed her on the path worn into the brown shag carpet that flowed down the steps from the second floor to the main floor and into the living room, where faded pink wallpaper, with blood red and pale blue blossoms, covered the walls. A long time had passed since I'd been in the house, long enough for me to be struck again by the stale, musty smell that permeated the air, as if the body of each person who'd lived there had left a trace of its odor. With each breath I inhaled time and saw its presence in the furniture that dated from my boyhood—the armchair, upholstered with an orange and brown knit fabric; the grayish-blond wood end table; the matching round coffee table, its luster dulled; and surrounding it, the three-piece couch, with a curved middle piece in the corner of the room.

We entered a pool of sunshine, in which dust motes floated and shimmered above the dining room table, the light entering the room from the two large windows in the alcove facing south and the two smaller ones facing east and west. A narrow table that matched the color and design of the tables in the living room filled the alcove, and on its surface, on either side of a glass planter and plants with heart-shaped leaves, stood school pictures of Patty's kids, Julie and Scott, and a wedding picture of Mom and Dad. Across from the alcove, a door to a small room stood open, revealing a rocking chair and the corner of a single bed.

The light from the dining room nearly disappeared when we entered the kitchen. There were no windows on the back wall, only one on the wall facing the highway and the chain-link fence, a small one on the opposite wall, above the sink, between a set of cabinets, and another in the door that opened onto a mudroom I'd passed through a few times over the years on my way out the side of the house to the driveway.

"Why don't you sit down," Patty said. "I'll make us some coffee."

"Okay."

She went over to the counter next to the sink to prepare it, while I walked to the other end of the gray Formica-top table, with a silver metal frame and legs, and matching chairs with gray backrests, the same table and chairs that had been in the kitchen when I was a boy, and I'd sit to one side of Dad, who was at the head of the table, and Mom would sit across from me. I looked back at the head—almost expecting to see him, even though he'd been dead for over twenty years—and sat down at the place that had become mine, at the opposite end from him, after Linda was born and sat in the highchair that had been Patty's, and Patty had moved from the high chair to my previous place next to Dad. I sat at that end until he told me to pack my things, leave, and never come back.

I became aware of the breakfast things left on the table—cereal boxes, bowls, a carton of milk, and a plate with smears of butter and jam—and looked up at the ceiling and around at the walls. Even though the kitchen might've been the biggest room in the house, I felt cramped. The stove and brick chimney on one side of me, the refrigerator on the other, the sink in front, and the counters and cupboards filling in the gaps—everything hedged me in. The ceiling sagged, as if the weight of all the generations that had lived on the second floor had accumulated and might come crashing down on me. Aside from the muffled drone of the traffic behind me and the sound of the water running in the sink, the room was quiet, and in that quiet I felt time—time that had silenced the voices of generations, caused the ceiling to sag, leached the brightness out of the yellow paint of the walls and the white paint of the cupboards, and left the linoleum that covered the floor a scuffed, dull gray.

I leaned back in my chair, took a deep breath, and looked up again. A tin plate attached to the chimney, about seven feet up, covering the hole to which a stovepipe had probably been connected, caught my eye. I imagined the old iron stove and the early inhabitants of the house, probably a multigenerational family, with kids of every size, like rungs on a ladder, and women canning fruits and vegetables and preparing large meals, banging pots and pans on the stove and slamming the oven door shut, a cacophonous mélange of voices talking about different things at different pitches all at once, and everyone sitting at a long table that filled the room, heads bowing in silence when the patriarch said grace, and then the voices exploding again. As the image of the family and the sound of the voices faded, I thought of Patty, sitting at the table with her two children, her head bowed, not by reverence for God, but by the weight of the mortgage and the utilities and all the other expenses she bore alone.

She sat down at my side, exhaled a long sigh that ended with the words, "Oh, God," and shook her head.

The ringing of a phone startled her. She rushed toward the sink, took the receiver off the wall phone on the side of a cabinet, and listened, shaking her head. "Ken, I promise, if she comes here, or calls, or if I hear anything, I'll call you right away." She nodded and said, "Okay. Goodbye."

"That's the third time he's called this afternoon." She sat down. "The police have posted a missing-person alert and they're looking for her, but . . ." She shook her head, bit her lip, and furrowed her brow. The coffee started percolating. She blurted, her voice tense, "He repeats the same things over and over—'Where could she be? What could've happened to her?'" She extended her hands, as if begging for help. "I don't know. I'm wondering the same thing. I . . ." She took a deep breath and shook her head. The percolating accelerated to a frantic pitch. "He's called me more over the last twenty-four hours than in the last ten years. I almost feel sorry for him." She bit down on something inside and leaned back. The percolating climaxed and collapsed, and the muffled drone of the passing cars filled the silence.

I placed my hand on hers, wishing I could tell her everything would be all right, everything, and gazed at her worried face as she stared down at the table. After a while I said, "Barbara told me to say hello." Patty looked at me, as if I'd wakened her. "She wishes she could've come, but she was at work, and we decided the best thing was for her to just finish the day and go home, and I'll call her as soon as I know something."

Patty nodded. "I haven't told Julie or Scott. I don't want them to worry. They were surprised this morning when they got up and found me dressed like this." She looked down at her bulky gray sweatshirt. "I told them I didn't feel well and wasn't going to work." She tried to smile again. "It would've been good to see Barbara." She sighed, "Oh, well," and glanced at the counter where the coffee maker stood. "Did I forget to make the coffee?"

"I think it's ready."

"It percolated?"

I nodded.

She shook her head and seemed to notice the breakfast things. "I didn't even think to put this stuff away." She got up and went back and forth between the table and the refrigerator, sink, and cupboards, clearing everything, except for the milk, and then filled two mugs with coffee, set one in front of me, and sat down at my side.

"Have you heard from Linda?" I asked.

"Not since I talked to her this morning. She hardly said a word. I think she's holding a lot in." Patty poured milk in her coffee and stared at the mug as she stirred. "I wish I could stop thinking. When I couldn't sleep last night, I tried reading, but I kept worrying about her. And when I tried to focus on what I was reading, so I could stop worrying," she shook her head, "I saw the book was about a woman who gets murdered. And then I lost it, just lost it, and couldn't stop crying." Tears welled in her eyes. "What if someone's done something to her?"

She set her elbows on the table, her face collapsed in her hands, and her blond hair fell across her fingers. Even though she was thirty-seven, she seemed so young, vulnerable, and I wished I could protect her, but I couldn't. Just as I couldn't twenty years before. She raised her head, wiped away her tears, and took a deep breath. "I'm not going to be good company." She forced a smile, her eyes shining through the mist. "You can leave if you want. Just check in with me from time to time."

"I'd rather wait with you."

"Thanks."

I nodded and took her hand in mine, to assure her I meant it. I let go, took a sip of coffee, and looked around, tapping the tabletop until I felt her eyes on me. "Every time I sit at this table, I feel like I'm back in the old house."

"That's probably why Ken and Mom gave it to me. I'm sure he wanted to get rid of it. Anything that might remind Mom of Dad."

A screeching cry tore through the house, the wailing of an infant upstairs. "Oh, poor Ashley. She's teething and can't sleep."

Ashley. The name puzzled me, and then I remembered the Christmas card Patty had sent, with a picture inside of Julie, about eighteen years old, holding Ashley, her baby, asleep with her mouth open, looking as if she'd just finished nursing. And I remembered Chantal holding Alan, his eyes under puffy lids looking up at her, and her feeling my gaze and looking up at me, her eyes radiant.

Ashley screeched again, Patty gasped, and I started. Another screech morphed into long wails followed by hiccup cries. Patty and I gazed upward as footsteps paced back and forth above our heads.

"You almost have to envy babies," Patty said. "They can express the pain they feel so simply."

A voice upstairs chanted in a singsong way.

"Oh, thank God!" Patty exclaimed. "Julie probably got her to nurse. She might even fall asleep." The chanting voice faded. "Poor Julie, she's hardly slept the last few days. But at least she knows she has a home. No one's going to try to push her out. And she never has to worry about a man taking over our family. No man's ever moving into this house." Patty shook her head. "Julie made the same mistake I did. But at least she didn't marry the jerk." Patty smiled, and for the first time her smile remained. "My little girls are safe here. This morning, Julie put Ashley in the stroller and took her for a walk, hoping she would fall asleep, and I stood on the front porch and watched. The sun was shining, birds were singing." She shook her head. "If only this hadn't happened." She grimaced, placed her hand on mine, and her voice trembled. "I'm so glad you're here."

"I am, too."

Tires crunched in the driveway along the side of the house, a car door slammed, and then the screen door, and someone walked through the mudroom and turned the door handle and stopped. Linda peered in through one of the three windowpanes. Patty opened the door, and Linda, in a black pantsuit and white blouse, her light brown hair cut in a pixie, stepped inside.

"Any word?"

"No."

Linda shook her head and sighed, "Oh God." She eyed me as I moved forward to greet her and said, "Don't you look cool in that black corduroy jacket. Goes really well with your blue shirt and jeans." We hugged, and when we pulled back and looked at one another, she asked, "Is that what you wear when you teach?"

"It's what I wore today."

"You're so different from the attorneys at work. They wear suits and ties and all look alike."

Patty asked Linda if she would like some coffee and got her a mug, while Linda sat down across from Patty's place at the table, and I returned to mine, opposite our dead father. Patty set a mug in front of Linda and sat down on my other side. Linda glanced down at her steaming coffee and up at me.

"So, how's your better half?" she asked.

I chuckled. She'd always referred to Chantal as my better half, and now she was doing the same with Barbara. "She's doing fine. How's your better half?"

"I am my better half."

"You've been giving me that response for years."

"Why would it change?"

"Our mother's gone missing." Patty glared at Linda.

Linda leaned back. "That's why I'm here. Did you talk again with her mistake?"

"Ken," Patty said.

"Did you talk with him?" Linda asked.

"He called a little while ago," Patty responded. "Nothing's changed, and he's going nuts."

"Going nuts." Linda sighed. "I remember going nuts . . . the last time she disappeared. Maybe she's found another man. It wouldn't take much to find someone better than Ken. You could pull a guy out of pretty much any gutter, and he would be a step up."

"At seventy-one, she's a little old to be looking for a new man. You know, you don't have to stay. I can call you as soon as I have news. I'm sure you'd rather—"

27

"I've already told Tom and Chris I won't be home for dinner. I need to know what's happened. And if it's anything like the last time . . ." Linda shook her head.

We waited, staring at the table or one of the walls, time moving so slowly I could feel it, like a corpse I was dragging behind me. I thought of checking in at a hotel but decided not to. This time, I would be with my sisters. If anything had happened to Mom, we would deal with it together.

Ashley's screech startled me, I flinched and gritted my teeth, and Linda started and exclaimed, "Oh, my God!" Wails came in waves, each one reaching a piercing crescendo, hollowing out, and collapsing as the baby exhausted her breath. Seconds later a new swell followed. And another. I remembered Alan teething and me trying to calm him, holding him, his body twisting in my arms while I walked back and forth, struggling to contain him as he launched himself in every direction, and giving him to Chantal who nursed him, his hand touching her breast as he suckled, his eyes fixed on her face as if it had hypnotized him, and his eyelids fluttering shut as he satiated his hunger.

"Poor Julie," Patty said, gazing upward, as if she could see her walking with the baby in her arms. "She hasn't been able to get a full night's sleep in days."

"It hurts getting those teeth," Linda said, "but she'll need them."

The waves of Ashley's wails waned to a few weak cries and died, while Julie, the ceiling creaking beneath her feet, sung a lullaby in a soft voice. Knowing the next tsunami of wails might rise and come crashing down on us at any minute, I decided it would help to have a sedative. Patty never kept alcohol in the house, not since she'd split from her ex, who'd had enough addictions to destroy the lives of everyone around him, but she did like to have an occasional glass of wine, so I offered to go to the liquor store.

Linda smirked. "Don't forget to come back."

I stood, heard a whispered "shh" coming from the dining room, and Julie entered the kitchen carrying Ashley. She stopped when she saw Linda and me and said, "Uncle David, Aunt Linda. I thought I heard someone talking down here."

Linda said, "Oh, let me see the little one."

Julie handed her Ashley, in her pink footie pajamas, and the baby, her mouth agape, gazed up with a puzzled look at Linda smiling down at her.

Patty headed for the mudroom.

Julie, with loose strands of brown hair straying from her ponytail, looked at me and said, "It's good to see you. Did Chantal and Alan come, too?"

"Barbara," Linda whispered.

"Oh, my God. I'm sorry. I meant Barbara."

I smiled. "It's okay. And, no, Barbara didn't come. I'm just here for a . . . a meeting with some faculty from the University of Minnesota. I thought I would stop by and see how everyone's doing."

Ashley began whining, and Julie took her back. "Well, say hello to Barbara for me." Patty wheeled the stroller in from the mudroom and followed Julie toward the front porch. They put Ashley in the stroller, and Linda and I joined Patty and watched Julie push the stroller up the sidewalk, along the edge of the shadows cast by the houses.

Patty and Linda went back inside. I got in the car and passed Julie and Ashley as I drove down the street on my way to the liquor store, where I picked up a couple of cabernets. I returned to the house and found my sisters sitting on the couch in the living room. Patty said, "I'll get the glasses," and headed for the kitchen. I followed her, set the bottles on the table, uncorked one, and we returned to the living room. I poured and set the bottle on the coffee table, within reach of my sisters. They leaned back, sipped, and stared off, absorbed by whatever was going on inside them.

I settled into the armchair, took a drink, and another. The drone of the traffic on the highway parallel to the fence was muted, and the near silence helped me to relax, until the thought of Mom missing pricked me, and I panicked. She'd disappeared, the woman who loved and protected me when I was a child. I looked out the window to my side, as if she might be there, and then at my watch. A little after seven. More than twenty-four hours had passed since she'd gone missing. What if she'd returned? I looked at Patty and asked, "Do you think Ken would let us know if she came home?"

"I hope so." She checked her watch. "I'll call him in a little while."

I leaned back and closed my eyes. Even in the dark I could feel the proximity of my sisters, of the couch on which they were sitting, of the table on which they were resting their feet. All this furniture, including the chair on which I was sitting and the table next to it, were in the living room of the house in which we'd grown up, a much larger room than this. When I was in high school, unable to sleep at night, I'd get up, go sit in this chair, next to the picture window, and read novels by the writers we were talking about in class, like Fitzgerald or Hemingway. And sometimes I would find Mom, in her blue silky house robe, already reading in the chair, so I would sit in the matching armchair, a few feet away, next to the door that opened onto a bedroom that served as Dad's office. Mom and I would usually read in silence, but it felt like something we were doing together, something that created a bond. Occasionally we would talk about our books—what they were about, whether or not we liked them, and why. Mom read a little of everything—mysteries, romances, books talked about in the media, like *Atlas Shrugged* and *Doctor Zhivago*, and books I was reading for school. If we did talk, our conversations would often stray to other topics, like the hours I was working at the supermarket, the car I was saving up to buy, or the English teacher who'd talked to me about going to college—an idea that had startled Mom.

"This brings back such horrible memories," Patty murmured.

I opened my eyes and saw her shaking her head. The big old living room had disappeared, and Patty's tight space, with the couch and the coffee table, felt even tighter. Linda finished her wine, refilled her glass, took a drink, and stared at the *St. Paul Pioneer Press* and the paperback book on the coffee table. She studied the front cover, turned it over, read the back, and asked Patty, "Are you reading this?"

"You can have it."

"Sounds grisly."

"What is it?" I asked.

Linda read aloud the synopsis about the tortured body of a beautiful woman found in a vacant lot in Los Angeles, a woman whom the press dubbed the Black Dahlia, and the two detectives obsessed with knowing everything about her, finding her killer, and possessing the woman in death. "How can someone possess a dead woman by knowing things about her? She would still be gone." Linda turned the book over, looked at the front cover and then at Patty. "Are you worried Mom might've been murdered?"

30

Patty took a deep breath, shook her head, and groaned.

"Let me see the book," I said.

Linda passed it to me. The cover bore the illustration of a woman with thick black hair and eyebrows, pale skin, red lips, and blue eyes. Light seemed to emanate from behind her head, creating an almost purple halo in the black background. Her face didn't resemble Mom's. I leaned forward and tossed the book on the table.

"The Black Dahlia's a tramp," Patty said. "Mom was never that."

"She was behaving like a tramp the last time she disappeared," Linda said.

"She was broken," Patty said. "And grieving. She's not broken now. Not unless something has happened to her."

"I can understand wanting to run away from something you can't deal with," Linda said. "But how do you leave your kids behind? How do you just walk out on them?"

"Let's not go there," Patty said.

Linda looked me in the eye and shook her head. "We came home from school one day, and she was gone. I was just thirteen. Patty, fifteen. We didn't know what to do." She paused, and her eyes drifted off, as if she were seeing that day. "We turned on the TV and watched *American Bandstand* and *The Road Runner*. We thought she'd be back soon. Maybe she'd just gone to the store. We looked in the garage. The car was gone. We got hungry, so we made ourselves peanut butter and jelly sandwiches and kept on watching TV. We fell asleep to *The Fugitive* and woke up to the audience laughing on *Johnny Carson*. All that noise, the laughter, the glow of the television in the dark and the silence made us feel so alone." She looked at me. "We wanted to call you, but we didn't know your number, and Information didn't have it. We checked the doors to make sure they were locked, went to bed, tried to sleep. We stayed home from school the next day and watched *Mr. Rogers* and more kids' shows, soap operas and all kinds of shit. We were so scared. Patty called some friends, just so we wouldn't be alone. They came over that night, and some of them invited other friends, and pretty soon we had a party, and the party took over the house. We played records—the Beatles, the Stones, Janis Joplin. Some older kids showed up with beer and whiskey, and the party got really wild."

"And then the doorbell rang," Patty said. "I went to the door, looked out

31

the window, and saw our next-door neighbor, the one with the black lab. I ducked before he saw me, turned the record player off, and told everyone to get out of the living room. The neighbor started knocking. I opened the door, and he looked down at me, and then toward the living room full of smoke, and asked if my mother was home. I said she was gone, but she'd be back. He asked when. I panicked, and then I said her sister was sick, she'd gone to take care of her, she'd be back in the morning."

"And then, a day later," Linda said, "Ellen showed up."

"Who?" I asked.

"Mom's friend, the divorcee, who lives down the street," Linda said.

I recalled the woman, a little older than Mom, with a couple kids older than me.

Linda continued, "Ellen said the neighbors had been watching the house and had started talking about the two girls living here alone, and maybe they should contact the state or the county and have the girls taken into custody. She left a note for Mom and took us to her house, and we stayed with her until Mom showed up a few days later. And when Ellen brought us home, he was there." Linda's nose wrinkled in a look of disgust, and she shook her head. "They'd gotten married." After a brief silence, she looked at me. "You disappeared. For two years, no one heard anything from you, except that one time, when Mom got a postcard and learned you were in Paris. She was so happy—so relieved you weren't dead." Linda shook her head.

I remembered what I was going through, and the postcard—a reproduction of an impressionist painting of a bridge over the Seine and people in late nineteenth-century gowns and coats strolling, and Notre Dame in the background, the white stone of the bridge and the cathedral walls glowing in the sun. And I recalled what might've been in the back of my mind when I'd bought the card—the night I'd sat on the balustrade of that bridge, drunk, my legs hanging over the Seine, reciting the entire voyage of "The Drunken Boat" to the moon and the stars. I stood up on the balustrade and walked along it, like I was walking on a tightrope, chanting the lines, "'Et dès lors, je me suis baigné dans le Poème / De La Mer,'" knowing if I fell, I was dead. That's what it was all about when I was twenty-two—playing with death. As I looked at my sisters, I decided again not to say anything to them about the kid who'd left the

32

country in '67 and sailed from New York to Southampton on a cargo ship, not knowing anyone in Europe, or if he'd ever return home. I couldn't talk about that kid without talking about Dad, and I wasn't going to do that. "Those years I was gone weren't all fun."

"Oh, I'm sure they weren't," Linda said. "But you didn't have to live with an addict, who happened to be your mother."

Patty shook her head. "After Dad died, Mom would go to her room almost every evening and lie in bed and cry. We never knew what to do. We'd just sit next to her. Sometimes she'd get up and try to look strong, try to smile, talk with us, but often she couldn't hear us, couldn't be with us. She was with Dad. Tranquilizers got her through the first couple years. She'd get doped up and fall asleep. And when she couldn't get her drugs anymore, she started drinking. She couldn't live without something to kill her pain."

"And it got worse," Linda said. "When she thought we were asleep at night, she'd go out. One morning, while she was making breakfast, I went into her room to see if she'd done the laundry and found a basket full of clean clothes. I started looking through it. And then I heard someone breathing. I thought, Mom's in the kitchen. I looked at the bed and saw a man lying on his side, his head just above the edge of the covers. In the same bed in which Mom and Dad used to sleep. It was like finding a huge turd, and that turd was Ken. I grabbed my clothes, went back to my room, and didn't say a word to her at breakfast. Didn't say anything to her for a long time, unless I had to."

"We'd lost her," Patty said. "She was still there, but we'd lost her."

"When Chantal and I used to drive out to the trailer to see Mom and Ken, she seemed happy. She had a full-time job at the insurance company, he was working, and neither of them were drinking. Of course, she loved Chantal, and seeing me with her made Mom happy."

"She still loves her," Patty said.

The front door opened, I started, thinking it was Mom, but Julie stepped inside, with Ashley asleep in her arms, her head resting on her mother's shoulder. Julie held her finger over her puckered lips, breathed a barely audible "shh," and headed upstairs. Patty brought the stroller in from the porch and then followed her. Linda poured the last of the wine, leaned back, and drank. I took the empty bottle to the kitchen, opened the second, returned to the living room, filled my glass, and set the bottle down on the table.

"Consider yourself lucky you weren't there," Linda said. "Can you imagine, if every woman who became a widow with kids at home behaved the way she did?" She looked away. I could feel her anger. She took another drink. "I think I might go home. You can call me when she shows up." She stared at the table. "Are you staying?"

"I should probably call a hotel and see about a room." I didn't move. Having a place to stay didn't matter, if I didn't know Mom was safe.

Patty came downstairs and said Julie was hungry, we might have a long wait, and suggested we order a pizza. Linda and I agreed, in spite of our talk about leaving, and Patty went to the kitchen and returned with the yellow pages, looked up a place that delivered, and we ordered a pizza and a salad. Patty refilled her glass, leaned back into her section of the couch, and looked at Linda and me.

"What were you talking about?"

"I was just wondering how it's possible for a woman to abandon her children," Linda said.

"That was over twenty years ago. Sometimes I think you've never forgiven her, even though your life turned out just fine. You're not the one who had to put up with him in that trailer when you were pregnant." Patty glared at the table and shook her head. "It was so humiliating; those last few months. Every time I would walk by him, in that hall between the bathroom and the kitchen, I would turn my back to the wall and try to shrink against it, but his body would bump against my breasts and belly, and he would look at me in a way that . . . that made me feel cheap."

"And where was Mom?" I asked.

"Oh, she was loopy," Linda said. "You know, the tranquilizers, and then the whiskey."

"He was usually drunk," Patty continued. "He reeked of beer and whiskey. And the bigger I got, the more he would stare at me and look me over like I was just a thing. I couldn't wait to get away from him. And that's just what he wanted—for me to marry Mickey and move out of the trailer when I was eighteen, so there would be one less kid, and he would have Mom more to himself." Patty sneered. "And I'm sure that's why he was only too happy to give Mickey and me the furniture from Mom and Dad's house. It wasn't to help us out, like Mom said, it was to get rid of things from Mom's life with Dad. Ken was such a baby, and he still is—a spoiled brat, who has to have his mommy all to himself."

While Patty continued talking, describing what it was like to be pregnant and go to school, and then drop out and have to spend more time in the trailer around Ken, because he was often not on the road, I thought about her comment that he'd wanted to give the furniture to her and Mickey to get rid of anything that might remind Mom of Dad. Perhaps that was the real reason Patty had hung onto the furniture all these years, why she'd hauled each piece from one apartment to another, and finally to this house, because it was all she had of her life with Mom and Dad, a life that in retrospect must've felt like paradise—a happy childhood, a home with a mother and a father who loved her, didn't use drugs, and seldom drank, and she could have friends over to her house and never worry about being embarrassed or humiliated. The very reason she'd held onto the furniture was the reason I wouldn't have. I had no desire to hold onto that past.

"That creep never touched me," Linda said. "He didn't dare. If he got anywhere near me, I would tell him to get away, and if he so much as looked at me the wrong way, I would look him in the eye and tell him to stop."

"I guess I wasn't gutsy, like you."

"And I let Mom know I wasn't putting up with any crap from either of them. I ran away a few times, and that scared the shit out of her. Above all that time the police brought me back, and she was sick at the idea she might lose me."

"Still, you have to give Mom credit," Patty said. "She got off the drugs and whiskey, and gave him an ultimatum—quit drinking, or get out of our lives. She didn't bend, and he did what she wanted him to do."

"And here we are, right back where we were twenty years ago, wondering where she is, if she's alive. And for all we know, she might've decided to start something with another man."

The phone on the table next to Patty rang, and she started. She answered. "Ken, she hasn't come back." She listened, and then said, "I promise, if I learn anything, I'll call you immediately."

35

There was a knock at the door, Patty answered, and I paid the man doing the delivery. She led us to the kitchen, set the pizza and the salad on the table, got some plates and silverware, and we sat down. Julie appeared, and her eyes bulged when she saw Linda and me still there. Patty told her we'd been talking and lost track of time. Julie bit her lip and nodded. She stayed with us for a while, and then went to bed. We didn't have anything more to say and spent the next couple hours reading the newspaper, wandering from one room to another, looking out the windows, in a silence far more stressful than Ashley's wails, until we were so exhausted, we couldn't do anything but go to bed.

Linda called Tom to tell him Mom hadn't shown up, and she was spending the night. While Patty took her upstairs and prepared Scott's bed for her, I called Barbara and told her what I knew. She wished she could do something to help. Patty came downstairs with sheets and a blanket, and we made the bed in the small room off the dining room. I followed her upstairs, hugged her goodnight, went into the bathroom and pissed, and returned to my room. Aside from the single bed, which was just a box spring and a mattress that functioned as a couch during the day, there was a rocking chair nearby that held the pile of cushions that Patty and I took off the bed. On the wall, a few feet from the door, hung more pictures of Julie and Scott, and a close-up of Ashley's face, her smile spreading her pudgy cheeks and lighting her eyes. I gazed at the pictures, thinking of Alan and how much he meant to me, and my total indifference to having children before I'd met Chantal. I stripped to my underpants and T-shirt, tossed my clothes on the cushions, switched off the overhead light, lay down, and stared at the ceiling.

I saw again the picture of Mom, emaciated, with that terrified look on her face. Dad's death had devastated her, and that devastation revealed the depth of her love for him. But her love for her children was just as deep. It had saved me from a childhood that might have been my destruction. As I thought about Mom and Dad, the same old questions returned. What made her fall in love with him? What did she see when she looked at him? How could she see his anger, his violence, and still love him? I was still wondering as my eyes closed.

Virginia (Ginny) Ann

I slowed to a crawl as soon as I noticed Julie pushing the stroller down the sidewalk and followed her from a distance as she walked home. I saw David's car parked in front of Patty's house, and Linda's in the driveway. I pulled over to the side of the street. David had to be anxious to drive all the way to St. Paul from Iowa City. Patty must've called him. Yeah. And she probably called Linda too. The three of them are scared out of their minds, worried sick something has happened to me. Julie pushed the stroller to the steps and carried Ashley into the house, and Patty came out to get the stroller. The sun was setting, the shadows of trees and houses covered the yards and sidewalks, and soon it would be dark. I can't let this go another day. Someone turned the porch light on. My kids are waiting. I have to tell them the prognosis. But that'll just make them more anxious. I have to reassure them everything'll be okay, even if that might not be true. They'll ask questions. Why didn't I go home after work yesterday? Where have I been? I won't tell them. I can't. Can't tell them I visited John's grave today. Can't tell them that after all these years I still grieve. Still fall apart.

I remembered the name—Resurrection Cemetery—and once I started driving, the route came back—every stretch of road, every stoplight, every turn. During those first few months after his death, when the girls were in school, I would visit his grave, and every day I would resurrect him. I would enter the cemetery, just as I did this afternoon, drive down the main road, turn

37

onto a smaller one, and when I would get close to the tree that provides shade in the summer, I would stop and get out. I immediately recognized the spot today, got out and walked around the car to a yellow lawn and passed two rows of headstones, turned at the third, and walked down the row, looking at the names partly covered by blades of grass that lay flat across the stones. After passing several graves, I realized that wasn't the row, went to the next one, and continued until I saw the engraved letters BERM. I pushed the grass out of the way with my foot, revealing the name, HABERMANN, and fell to my knees. I pulled out the grass growing across the stone and stood up and kicked the sod away. I got back down on my knees and ripped up chunks of sod until I could see the entire stone—a cross carved beneath our family name, and on either side of the cross, a rectangle. In the one on my right, the word FATHER, and JOHN A below it, and the years of his birth and death beneath his name. The one on the left remained blank. That's where I would be buried. He'd always slept on the side on which he'd been buried, and I on the other, and that's the way we would lie until nothing remained of us.

I rolled off my knees, sat in the sun, and ran my fingertips across the engraved letters. When I used to come here, I would look at the stone, at my place next to his, and I would remember what it was like to lie with him and feel his body pressed against mine. I would sit here for a long time reliving our life, until I could no longer ignore the thought that was always stalking me— he was dead, and I could never have him back. And then I'd get angry and leave.

Death had separated us. Now it would reunite us. I looked around, as someone who had bought a house might look at the new neighborhood into which she was about to move. Beyond the row with our grave were three more rows of headstones, a row of small mausoleums, and beyond them a stone wall, some leafless trees, a road, and in the distance more trees bordering the bluffs above the Mississippi. It was good to know I would be here, in a place that already felt like home.

I looked down at the headstone, at the dirt that had accumulated over the years and had given the stone a grayish hue. I ran the side of my index finger beneath each eye, pushed away the tears, and with my wet finger wiped away some of the dirt, revealing a bluish-purple surface. I went to the car, drove to a

Super America, bought a roll of paper towels and a bottle of water, returned to the grave and sprinkled water across the stone. As I wiped it, working the towel deep into the carved grooves to get out all of the dirt, the colors and the engravings of the names, the dates, and the branches with leaves in the top corners became just as clear as the first time I'd seen them. I lay down on my side, facing the headstone, my hand resting on the ground above his body. If he were alive and lying next to me, I would be facing him, tracing his lips with the tip of my finger to make him smile, and his eyes would look up at me. Only I knew this man.

David, Patty, and Linda, they never really knew him. Do kids ever know their fathers? Can they even imagine what he was like when he was young? A beautiful boy with black, wavy hair, green eyes, and a smile that made my heart dance. His family lived in New Devon; the town closest to our farm. We were about five miles out. My sister and I began our education in a one-room school, close to home. When it came time for Gerda to go to high school, Papa arranged for her to live in town, in a doctor's house, where she earned her keep by doing the cleaning and the laundry and the dishes. Two years later, he made a similar deal for me, only in a hotel. Living at home was out of the question, because there weren't any school buses in those days, at least not in that part of Wisconsin, and even if there were, I don't know how, after a snowstorm, a bus could've gotten five miles down the narrow highway from town to the gravel road, and then another mile down that road to our driveway.

My first year in high school was John's last. I'd see him sometimes in the hall, standing by his locker, or goofing around with some of his buddies, and occasionally, I would notice a girl talking to another girl, and they would gawk at him, and then look down or at one another if he looked back. I asked one of my friends if she knew his name, and she asked, "Why?" And I said, "Just curious," and she said, "Yeah, sure," and grinned and told me.

The first time John looked at me was in the bakery. Gerda and I moved back to the farm after my first year in high school, with the understanding that in the fall she would return to the doctor's house and I to the hotel. One day Papa had to take some corn to the co-op to get it milled, and I went along, because I wanted to go anywhere he went. I liked to think he was all mine. I'd felt that way since I was a little girl, old enough to know he was the only grown person in my life, because Mother had died a year and a half after she'd given birth to me, during the flu pandemic of 1918, and Gerda had gone to live with family somewhere else, and the woman I called Mama he married when I was five. So, I often went with him when he did chores, wore bib overalls like his, and Mama cut my hair short, so it hung straight, barely reaching my neck, making me look like a boy.

I helped Papa fill the bed of his old Tin Lizzie with corn, and we set out for town, the crankshaft whining as always, like this trip might be the truck's last. When we got to the co-op, he gave me a nickel, told me to go to the bakery and get a treat. I walked from the mill, along the gravel path that bordered the river, the branches of willows streaming on the water, until I reached Main Street, and then turned and walked across the bridge, my hand gliding on the warm surface of the green metal railing and the crusty rust spots where the paint had flaked off, sunlight sparkling on the river below. I crossed First Street and continued along Main, walking past the large red brick building that housed the post office and Western Union, and then the Donna Jean Salon, and the pool hall, where fellows stood chalking their cues and watching their opponents bend over to take a shot, and then the bakery. If I'd kept on walking, I would've passed the Jewel Theater, the Cozy Nook Cafe, the bowling alleys, and in another big building on the corner, McNally Furniture and Undertaking, McNally Drug, and around the corner, on Second Street, the McNally Hotel, where I'd roomed and would again. All through high school I heard the joke that this block on Main had everything you needed: Donna Jean to get you ready for your wedding, the bakery for the cake, the pool hall and movie theater and bowling alleys for a good time, and the undertaker to put you to rest. But getting married was the furthest thing from my mind when I paused in front of the bakery and looked in the window at the cakes and pastries on display.

I pulled open the screen door, inhaled the warm, sweet smells, and took my place behind two women. They looked back at me and smiled, and the one closest asked how my mother was doing and nodded when I said she was fine. I looked at the display cases and the cakes, the cookies, the doughnuts, and the Danish, with fruit fillings covered with creamy white frosting, and wondered what I should get. A girl with red hair took a loaf of bread from the display case behind the counter, ran it through the electric slicer, bagged it, and handed it to the first woman.

While she was talking to the next, a boy in a white T-shirt, pants, and a baker's cap came in carrying a long narrow tray of Danish. He turned his back to me and set the tray on the counter beneath the bread, and when he turned toward one of the display cases, I recognized John. He bent over and rearranged some of the Danish from one tray to another, took the empty tray out and replaced it with the full one, and stood up and noticed me watching him. He looked at me for a second, smiled, and said, "Haven't I seen you in school?"

I grinned and felt my face blush. For the first time in my life, I would've liked to have been pretty, with long hair and curls, and wearing a dress instead of overalls. All I could think of saying was, "Yes."

"Well, *Yes*," he said, as if that were my name, "what would you like? A Danish?"

"Yeah."

"What kind?"

"I don't know. Which is best?" He shook his head, and his eyes twinkled, like he was toying with me. I didn't want to be his toy, so I looked over the different colors of fruit fillings and said, "Raspberry."

He took out a raspberry Danish and put it in a little bag. "What's your name?"

"Ginny."

"Are you Danish?"

"Yeah."

"Here, Ginny," he handed me the bag over the display case. "There's no charge for a Danish girl."

The redhead's face snapped in his direction, but he ignored her.

"Thank you," I said two or three times as I walked backward, turning just in time to bump into a woman who was entering. I got around her and hurried out the door.

For once I didn't care that Papa drove twenty miles an hour along the two-lane highway so he could look out the window at his neighbors' crops and see how they were doing, because I wanted to go slow and look out the window too and fantasize about the boy in the bakery. He'd already taken root, grown inside me, and filled me with warmth, just like the fields of corn and wheat basking in the sun. The warm breeze breathed across my neck and face, and I wanted to open the door, get out, and walk into those fields of yellow, green, and gold, and feel the wheat brushing against my thighs and the tall rows of corn folding over the boy and me and concealing us from the world.

Papa swung Lizzie onto the gravel road that crunched under the tires and rose and fell with the flow of the fields. The crunching disappeared for a second, replaced by staccato bumps as we crossed the thick wood planks of the bridge over the creek. We turned onto our dirt driveway, and I watched the wheat field flow by on the other side of the barbed wire fence. As the truck followed the curve, the cow barn appeared a couple hundred feet off, and when Papa turned and pulled to a stop in front of the back door, the faded red machine shed, and the outhouse were off to the side. I got out, followed him through the washroom to the kitchen and the living room, and floated up the stairs to my room and lay down and stared at the ceiling, still in that field with John.

I returned to the bakery a couple weeks later and saw the redhead behind the counter. I tried to appear calm as I looked over the pastries before ordering a doughnut. As she handed me the bag, and I handed her the money, I asked if John was working.

"He doesn't work here anymore."

"Where does he work?"

"I heard he got a job in a bakery in St. Paul." She smirked. "Why do you ask?"

I shrugged. "Just curious."

"Did you know him?"

"We were kind of friends in school."

I felt her eyes on me as I walked out, glancing at the window as I turned onto the sidewalk toward Second Street, catching a glimpse of her bemused look.

Mama wanted to cut my hair, but I told her no, I wanted to let it grow. She tilted her head and stared at me. I asked, "What?" She smiled as if she could see what was going on inside me and said, "Okay." I'd seen plenty of pictures of movie actresses, and none of them had hair like mine. Not that I wanted to be an actress, but I did want to be a woman, and even Mama had enough hair to curl. I was looking forward to moving back to the hotel, in spite of the work I had to do to earn my keep.

I was a farm girl, so work didn't scare me. I was used to helping Papa milk the cows in the morning, before breakfast, and again at night, walking back from the barn to the house in the dark with him, and driving tractor with the baling and threshing crews—at least until I was about twelve, when Mama decided it was time for me to learn the work a woman does. The first thing Mama taught me was to cook, so I could help make lunch for the threshing and baling crews that our neighbors formed to harvest one another's crops. I helped with the baking of the breads and pies, the roasting of meats, the preparation of corn on the cob, salads, and potatoes and gravy, all in quantities large enough to feed about fifteen men and boys, and us women, too, when we finally got to eat after they'd finished.

When it came time to move back to the hotel, I felt sad leaving Papa and Mama and my little brothers, even though I knew I wanted to go. I let my hair grow to my shoulders, permed it so it would be just right, started wearing dresses, making friends, and exploring the town. There'd never been much of anything to read at home, other than some books on Holsteins, and the newspaper, with comic strips like Little Orphan Annie and Popeye. But I could stroll over to the library from the hotel in just a few minutes and check out books, like *Black Beauty* and *Jane Eyre*. In my third year, I started going on dates. I gave myself fancy eyes, soft rosy cheeks, and luscious red lips, like in the movies, and when I would finish putting on my make-up, I would pucker up like I wanted to kiss myself in the mirror. The boys would arrive, always on time, or maybe a few minutes early, dressed up in shirts, ties, and jackets, looking a little stiff, and we would go to the Jewel, where we saw the films everyone was talking about—*It Happened One Night*, *The Thin Man*, and *Bride of Frankenstein*. The next year, I clutched a boy's hand as we watched *The 39 Steps*, laughed through *Modern Times*, and could barely sit still through *Born to Dance*, because it made me want to get up and dance, but not with the boy I was with.

Oh, no.

By spring of my last year in high school, Prohibition had been over for two years, the town had pulled out of the Depression, and we'd survived the worst snowstorms anyone had ever seen, with drifts ten feet deep, and everyone was ready to party. Bars and saloons sprung up on both sides of Main Street for six blocks, all of them packed on Friday and Saturday nights with curious girls and cruising fellows drinking beer and whiskey. Sometimes my date and I would end up in one of those dens of iniquity, as the religious crackpots called them, and if there was a band we would polka until we worked up a sweat, and later we might park somewhere and play around until things got hot.

One weekend Gerda took the train from St. Paul to New Devon, and Papa and I met her at the station, and he drove us home in his new Ford V-8. Now that he and Mama had three boys—the oldest was eight and was already helping Papa with the chores—old Lizzie wasn't big enough anymore, and he just used it for hauling. After Gerda and I spent some time with the family, and Papa left with one of the boys, she and I went upstairs to our room and sat on one of our beds, and she told me stories about the fun things to do in St. Paul— like going to the parks and beaches, where you could picnic and swim; and to the movie palaces, where you could see all the best films, not just some, like in New Devon; and to the clubs where bands played polkas and swing music and you could dance. When I asked her about all the shootings and holdups people talked about, she said there was no need to worry, now that Dillinger and Ma Barker and all the other gangsters were gone, and St. Paul wasn't crooks' haven anymore.

I told Gerda I'd bought an outfit I wanted to show her. I went to the closet and put on my black silk dress, with blue and purple and red bands arranged diagonally across the bust, a black bolero jacket, a pair of black shoes with Cuban heels, and a black velvet cloche hat, with a red bow on the side. I turned toward Gerda and swaggered back and forth in front of her, swaying my hips and looking off, as if in another world. She said I resembled a gun moll. Then her face lit up, and she said Papa's car looked just like the one in the photographs of the car Bonnie and Clyde had been driving when they got shot—pictures that kept popping up in articles about gangsters and their gals. She suggested I pose in front of Papa's car the way Bonnie had, and she'd get

Mom's Kodak Brownie and take a picture. While she went downstairs to talk to Mama, I put on lipstick, rouge, and eyeliner, and when I strutted through the living room, Mama and my two youngest brothers stared at me, and Mama shook her head and grinned as if to say, *Well look at you*. We all went outside, and I posed at the front of Papa's car, with my left elbow on the headlight, my left foot on the bumper, my right hand on my hip, a cigarette hanging out of my mouth, and a cocky look that made Mama and the boys giggle. Gerda took two shots and said she couldn't wait to get them developed, I just might be the new Bonnie Parker. Mama screeched, "Oh my God!" And Gerda and I burst out laughing.

After graduating high school, I stayed at the hotel, instead of moving back to the farm, and worked full-time, saving every penny I could, because I was determined to move to St. Paul. Gerda had moved two years before and had found a job and a place to live, and she told me I could stay with her. I'd had it with New Devon. Townsfolk liked to talk about how great it was to live in a place where everyone knew your name, but nearly everyone gossiped too, and stories had gotten back to Papa and Mama about their girl drinking and having too much fun. And they talked more about me, because I wasn't really one of them. I came from a farm and lived in a hotel and did a maid's work. I wanted to move to a city, where everyone didn't know my name.

Papa drove me to the station. He gave me a hug, and when he let go, I hung on, clutching his sleeves. Tears filled my eyes. I bit my lip, took a deep breath, and looked up. His blue eyes smiled down at me. "I'm gonna miss you, Ginny. But a new life in St. Paul, maybe that's the best thing. And you'll be close to Gerda." His smile faded. He brushed my tears away, hugged me again, and kissed me on the forehead. I turned and got on a train for the first time in my life. I found a seat on the side facing the station and looked out at Papa, standing in front of the little red building, his brown hair lifting in a breeze. The train lurched forward, metal clanked, I started, and it lurched again. I waved to Papa, standing on that concrete platform, his eyes squinting in the sunlight, his hand waving back and forth until it fell to his side.

I settled into my seat, closed my eyes, and saw him standing there, watching me leave him. When I opened my eyes, he was gone. I stared out the window at the fence posts and barbed wire flashing by, the fields covered with gold stubble where the wheat had been mowed and threshed, and the gravel roads that led to rows of trees sheltering farmhouses in the distance. I wondered if I really wanted to move to St. Paul. I had the money to buy a ticket when I got there and turn around and come back. I thought of the kind of life I would have if I did return—a farmer's wife or living in New Devon. I pulled Gerda's letter out of my purse and read about how fun it was to live in the city and went over the list of things she told me to do as soon as I got to St. Paul. I leaned my head back, and the clicking of the wheels on the tracks and the rocking motion of the car lulled me to sleep. When I woke, the train was running alongside a huge river, the Mississippi, which I'd never seen before.

As the train approached the depot, I was surprised to see so many tracks and to find, as it slowed down, that there was another train outside my window. For a second, I felt as if the train I was in had stopped, and the other one was moving, presenting me with a fleeting view inside each compartment of the passengers—a man reaching up for a suitcase, a woman packing her knitting into a shopping bag, and another woman glaring at me as if I'd surprised her doing something I wasn't supposed to see. I felt guilty and looked away. As I descended the steps of the car and merged with the crowd flowing down the platform between the trains, I heard a strange mix of sounds—the clank of metal against metal, engines releasing steam in heavy hisses, voices talking and shouting and laughing—and all those sounds echoing in a huge cavernous space.

We passed one platform after another, each with a train on both sides, and went into a building, up a flight of stairs, and down a corridor with a gold ceiling and giant skylights. I peered over the shoulders and between the heads of the people in front of me and saw that the hallway was as long as a block in New Devon. When we approached the end of the hall, it opened up and extended to one side, like the bottom of an L, where people were lined up at ticket counters. I stopped and looked up a good hundred feet at the ceiling and skylights and down at my feet standing on marble and turned in a circle, seeing faces milling around me and hearing echoes of voices and feeling like a wisp of straw in a river. The river swept me away, and I found myself standing outside, next to a gray column as thick as a dozen of me, and my eyes followed

46

it up to the overhang and the dark clouds looming above. A gust of wind blew, and I knew a storm might be brewing. I needed to get to Gerda's apartment.

Lugging my suitcase with one hand and clutching my hat to my head with the other, I rushed down the steps and the sidewalk along the drive, where some passengers were being picked up. I crossed the cobblestone street, almost stumbling on the streetcar tracks when I looked up at the black cables and joined the other people standing at the stop. A yellow streetcar came clanking toward us, a steel pole reaching from its red roof to the cable above, and a steel mesh basket on the front. Everyone in New Devon called the things on the front of trains cowcatchers, so I figured these must be people catchers. The motorman brought the train to a stop, and the conductor, standing on a platform in the rear, pushed open a wire gate. I followed the others on board, dropped my fare in the box, and sat down on one of the rattan seats.

A bell rang, and the car accelerated, its metal wheels making a deep humming sound on the steel tracks. I took Gerda's letter out and checked the directions to her apartment and the list of things I would see along the way. I looked out the window at the tall gray-stone and redbrick buildings that felt like the cliffs of a canyon, leaving little room for the cars driving between the streetcar and the sidewalk. No matter how much I leaned forward and twisted my neck to look up, I couldn't see the top of the tallest buildings. From time to time the wind came whipping around them, rattling the streetcar's windows and hurling trash across the streets, and I remembered Papa, fear in his eyes, describing the winds in North Dakota sweeping grit across the plains and hurling it against the walls of the sod hut he'd built, rattling the planks like it was about to rip them apart, the whole world turning dark. The streetcar passed a park, the tops of the trees swaying back and forth, and a large building on the other side, with a clock tower that reached into the clouds. And then the park disappeared, and cliff-like walls surrounded us again.

A sign covering the upper pane of one of the windows caught my eye. It had a picture, a drawing of an elderly man with a big smile and a cap with the word *MOTORMAN* just above a black visor. He could've been Papa, he looked so kind, except he had a pipe sticking out of his mouth, and Papa didn't smoke. Next to the picture were the words, BILL, the Motorman, says: Here's something for Believe-it-or-not Ripley—Since 1920 we've carried over 2 billion passengers without a single fatality. The message was signed, Bill. The picture and the words, superimposed on a photograph of a crowd, made me feel safe, until the wind blew again, and the windows clattered and the sky seemed to darken even more. The streetcar entered the black hole of the tunnel that went up Cathedral Hill and slowed as it strained, and I felt my body tense even more. The constant deep ringing sound of metal wheels on metal tracks got louder, the racket reverberating through the cavernous space. The opposite side of the tunnel lit up, and just when I wondered what could be happening, a streetcar flashed by us going down, and some of the people inside looked out their windows at us, while others stared ahead or looked down, and I remembered entering the train station and feeling there were so many people in this city, so many different worlds. The car disappeared, the space beyond the window turned black again, and I saw my reflection, my eyes bulging and my mouth hanging open, and the motor seemed to screech and grind as the car strained to climb the hill. I clutched my seat, wondering if we would make it.

And then sunlight. We pulled out of the tunnel, and I sighed, *Thank God*, as I stared out my window at a tall picket fence. I looked back and saw the cathedral that Gerda had told me about. The gray-stone building looked so huge it seemed to have come from another world. We continued past a row of two-story houses and three-story apartment buildings, with pillars that supported the roofs and framed the porches. The wind rattled the windows again, whipping one way and another the limbs of the tall elms that lined Selby Avenue. We passed more apartment buildings and fancy wood-frame houses, painted two or three colors, with towers and balconies and wrap-around porches, and I recognized in these houses that looked like they belonged in a fairy tale the painted ladies Gerda had talked about.

The streetcar came to a stop. I noticed a red stone and brick building, with arched doorways and windows, and looked at Gerda's letter. Sure enough, this was the Dacotah, which she said had beautiful apartments on the upper floors, with fireplaces and fancy plasterwork and electric doorbells, and shops on the main floor. I continued looking back and forth, from the letter to the corner, and as the streetcar lurched forward and crossed the intersection, another red stone and brick building came into view—the Angus Hotel, with arched doorways, bay windows, carvings in the stone, and shops along the main floor, just like the Dacotah. According to the letter, I was close to her street when I reached this intersection. A couple blocks further down, the conductor called out, Mackubin! And I grabbed my suitcase and hurried toward the door.

The streetcar rolled away, and I crossed the intersection, struggling with the weight of my suitcase in one hand, and holding my hat on my head with the other. The wind died down when I entered Gerda's street, lined with elms that arched above my head. I felt protected as I looked around at the apartment buildings and houses, all of them nice, but not lovely like the painted ladies. I found Gerda's address a block from Selby, on a brick building similar to others in the neighborhood, and as I headed for the door the sun caught my eye, and I stopped to look up at the shafts of sunlight that tinted the edge of the clouds a rosy gold. I climbed the red-carpeted stairs to the third floor and headed down the hall and knocked on Gerda's door.

Footsteps approached, and Gerda opened. I dropped my suitcase, and we threw our arms around one another. I pulled back to look at her face lit with joy and cried how happy I was to see her. She led me in, and I inhaled the warm smell of roasting meat while looking around the living room. Pale blue wallpaper with rows of white and gray leaves covered the walls, while the worn furniture and the bare wood floor, with just a throw rug in front of the door, reminded me of how little money Gerda had.

She took my suitcase, but the weight of it yanked her arm down. "What in the world do you have in here?" she asked.

"Everything I could pack. Here, let me take it."

She hung up my coat and led me through the dining room and down the hall, past the kitchen and the bathroom, to her bedroom, where a window looked out onto a brick building several feet away and another onto an alley. I plopped my suitcase onto her bed, scanned the room, which contained nothing but a chest of drawers and a night table next to the bed.

"This is it," she said.

"Wow! Your own apartment."

She nodded and smiled, and I could see she felt proud.

She took my arm, and we went into the living room, sat down on the couch, lit up our cigarettes, and talked about Papa, Mama, and the boys, and the spring melt from the snowstorms that had saturated the ground and filled the streams and ponds, and how good the harvests had been. They'd made Papa so happy he'd taken the boys fishing several times in the creek that flowed near the woods.

The light through the windows had begun to fade, and Gerda suggested we eat dinner. I followed her to the kitchen, and as she handed me the dishes and silverware to set the table, I noticed a bottle of whiskey on the counter and wondered whose it was, because I couldn't imagine her buying it. Mama didn't drink, Papa drank schnapps and beer, and I couldn't remember ever seeing a bottle of whiskey in the house. I set the table, discovering the milk bottle with a red rose that Gerda had set in the middle to welcome me. I helped her dish up the food, and we sat down to a dinner of roast beef, carrots, potatoes, and gravy. I told her the food was delicious, and she said that was one of the things we got from Mama—how to make a good meal.

And then she asked, "Did you get the letter from Mrs. McNally?"

"Oh, yeah. She wrote such a nice letter. Talked about the work I did at the hotel and how I helped take care of the kids. Even if I look for a job as a waitress, I think it'll help."

"I wonder if getting a job as a waitress is the right thing to do. You know, you'll have to come up with money for rent and groceries and everything else. I was thinking, maybe you should look for a job as a maid or a nanny, in a big house, where they give you room and board. And then you can save your money and get your own place." She paused. "That's what I did. I worked as a maid in a house for a year."

I nodded, but I was confused, because she'd told me I could stay with her as long as I needed, and she hadn't said anything about working as a maid.

"And once you have your own place, you can have friends over, do whatever you want. Wouldn't you like that?"

"Sure."

"But, while you're staying with me, let's have fun. All right? I have Sunday off. Maybe we can go for a walk down Selby and look at the shops and restaurants and everything."

We talked for a while after dinner about my plans for the next day. I said I was going to start looking for a job, and she said I should get a copy of the *Pioneer Press* at the grocery store. We went to bed and continued talking as we lay side by side in the dark. She said, "I think I've found my fellow. His name's Hans. He's a housepainter. Loves to go to taverns, polka, have a good time, and . . ." A moment of silence, and I heard a snore.

I closed my eyes. A minute later, they snapped open, and I found myself gazing at Papa, a blur beyond my tears, waving slowly, his hand falling to his side as the train pulled further away from the station; and staring out the window of a moving train or streetcar at people staring back, or at something in their own world, before disappearing; and looking up a hundred feet at a skylight and down at the marble floor, feeling dizzy, and then afraid as the torrent of people carried me off like a wisp, their shouting and laughter blasting through the station; and gaping at the pitch-black tunnel, at my face reflected on the streetcar window, my mouth open like I'm about to scream, and I remembered the screeching, grinding sounds of the streetcar echoing louder and louder; and the burst of sunlight as the streetcar enters a new world with streets lined with trees and painted ladies. I said to myself, the way Papa might've, You're starting a new life, be patient. That relaxed me, and I smiled, until I remembered Gerda suggesting I take a job that provided room and board, so I'd be gone, and her fellow could move in. Well, I thought, I'll show her. I'll have a job within days. I glanced over at her, sleeping on her back, an occasional faint snore rippling from her lips, and I thought, It feels a little strange sleeping with you.

Gerda took her bath in the morning, and then I took mine. When I came to the dining room, she told me she was in a hurry, gave me a hug, and ran out the door. I glanced at the table, where Gerda had set a bowl and a box of cereal and a bottle of milk and went to the kitchen and poured myself some coffee. I looked out the window at the next building and saw a woman dressing her little girl. Surprised at how easily I could peer into another person's life, I turned away, afraid she'd think I was a peeping Ginny. After breakfast, I walked to Selby, found a grocery store, and bought a copy of the *Pioneer Press*.

I got back to the apartment, spread the paper open, and right away a headline grabbed me—something about cornstalks offering the only shelter from machine guns. I read the article about the war in Spain and people trying to survive by hiding in a field and shook my head as I wondered how people could be so cruel to one another. I skimmed the paper, looking at articles about FDR, the state fair, and the Tunnel of Love, and at ads for department stores, with pictures of men gazing off as they modeled suits on sale for twelve dollars, and of tall slender women posing in everything from wash frocks to printed linen and crepe suits and dresses, and of one woman in an elegant black gown.

I stared at an ad for *Swing Time,* with a picture of Fred Astaire holding Ginger Rogers with one arm, and with the other pointing up through the title to their names at the top, both of them looking so happy, and at an ad for Cab Calloway and his band performing at a place in St. Paul called the Castle Royal, where you could have a night of dinner and dancing for a dollar. A picture showed women at the Castle dressed in elegant gowns, and I imagined myself in the black dress I'd seen in the department-store ad, taking the place of one of them, standing on the edge of the dance floor, next to one of the tables with white cloths. But not having a fellow whom I could put in my fantasy, I thought, Oh, well, turned the page to the want ads, found the *Help Wanted-Housework* section, and took my pencil and started circling ads for maids and nannies.

I got hungry, looked at the clock on the wall, and saw it was noon. I opened the refrigerator and found leftovers from dinner, as well as baloney and cheese, but no bread. I put on my coat, walked down to Selby, went into the first bakery I saw, and got in line behind some women. I was staring at the hats and hairdos in front of me, when a young man in a brown leather jacket and a brown fedora appeared in the narrow entrance from the backroom to the sales room. He was talking to someone I couldn't see, but when he turned, I saw his intense eyes and recognized John. He walked behind the women waiting on customers and past the display cases along the back wall toward the passage between the end of the counter and the sidewall. The heads of the women ahead of me in line turned, their eyes following him as he walked past the counter and toward us, and I remembered how the girls in high school would gape at him and look away if he looked in their direction. When he was about to pass me, I said, "John?" He glanced at me as he kept on walking, and I cried, "John!"

He pivoted, peered at me, and asked, "How do you know my name?"

I said, "I'm Ginny. Ginny from New Devon."

"Ginny?" His black brows furrowed, like he was going through the memories in his brain but couldn't find one for me. "I don't remember—"

"One day, in the bakery in New Devon, you waited on a fifteen-year-old girl. She was wearing overalls and had short brown hair. You asked her what she wanted, but she couldn't tell you. I think she was . . . a little flustered." It amused me to see him tilt his head as he studied me and tried to remember what I recalled so clearly. "She wanted a Danish, and you helped her select the kind she wanted—raspberry. You asked what her name was, and she answered, Ginny. And then you asked if she was Danish, and she said yes. And you put the raspberry Danish in a bag and handed it to her and said, 'Here, Ginny, there's no charge for a Danish girl.'"

He shook his head. "Looks like the little Danish girl grew up."

"And moved to St. Paul."

"Well, Ginny, it's nice to see you." He paused. "I was just going to get some lunch down at Bud's. You wanna join me? You can tell me what's going on in our hometown."

"Bud's?"

"Bud's Coffee House, best diner on Selby. Or did you want to ah . . . stay in line and buy something?"

"No, I'm hungry." And then I remembered how tight I had to be with my money, not knowing when I'd find a job, and I probably should just get the loaf of bread and go home. But he stood there, waiting, looking at me as if to say, *Well?* And I said, "Let's go to Bud's," thinking I'd just eat less the next few days.

He pulled the brim of his hat down, opened the door for me, and we walked out into the sun and down the sidewalk. I asked him how long he'd been working at the bakery, and he said about three years. He'd saved most of the money he'd earned the last summer he'd worked at the bakery in New Devon, when he gave me the Danish. He shook his head and smiled, as if he couldn't get over the idea I'd grown up and was walking next to him. And then he said, "Here we are," and I saw a huge window covered with menu items and prices printed in big white letters on the glass, and signs, like little blackboards, leaning against the windows, with more menu items printed with chalk. I stopped to look, wondering about the oatmeal for a nickel, ham and beans and coffee for fifteen cents, and meat loaf and mashed potatoes and gravy for twenty. We went in. The place was packed with men in jackets and overcoats hunched over their meals, their hats still on, and women in their frocks and coats. There were a couple of empty stools at the counter, where people sat elbow to elbow, and we squeezed in. I leaned toward John, touching his elbow, so I wouldn't touch the fellow's on my other side.

A waitress stopped in front of us, raised her pad to write our order, looked at John, smiled, and said, "Well, here you are again."

And I thought, Women are always eyeing him.

"Yeah, that meatloaf's just too good to pass up. Can't stay away."

"So, meatloaf for John," she said, writing on her pad. "And what'll you have, dearie?" She smirked and glanced back toward John.

"I don't know." I was wondering if she had a thing for him. "Can I see a menu?"

The waitress stepped aside and pointed toward the wall, where the menu was printed in black letters. I ordered the ham and beans.

John pushed his hat back off his forehead, a wave of black hair fell across his temple, and he sighed, like it felt good to finally sit down and relax after a long morning of work. He slid his hand under his jacket, pulled out a pack of Pall Malls, offered me one, and lit a match for both of us, cupping it in his hands. He drew the smoke deep into his lungs, and I heard the fire burn the paper and the tobacco. He exhaled a long raspy stream. "So, what brought you to St. Paul?"

I exhaled. "Boredom."

He chuckled and nodded. "Where are you staying?"

"With my sister, Gerda. She's got an apartment over on Mackubin."

"And you're looking for a job."

"How did you know?"

The waitress set our coffees on the counter, her eyes lingering on John for a second, and then walked off, without even glancing at me.

"My younger brother's staying with me. He's got a job now. And he's finally saved enough money he can get his own place." John took another puff. "What kind of job you looking for?"

"Something that would include room and board, like a maid or a nanny, until I can save up enough money to rent my own place."

He nodded.

"How do you like working in that bakery?"

He took one more puff, jabbed his cigarette into the ashtray, and leaned forward, his hands circling his cup, his eyes fixed on something only he could see. "I started working in the bakery in New Devon when I was fourteen, so I'm used to it. Here, I get up every day at three and start work by four. First thing I do most mornings is haul up a sack o' flour. That wakes me up, grabbing a hundred-pound bag down in the basement, hoisting it up on my shoulder, and carrying it upstairs."

I looked at the hands concealing the cup and imagined them gripping the sack and holding it tight enough to pick it up. Hands that could hold onto something and never let go.

"And then I start mixing the different kinds of dough. They've gotta be ready by six, so when the owner arrives, we can start cutting and scaling, shaping and rolling the loaves, putting them in bread pans, and the pans in the steamer, so the dough can rise. And while it's rising, we fry the doughnuts and make the pastries." He chuckled, and his eyes twinkled. "Like the Danish, for the little Danish girl."

He took a sip of his coffee and asked me if I'd had a chance to get to know the neighborhood. I said I'd just arrived the day before, but I'd spent time this morning looking at the paper and told him about the ads and the movie listings I'd seen.

"Movie theaters. Selby's got three. You walk down this street, and you see taverns and restaurants and places where you can go bowling and dancing and . . ." He clenched his jaw, and his green eyes shined with determination. "Someday I'm gonna own a business on this street. There's no better place in St. Paul."

The waitress set our plates in front of us and filled our coffee cups. John didn't bother to look up at her; he was staring at that business he was gonna create. She asked if we wanted anything else, we said no, he gave her a quick smile, and we dug in. Between forkfuls of meat loaf, mashed potatoes, and peas, he asked me if I knew anyone in town, aside from my sister. I said, no. And he said, "Well, you know me, so now you know two people."

When it was time to go, John paid for both of us. He offered to see me home, so we strolled down Selby, the sidewalk bustling with people. We turned onto Mackubin, and I heard birds singing and calling to one another. I looked up at the sun shining through the elms and felt a light breeze feather my cheeks. He said he'd like to see me again, but couldn't that night, he had to get to bed early. But he was free Saturday night and wanted to know if I'd like to get together for dinner. I glanced over at the side of his face, between the upturned collar of his jacket and the brim of his fedora, remembered how the waitress had looked at him, and wondered why someone so handsome wouldn't already have a date for Saturday. But I kept that thought to myself and said, "Yes."

That night, as I lay in bed next to Gerda, after she'd laughed and repeated for the hundredth time, "Come all the way to St. Paul to meet a fellow from New Devon," and had fallen asleep, I remembered the little girl who'd left the bakery with a Danish in her hand and found her papa. As she rode with him in the tin Lizzie, everything seemed to slow down, and she felt she could step out of that truck and take John's hand and walk into the fields and disappear with him in a warm space. Now that space was in me, and he was inside of me. No longer a boy, a man, with black stubble on his cheeks, strong hands that could lift a hundred-pound bag, and the drive to do things, a drive that I could see in the way his eyes would focus on something in his mind, and the way he smoked, his cigarette burning with fire when he inhaled. A man who knew exactly what he wanted, and I knew he'd get it. I wanted him to, and wanted to be with him when he did. I wanted him, because I could feel his kindness. And I could feel in the way he looked at me that I was still the little Danish girl—who'd grown up.

Saturday afternoon, I went into the bedroom, put on my gun-moll outfit, strutted into the living room and swaggered back and forth, clicking my Cuban heels in front of Gerda, who was sitting in her bathrobe, reading the paper and smoking. I stopped and gazed off, the way the models in the newspaper ads did, as if I were dreaming about my beautiful future, and then looked over and saw her, leaning forward in the chair and watching me, the cigarette hanging out of the corner of her mouth. "Well, what do you think?"

She snickered, coughed, and choked on her laughter. "Oh, my little baby sister, is he taking you to the Castle Royal?"

"I don't know. He just said dinner." I looked down at my dress and back up at her. She was smiling, my big sister, always concerned about me. "Is there something wrong?"

She shook her head. "You're fine. He'll get all cow-eyed when he sees you."

"Good. That's just what I want. That he gets all cow-eyed."

Gerda smirked. "Just hope he doesn't start chewing his cud."

We had a good laugh, and then she got dressed and left for work.

A couple hours later, when I opened the door to John, my first thought was that he was so handsome, standing there smiling at me, in his topcoat, with his fedora pulled down over his forehead, and my second was that his eyes were much too green to resemble a cow's. When we started walking down the street, I slipped my hand onto his arm, like we were already a couple. It was a beautiful evening, the sun was setting, and the clouds had absorbed its light and transformed into a crimson haze. After we talked about his day, he asked about mine, and I said, "Oh, Gerda and I chatted and got caught up, until it was time for her to go," saying nothing about my little show.

We turned down Selby, passed windows that looked in on bars, a coffee shop, and a pool hall, came to a building with a sign that said *Rhinelander*, and stepped inside. The restaurant seemed little more than a long bar at which fellows in suits, with fedoras pushed back from their brows or newsboy caps pulled down over their foreheads, and a few girls, in frocks and coats, stood in front of a beer or a whiskey, a cigarette in the corner of their mouths or held between their fingers. On the other side of the bar, a couple of fellows in shirts, ties, and white aprons were drawing beer or pouring shots for the customers, who filled the narrow space between the bar and a row of booths that lined the wall. A thick cloud hovered over heads, and barking laughter and screaming voices reverberated in the tight space.

John took my hand, and I followed as he weaved through the crowd, nodding hello to some fellows on the way, a few girls smiling up at him as he passed. A waitress finished serving drinks to people in a booth and was about to walk off when she saw him and smiled, too. She said she'd saved us a place, and we followed her to an empty booth. She laid her hand on John's arm, like they were old friends, and asked him what we were drinking. He asked me what I wanted, I said a highball, and he ordered a whiskey and ginger ale for me and a beer and a whiskey for himself. We tossed our coats into the booth and swung our bodies down on either side of the table. John looked around the restaurant and at me and said something with the word *good* that I couldn't hear, so I leaned forward, and he started all over. "Good food, good beer, good whiskey, good cheer, what else could you want?" He chuckled and added, "The owner comes from the same part of Germany my great-grandparents came from—the Rhine valley."

The smell of the beer, the whiskey, the cigarette and cigar smoke, and the food blended like the voices of all the people talking and laughing, and the restaurant felt like such a happy place. It was so loud, every time John said something, I had to lean forward and shout, "What?" He moved around to my side of the table, our legs touched, I pulled away, and then relaxed and allowed my thigh to lie against his. He offered me a cigarette and smiled at me as I held it in my mouth and leaned forward. I inhaled the smoke deep into my lungs, he did the same, and we exhaled into the cloud above. It seemed at that moment we'd let ourselves go and become part of the crowd, and I started laughing, I felt so good. The waitress came back with my highball and John's beer foaming at the top and his shot of whiskey. I looked at the menu, with all the dishes I wasn't used to eating, like sauerkraut, schnitzel, and goulash, and asked him what he was going to order, and told him he could order the same for me. I tasted my highball, John drank his shot and washed it down, and we leaned forward on our elbows.

I said, "You're so popular with the ladies." He looked at me, and I fixed my eyes on his. "They all smile at you, like you're someone special."

He furrowed his brows. "What ladies?"

"The waitress at the diner yesterday, the one who just waited on us, and some of the girls we passed when we came in."

"I go to that diner and come to this restaurant often, and I know the people who work in both places, and some of the customers too."

I felt stupid for talking about this, but I continued. "I'm surprised you didn't already have plans for tonight."

"If you must know . . . I was seeing a girl, but we decided to stop."

"I'm sorry. That's none of my business."

"It's okay." He took a drink, looked away for a few seconds, took another drink, and peered at me. "I don't know anything about you, except we went to the same high school, you're a few years younger than I am, you came to the bakery where I worked three years ago, and you came again yesterday. That's it. So, tell me what I don't know."

I was too interested in him to want to talk about myself, but he might not be interested in me if I didn't, so I talked. "I learned how to do a man's work on a farm by following my father and doing everything he did. I can ride horses bareback, drive tractors, plow fields, pitch manure, milk cows, and shoot a cat's mouth with milk from a cow's teat ten feet away." He laughed. "But I've never castrated a pig or a bull. I'm a lady." That got another laugh out of him. "My mother made sure of that. She taught me to cook and bake and sew and take care of the kids and the house. And that's what got me the job in the hotel." I didn't tell him about my mother—my real mother—dying so soon after I was born, or about those early years in southern Minnesota, after the Great War, when Papa was recovering from the flu and trying to begin a new life, and how he eventually remarried. That would be for another time.

The waitress set two dinner plates in front of us, and the steaming smell triggered my appetite. He ordered another beer, and we dug in.

After tasting a little of everything and commenting how good it was, I said, "So, your family came from Germany. How did you end up in New Devon?"

"I'm not sure. My father grew up in the town where my grandparents still live."

"New Devon?"

"No, this is a town made up of three or four families," he answered. "My father homesteaded a farm, and that's where he and my mother were living when I was born, and then they left and moved to New Devon when I was little, and he got a job as a policeman."

"A policeman? So, everyone in town must look up to him."

He took a drink and stared at the table. "Yeah. They do."

He seemed reluctant to talk about his father, so I asked, "How did you end up becoming a baker?"

"Over the years, my father got to know the folks who owned the businesses. When I was fourteen, he talked to the baker about me maybe working in the bakery in the morning before going to school, and all day Saturday. And I began working and paying my keep, which meant giving nearly all the money I earned to my father." He stared ahead, and his voice took on a hard edge. "When I finished high school, I talked him into letting me hang onto the money I was making, so I could move to St. Paul, and he'd have one less mouth to feed. He agreed, and I moved. My younger brother, Bobby, took my place in the bakery and started paying him." John leaned back, leaving his hands resting on the table. "My father believes kids owe their parents for bringing them into the world and taking care of them. I still owe him." His hand closed into a fist, and his jaw clenched. "I don't know if you can ever pay back a father and a mother for bringing you into the world. I helped my brother and a sister move to St. Paul, and with each move, it was one less mouth for my father to feed. My older sister stayed with me for months . . . waited on tables until she got married. Bobby stayed with me until he got a job in a bakery, saved up enough money to get an apartment, and now he's on his own. But I've got some younger sisters who'll probably want to move to St. Paul."

Whatever it was that seethed inside him, it made me anxious. I rested my hand on his fist. It felt like a rock, capable of smashing anything that might try to stop him.

"Within a year, I'm going to have my own bakery." He looked at me, his eyes shining, raised his fist a few inches off the table, and I pulled my hand back. "Karl, the fellow I work for, he's getting ready to retire. All his kids are married, and none of them want the bakery. He and I've gotten to know one another these last three years. He wants me to have it. We've got it all worked out. And by the time I'm twenty-two, I'll own it, and I'll be my own man." He laughed and shook his head, and while he continued talking about his dream of owning the bakery, giving me some of the details, I felt he had what he needed to make that dream come true.

I thought of Papa, fifteen years old, setting out from a small town in southern Minnesota after both his parents had died, getting a job working on the railroad and traveling through Minnesota, Wisconsin, and the Dakotas, marrying my mother, who came from another small town in Minnesota, and the two of them homesteading a farm, living in a sod hut outside a town of two hundred people in North Dakota. That was where I was born, where my mother died, and where Papa nearly died, too. We lived with her parents until he could get back on his feet. He remarried, homesteaded a farm in Wisconsin, the one I thought of as home, and created a life for him and his wife and Gerda and me and the boys. I saw something of Papa in John—the strength, the determination to build a good life, the warmth and the kindness.

We finished our main course and continued talking, and sometimes our eyes would meet, and we'd fall silent and just gaze at one another. While we ate our apple strudel, he looked at me between forkfuls and told me about the wonderful pastries he could make—strudel, of course, but every other kind of dessert, too. Black Forest cakes, plum cakes, rhubarb pies, Danish, any kind of Danish, anything sweet I might ever want. We finished eating, pushed our dishes away, leaned on the table, our elbows and thighs touching, and went back to just looking into one another's eyes.

"You're beautiful," he said.

I grinned, blushed, and shook my head no.

"I'll argue that with you."

I slipped my hand through his arm and leaned into him. "I don't want to argue."

We wanted some quiet, so after he paid, we put on our coats, and he led me back through the crowd, out the door, and into the night. It felt so good to get outside, like all the shouting and laughing inside had become an unbearable weight that disappeared the second we closed the door behind us. I felt a breeze graze my face, took a deep breath, slid my hand onto his arm, and we strolled up Selby, walking closer to one another than before. I felt so happy next to him, I didn't even notice the pool hall and bars as we passed them again. We turned onto Mackubin, the moonlight shining through the elms and lighting up the sidewalk. The cool air carried distant sounds in the night—a woman's voice, music bursting from an apartment and disappearing, a breeze fluttering leaves above our heads. When we neared Gerda's place, I knew I'd have to let him go and say goodnight, or else bring him in and share him with her, so when we arrived at the walk leading to her building, I stopped, looked up at the limbs of the elms above our heads, and said, "It's such a beautiful night. I hate to go inside."

"Well, let's keep on walking."

"Let's."

We continued down the street, past apartment buildings and houses, and then just houses—big houses, glowing in the dark. In one of them, all lit up inside, some people were standing in the living room, while others sat at a dining room table, with candles and a chandelier, talking and laughing, their happiness seeming to flow in the light onto the porch that extended the width of the house, with a tower at one corner that made me think of a castle and feel like I was looking at a fairy tale. As John and I looked on, I wondered what the people were talking about, what made them laugh, what it was like for a woman to live in such a house, with her children and husband. I pulled closer to John.

We started walking again. The street came to an end at an intersection, and we turned and passed mansions that made the houses we'd been looking at seem small. Chimneys rose in the dark above the roofs of the massive forms, sometimes four to a building, and here and there I could make out arches and bay windows and columns.

"This is Summit Avenue. It's where the rich live. The houses are all built of stone. Or stone and brick. They look like they'll last a thousand years."

"Between the houses, I just see the sky. No other houses."

"The bluffs are on the other side. They fall to the flats. That's a different world down there." He looked at me. "You wanna live up here."

As we continued down Summit, the mansions got even bigger. There was something intimidating about those dark forms rising in the night, something that made me feel I should remain silent. John must've felt the same way, because he didn't say a word. And I wondered if that was why the rich wanted to have such big houses, to silence everyone else. There were no taverns, restaurants, or shops on Summit. Everything was still, just a few lights glowing in the houses. We came to a gray-stone mansion with a fence of black metal spears that took up an entire block. I'd never seen anything like it, except in movies.

"This place used to belong to a fellow by the name of Hill. One of the richest of the rich. He built a whole bunch o' railroads. But he started out as just a bookkeeper. When he died"—John turned away from the house and nodded at the Cathedral, its gray-stone walls looking like the side of a mountain in the moonlight—"he left it to the Church. And you see that street, to the left of the Cathedral? That's Selby."

"Selby? Really?" I remembered my first day in the streetcar, coming out of the tunnel, past the tall picket fence, and looking back at the Cathedral, so gigantic it seemed unreal. But it was definitely part of this world. It was the point where Summit and Selby merged. And among all the people who lived between those streets, I wasn't much more than a speck of dust, in a little apartment with my sister. The rich and powerful lived in mansions, and something about the size of the mansions and the Cathedral told me they were all somehow one.

John took my hand, and we walked a little ways, stopped, and he pointed at the city at the bottom of the hill, hundreds, maybe thousands of lights glowing in the dark. "All that down there—the hotels and the restaurants and the department stores and the train depot and everything else—all that belongs to the people up here," he said, turning around and looking down Summit toward the houses we'd passed. "If a fellow works hard in this city, he can make it."

"And you're that fellow."

He turned, his eyes seeming to glow in the dark, and drew me toward him. I closed my eyes, feeling light-headed, and his soft lips touched mine. I was trembling when he pulled back. I heard him take a deep breath, and another, and he pulled me close, and our lips and bodies joined again. And again. We have to stop now, I told myself, or we won't be able to. I pulled back, took a deep breath, and another, and said, "Maybe it's time to go home." He held me tight, his arm wrapped around my back as we wandered along the streets, swaying, like we were tipsy, often stopping for another kiss. After we got back to Gerda's apartment, I let go of him, went in and undressed and lay next to her in bed. I saw his eyes glow in the dark. I closed mine and felt our bodies touch again.

While Gerda and I were sitting at the dining room table eating breakfast, I told her about dining at the Rhinelander with John and our walk afterward and our kisses on the way back. I probably sounded like a little girl, who'd gotten everything she'd wanted for Christmas. Gerda nodded and smiled. But, when I finished, she said, "By the way, how's the job search going?"

"Oh, I haven't thought about it since," I shook my head, "since Friday morning."

She bit her lip, then put her hand on mine. "That's all right. You're welcome to stay here as long as you want." She tried to smile. "You need to find the right job."

"You know, the last three days have been so busy . . . I'm going to do what you suggested, see if I can find something as a live-in maid, or nanny."

Her lips spread as she sighed. "Take whatever time you need."

We cleared the table and did the dishes, and then I went to a pharmacy, bought the *Pioneer Press*, came back, opened it to the *Help Wanted-Housework* section and got to work, circling every ad that looked promising. Gerda advised me to wait until the afternoon, to give people time to get home from church. I waited, and then called, but had no success, other than being told to call back again tomorrow. I started the search again the next day, got some appointments, and set out.

The second address on my list belonged to a house on Summit that John and I must've passed in the dark. I walked down the sidewalk, past the mansions, and came to a house so big it had two chimneys on one side, one toward the front and the other toward the back. I stopped to check the address I'd written down and the one above the door. I took a deep breath and went up the steps, looking at the stained-glass windows that framed the door above and on either side, wondering what some poor farm girl was doing here as I rang the bell.

The door opened, and an old man in a black suit looked down at me. I said I was here to see Mrs. Whiting about employment. He invited me in. I noticed a woman walking toward me from down the hall. She had brown hair falling into a froth of curls above her neck, pale skin, arched eyebrows, and wore a dark blue dress. I felt her looking me over, like she was appraising my worth, and hoped my dress and hair and everything about me was good enough. I introduced myself, mentioned I was here for the job of nanny we'd talked about on the phone, and took the reference out of my purse and handed it to her.

She told me to follow her. We walked down the hall on a carpet of rich colors, past a room full of books and a grand oak staircase, and entered the living room. She pointed toward one end of a couch and told me I may sit down, while she sat at the other and read the letter. I peered at the room with the bookshelves across the hall, amazed to see so many books, until I felt her staring at me.

She had a cold look, but then her eyes warmed and she said, "I talked with Mrs. McNally. She told me you're an excellent maid, and you often took care of her children. You could be both a maid and a nanny. That's why I thought you might be the right person for this position. And, you know, I like hiring country girls. They work hard, and they're honest. Our nanny, the one you might replace, is a girl from the country too. She worked very well for us, until she ended up in the family way. I can't have a girl in her condition taking care of my children."

I nodded as she talked about her three children and all the demands on her time, what with the meetings of the civic and charitable organizations to which she belonged. As she described how wonderful these organizations were, my eyes wandered across the beautiful woodwork, the marble fireplace and carved wood mantel, and the chandelier hanging above the coffee table in front of our knees. I heard her talking about where she attended the meetings, and while some of them were here, over tea, most were at the Cathedral, or hotels, or the Castle Royal. I remembered the ads for the Castle that I'd seen in the *Pioneer Press* and the conversations I'd had with Gerda about the restaurant in a cave having been a speakeasy during Prohibition, where gangsters like Dillinger and the other crazies went to do their drinking, and sometimes murdered one another. It seemed funny that Mrs. Whiting's clubs would meet in such a place, just as it had struck me as funny that Summit Avenue, the street of the wealthy and powerful, led directly to the Cathedral, and met Selby there. My eyes had returned to the fireplace and the red carpet with yellow and blue flowers and green stems, when I noticed Mrs. Whiting had stopped talking. She said, "I can see you're not used to beauty and elegance. You'll get used to them—at least enough so you can listen to me when I talk to you."

She handed me my letter and explained the terms of employment, which included free room and board, a salary, and I had to be available all day, every day of the year, except for one Sunday off every month. So, I'd be a prisoner in this beautiful house.

Wanting to show me my room and introduce me to her children, she stood up, and I followed her down the hall, past the dining room, and through a door to the pantry and the kitchen, where windows looked out on an open-air porch. She led me up a narrow flight of stairs off the pantry to the third floor and a room at the back of the house, knocked on the door, and pushed it open. It was the nanny's room, which included a single bed, a chest of drawers, and a chair. I walked over to the dormer window and looked out at the sky and down at the flats far below the bluffs, west of downtown, and the railroad tracks that ran alongside the river, and the houses that looked like match boxes—tiny, fragile little things inhabited I'd heard by multigenerational families. I felt like a queen looking down on her subjects. It was a sad feeling. Immediately below the window, the roof of the porch spread out, covering the entire back of the house. I imagined the lady of the house and her husband sitting like royalty on that porch and looking out on the people below, while drinking a glass of wine or brandy.

She led me down to the second floor, toward the open door of one of the children's rooms, and I saw the nanny. A girl about my age, her hair pulled back into a bun and no make-up, she was sitting on a rocker, holding a little boy on her lap and reading a book with a blue engine against a yellow background on the cover. I recognized *The Little Engine That Could*, which I'd read to my brothers and to Mrs. McNally's kids—the book that told children if they just tried hard enough, they'd succeed. Her voice sounded disinterested and remote, as if her mind were in a different place.

I stopped and said, "Mrs. Whiting."

She turned around.

"I don't want the job. I don't want to work someplace where I can't have my own life."

She glared at me. "Well, you should've told me that when I explained the position to you. The trouble with you country girls is you don't have any idea of what you want. And you have no backbone." She walked past me and snapped, "Follow me."

The nanny smiled, I smiled back, and followed Mrs. Whiting downstairs.

She called the old man and told him to show me out.

I returned to Gerda's apartment with a light heart, even though I'd have to come up with a new plan. When she got home from work, I told her what had happened, and she was surprised the only time I'd have off would be one Sunday every month.

"So, this is what I want to do—dress up in my gun-moll outfit and take the streetcar downtown every day, go to all the department stores and clothing stores, and look until I find a job. And, Gerda, until I can get my own place, I'd be happy to sleep on the couch if sometime you'd like to bring Hans home."

She blushed. "I'm sorry if I gave you the impression I wanted you to move out. You can stay as long as you need to, everything else can wait."

But I knew what she wanted.

The next day, I put on my outfit and caught the streetcar on Selby. As I sat on the rattan seat, I remembered the day I'd come up Cathedral Hill and the deep ringing sound of metal wheels on metal tracks and the screeching and grinding as we reached the top. Now, as the streetcar approached the mouth of the tunnel for the descent, my hands tensed, my fingernails dug into my skin, and I prepared myself for the worst. Taking one deep breath after another, I looked up and saw the picture of Bill the Motorman and read and reread his message that since 1920 the streetcars had carried over two billion passengers without a fatality. I was ready for the worst, knowing I'd survive. But now, inside the dark tunnel, I didn't hear the sounds I'd heard before. Or rather, I heard the ringing, screeching, and grinding as simply irritating, and as I reflected about what was happening, I was grateful for the tunnel, so I didn't have to look out at the steep hill as we descended. In no time, the streetcar was rolling through downtown, where the sun penetrated the shadows between the buildings that still made me feel I was in a canyon.

I went from one department store to another, asking about employment, and people shook their heads and said, "Sorry," until I got to Schuneman's, one of the stores that placed ads in the *Pioneer Press*. The woman to whom I was referred seemed quite impressed with my appearance and bearing and offered me a job in the women's clothing department. In no time, I was using words like *chiffon* and *crêpe* and *mousseline de soie* and pronouncing them correctly, or at least as I'd been taught, and in the evening I taught them to Gerda, and when we got to *soie*, I said, "Just pretend you want to swat a fly and then drop the *t* and say *swa*," and she did it and snorted one laugh after another, her nose wrinkling and her cheeks dimpling. Some of the dresses cost thirty to forty dollars. I was amazed anyone could afford clothes that expensive. One day Mrs. Whiting appeared, looking at the dresses on the mannequins, and I went up to her as she fingered a sleeve and asked if I could be of any help. When she saw it was me, she smirked and said, "I don't think so, dearie," and moved on.

Another Saturday evening, John and I ate again at the Rhinelander, and the next day we went downtown to the Paramount Theater—or the Paramount Picture Palace, as everyone called it then, because it *was* a palace, with pink and red marble in the lobby, and a fountain, like I'd only seen in films, and chandeliers and balconies, and paintings on the ceiling. A red curtain opened when the movie began, as if to reveal something magical, and that's what *Swing Time* was. Whenever Ginger Rogers and Fred Astaire danced, I wanted John's hand, cupped in both of mine, to pull me up and take me dancing too. I fantasized us holding one another, his body pressed against mine. I got so excited, I squeezed his hand, and he leaned over and kissed me, until a man behind us cleared his throat. As we walked out after the movie, I asked if he liked to dance, and he said he did, but couldn't dance very well. I said I couldn't either, but I liked to. So, two or three Saturdays later, we went to Curly's Tavern and Dance Hall on Selby, where Whoopee John Wilfahrt and his band were playing.

John and I were the first to arrive at Curly's, where we were supposed to meet Gerda and Hans, and Bobby and his new girlfriend. We peered through the thick smoke and saw that nearly every table was occupied. We walked past the men and the girls at the bar, which ran the length of one side of the room, and cut across the edge of the dance floor toward the opposite side, turned, and went in a few rows toward an empty table and sat down, facing the dance floor and the stage. We were sipping our drinks, looking around from time to time to see if the others had arrived, wondering if they'd be able to find us so far off to the side, when a big fellow with a pudgy face, sandy brown hair, and a thick chest and shoulders that filled out his three-piece suit, emerged from the drinkers at the bar with a girl in tow, and John said, "There's Bobby." He paused and scanned the crowd, and I recognized from high school the look on his face when he'd lean against a wall, one hand in his pocket, the other holding his books, and he'd stare and smirk at a group of girls, like he knew something the rest of us fools didn't. And I remembered, too, that he had a reputation for being a hell of a boozer. John stood and said, "Hey, Bobby," and waved, and for a second I saw the two men as little boys, coming out of a house, and John crying, "Hey, Bobby, follow me," and Bobby was still following. The brothers hugged, and the girl approaching me stopped to look back at them.

Bobby gave John's jaw a little nudge with his fist and said, standing about three inches taller than John, "How's *my* little brother?" And laughed so hard some of the customers stared at him.

Bobby introduced Marlene to us, and we sat down across from one another. When the waitress came for our order, Marlene asked what I was drinking and ordered a highball, too, while Bobby ordered whiskey and beer, same as John. I asked her if she was from St. Paul, she said yes, and went on to say she'd met Bobby at a diner where she waitressed. She was a lovely girl, with a smile that dimpled her cheeks and warm brown eyes that made me feel happy just looking at her. I could see from the way she sat close to Bobby and looked up at him and beamed any time he looked back that she had a crush on him. She was young, younger than me—hadn't even finished high school.

Someone touched my shoulder, and Gerda's face grinned down at me. Hans stood next to her. He always made me think of a squirrel, the way his eyes darted back and forth, like he had to be on the lookout to not get caught for something he'd done—not something bad, just impish, like drinking from a flask in church. Gerda sat at the end of the table next to Marlene and me, and Hans at the other, next to John and Bobby. Hans waved the waitress over and ordered drinks for him and Gerda. Bobby added another round for himself, and when the waitress returned with the drinks, we ordered dinner.

We started talking about Whoopee John Wihlfart, whom we'd all heard on the radio but had never seen, with the exception of Hans, and wondered how he'd gotten his name. Bobby said with a grin, "He makes whoopee all the time," and we laughed.

"No, no, no," Hans said, leaning forward so he could look at all of us, his face flushed with excitement. "The reason they call him Whoopee John is because he shouts, 'whoo, whoo, whoo,' when his band's playing. He's the steam in the engine that makes the train go, the king of music, the kind of music people dance to in the old country, the—"

"The king?" Bobby asked. "With a name like Wilfahrt?" He laughed, injecting fart-like sounds in his laughter, and made one joke after another about Whoopee John's name, while Hans continued to sing his praise. I looked at my John, grinning at Bobby and Hans as they tussled, and John felt my eyes on him and smiled at me, his hand holding mine as it rested on my lap. And then he let my hand go and caressed my thigh. I leaned against him and looked around the table, not wanting anyone to know what was going on underneath. The waitress arrived with the roast pork and dumplings and sauerkraut, and Bobby and Hans ordered another round of drinks. By the time we'd finished eating our strudel—the thing that Czechs seem to love as much as Germans—Bobby and Hans were shouting and laughing drunk, the rest of us were tipsy, and we were all ready to dance.

Several men appeared from off to the side, crossed the dance floor in front of us, and set black cases of various shapes and sizes on the stage. One of the men wore glasses with black rims that matched his moustache, a red Alpine hat with pheasant feathers rising from one side, a billowing white shirt crisscrossed by suspenders that held up his blue knickers, and white socks and black shoes that looked like clogs. I'd seen outfits like that in storybooks and wondered if people in the old country still dressed that way. He slung the straps of his accordion over his shoulders, and I knew he was Whoopee John before Hans shouted his name.

The band opened with a polka that Whoopee John introduced as the "Laughing Song." My John and I got up to dance. I put my hand on his shoulder, and we shuffled across the floor, one and two, three and four, and then he twirled me around, I swung back into his arms, and we continued, sometimes bumping into other couples. And we laughed with everyone at the silly lyrics Whoopee John sang about being a lad, whose pappy called him fool, and meeting a girl full of devilry, and being around her so much he turned monkey too. The refrains were nothing but Whoopee John laughing, and they made people throughout the tavern laugh. The song was silly and funny, and went well with the beer, the whiskey, the schnapps and the cheers.

Then the band played a waltz, and John pulled me close, and I let myself go, responding to the movement of his body, the flow that it created. Sometimes I would look up, see his warm green eyes, and catch my breath, and at one point my eyes filled with tears, I was so happy. He bent his head and whispered, "I love you," and I said, "I love you, too." I don't know if we were dancing as beautifully as Ginger Rogers and Fred Astaire, but the characters they played in that film didn't have what we had.

We danced to one song after another, glimpsing Gerda and Hans and Bobby and Marlene as they passed. The tavern was getting louder, more people had arrived, the dance floor had become crowded, and the crowding was causing more collisions, so John and I took a break and weaved our way past the tables covered with bottles and glasses, trying not to bump anyone or knock over a drink. We sat down, he put his arm around my shoulder, I rested my hand on his thigh, and we watched the dancers. I must've been hearing things differently, now that I was no longer out there, because the rhythm and tone of the polkas and waltzes seemed sodden with booze and a little weepy.

A polka ended, and Gerda and Hans walked toward us from the dance floor. Gerda sat down next to me, flushed and sweaty, and fanned her face with her hand, while Hans pulled over a chair from another table and squeezed in next to her. He looked at the empty glasses and said, "Hey, we need another round. This one's on me."

John said to count him out, I said me too, and Gerda leaned toward Hans and whispered something.

Hans said, "Enough? The party's just getting started. It's time to have some fun."

And then Bobby, with one arm around Marlene's shoulder, came swaying toward the table, his jacket, vest, and the top of his shirt unbuttoned, his tie hanging loose, and his flushed face covered with a grin. He shouted, "Whoopee! That's why they call him Whoopee John. Whoopee!"

I leaned toward John and whispered, "He's totally crocked. So's Hans."

John whispered back, "I know." I was hoping he'd say we were leaving, but he didn't.

Bobby and Marlene sat down across from us. He looked John in the eye, laughed, and rocked back and forth in his chair, and John nodded.

Hans shouted over the music, "There's the waitress. How about another, Bobby. It's on me."

And Bobby shouted, "Oh, twist my arm! You gotta twist my arm!" And shook with laughter.

Marlene stiffened, and her eyes bulged as she stared at him.

Hans stood up and shouted, "Hey, over here!" at a waitress as she passed. She came and asked him with a smirk if he needed something. He ordered another round of beers and shots for him and Bobby. And while that was going on, Bobby was staring at John with a cocky look, like he was thinking, See, I get what I want. He pulled Marlene close and swooped down to give her a kiss. When he pulled back, she peered at him out of the corner of her eye, her mouth open. A few minutes later the waitress set the beers and shots in front of Bobby and Hans, and they clinked their glasses and guzzled their drinks. When the band started a new waltz, Bobby grabbed Marlene's hand and pulled her onto the dance floor.

John asked me if I wanted to dance, and we got up and followed Bobby and Marlene until they merged with the crowd. We were dancing among couples bumping into one another, and then the bodies on one side leaned toward us, pushing us away, like a huge wave had struck them, and everyone was screaming as the dancers who'd leaned tried to right themselves and push us away so they could regain their footing. John let go of me and pushed between them toward whatever explosion had produced the wave. As I tried to follow, I heard a man's voice shout, "Come on, come on," and a woman's voice scream, "Stop!" I reached an opening in the crowd and saw some men holding back a fellow with a bloodied face, and John trying to grab Bobby's arms, and Marlene standing in front of Bobby and screaming at the bloodied fellow to stop.

Bobby quit trying to lunge, while John held his arms down, saying, "Come on, Bobby, come on." Bobby allowed John to turn him around, and the crowd split and made a path for them. I caught up to John at the edge of the dance floor. He took out his wallet, handed me some bills, told me to pay the check and grab their coats, and walked Bobby out the door, with Marlene close behind.

I headed for our table, where Gerda and Hans sat staring at me, their mouths agape, and explained that Bobby and Marlene apparently bumped into another couple, the men got into an argument, and one thing led to another. Hans flagged down the waitress and got the check and was pulling out his wallet when I tried to give him the money John had given me, but he refused, saying, "It's on me, on me."

Gerda shook her head and leaned over and whispered, "Just give me the money. I'll put it in his wallet when he's asleep, and tomorrow he won't remember a thing."

We put on our hats and coats, grabbed John's, Bobby's, and Marlene's, ran out the door and found them standing at a corner, under a street light, and hurried toward them. Bobby was swaying back and forth, slurring the words he was shouting. John whispered, "I think he's gonna get sick. I'll take him back to my place. Can you take Marlene home?"

John walked Bobby down Selby in one direction, Gerda and Hans headed in the other, and Marlene and I started walking north of Selby toward Iglehart Avenue, where I was renting a room in a house. We'd only taken a few steps when I realized she was crying and put my arm around her back. She stopped walking, I let go, and she took a handkerchief out of her purse and wiped her eyes.

"I'll be okay. I'm sorry you have to take me to your place."

"It's not a problem. And it's not your fault."

We started walking again.

"Bobby's so wonderful," she said. "I've never met a fellow like him before—funny, caring, sweet. He's always thinking of me. Takes me out to dinner and movies, surprises me with chocolates and bouquets of flowers and . . . If only he knew when to stop drinking—because this kind of thing has happened before. And it's scary."

We reached Iglehart, and I guided her to the house where I rented and led her inside. We took off our heels, tiptoed up the carpeted stairs and down the hall to my room. I looked at the bed, remembered what it was like sharing one with Gerda, and wondered what it was going to be like sleeping with a woman I'd just met.

That was the first of many wild Saturday nights, when John and I'd go out with Bobby and Marlene, or Gerda and Hans, or all four of them, and we'd end up in some tavern or bar, with John usually sober and Bobby totally swacked and rambunctious and graceful as a bull that always managed to bump into tables and knock things over, shouting vulgar jokes and laughing like a jackass, or looking at someone with a smirk that irritated the person, or dancing with Marlene and slamming into people. More often than not a fight would start, and John would do whatever it took to save his brother, whom he treated sometimes like a son. And if Bobby didn't get into trouble, Hans would, and John would be there to save his ass as well. Always the father, the big brother, and me as his helper.

Marlene didn't snore, I got some sleep, and in the morning we tiptoed down the stairs in our stocking feet to the front door, hoping to get out without the landlady seeing us, but just as my fingers touched the handle, she shouted, "Stop right there." Her words turned us into statues. She came toward us from the living room, giving us a look that said, *This had better be good*. I introduced Marlene, who said hello in a timid voice, extending her hand, at which the landlady stared.

"Marlene's fiancé was hit by a streetcar last night," I said, "and they took him to the hospital. He's in such serious condition, they wouldn't even let us see him. I couldn't let poor Marlene walk home in the dark and spend the night alone."

"Well, maybe this time, but . . ." The landlady shook her head. "Poor girl, do you know how he's doing?"

"We're on our way now to catch the streetcar downtown to the hospital." And then Marlene's brows furrowed, and her eyes filled with tears, like she was going to cry. "It's so hard to even think of getting on a streetcar after what happened."

"Oh, dearie." The landlady took her in her arms.

"We really have to go," I said.

"I do hope your fellow is going to be well."

Once we got out of the house and far enough down the sidewalk so the landlady couldn't see or hear us, I asked, "How did you ever learn to lie so well? And cry too?"

"My mother's a fool for tears."

We burst out laughing, like a balloon had popped inside us.

And then the joy drained out of her, she got a worried look on her face, and we went straight to John's apartment. He opened the door, stood before us in his gray slacks and undershirt, rubbing his eyes, and let us in. Bobby had gotten sick and was sleeping it off, so I offered to make breakfast for us. I could do that because I'd already gotten into the habit of meeting John at his place in the evening, after work at Schuneman's, and we'd cook dinner and talk and eat at the little kitchen table, close and intimate.

After dinner, we usually ended up on the couch in the living room, kissing and caressing one another, and when we would come up for air, I would shake my head and try to get two ideas straight—his, that we shouldn't make love until we were married, and mine, that we shouldn't until I knew he would marry me. We would get up, pull ourselves together, and he would walk me the six blocks home, in the chill of October or early November, wrapping his arm around my back as we would cross the dark spaces between the streetlamps, where I felt anxious when I walked alone at night, but never when I was with him. In the morning, I would take the streetcar to work at Schuneman's and return to his apartment in the evening.

One night, a Friday, the worst night possible for what we did, because John had to get up at three in the morning, I couldn't stop the kissing and fondling, because I didn't want to, and neither did he. I let him undo the buttons of my dress, pull it and my slip down to my waist, and unhook my brassiere and toss it aside. I tried undressing him too, but his hand on my breast got in the way. I lay down on the couch, he pulled my dress and slip over my hips, and tried to figure out the garter belt. I laughed, unfastened it for him, and pushed it and my panties and stockings down my legs. Before he could climb on top of me, I sat up and said, "Let's get in bed." We went and lay down and made love, and the moment he came he pulled out and collapsed, gasping as if he were struggling for his last breath, and I cried, "John, oh John!" My arms slipped off his back and flopped to either side, my chest pushed up against his as I breathed, and with each breath I released I hummed and felt my happiness.

He rolled onto his back, and I came unmoored and drifted off like a leaf in a warm breeze. But a few minutes later, I felt the love juice trickle down one side of my belly and between my thighs and got up and headed down the dark hall to the bathroom. I sat on the toilet, wiped myself, and looked at the blood mixed with his juice and mine. I wondered, What do I say to him? How do I behave? Walking toward the light cast by the lamp on the night table, I saw he'd pulled the sheet and blanket up from the foot of the bed and was leaning against the headboard, smoking a cigarette. I went around to the other side, slid in close to him, and said, "'Cigarette me, big boy,'" trying to sound like a movie star.

He snorted a laugh. "Where'd that come from?" He handed me a cigarette. "A movie."

"Which one?" He clicked his lighter.

I leaned forward and lit up. "I don't remember."

"'Cigarette me, big boy'—that sounds familiar. Could be a line from a Ginger Rogers film. Maybe . . ."

Anxiety seeped into my thoughts, and I stopped hearing what he was saying. I didn't notice he'd stopped talking, until I felt his hand on my thigh. I looked at him, at his face as he stared at the ashtray on his lap and stubbed out his cigarette. I wondered whether I should say what was on my mind and run the risk of ruining the evening, imagining how he might respond. I felt ash fall on my fingers and looked down at the cigarette and its hot tip that was close to burning me.

"You know, you didn't wear a rubber. I didn't use any protection, either." I waited for him to say something, but he didn't. "I could get pregnant." He still didn't say anything. "I would be an unwed mother." I'd heard of pregnant girls disappearing, being sent or going off to homes for unwed mothers, and those mothers giving their children up for adoption and never seeing them again.

He touched my chin and turned my face toward his. "Ginny, you're not going to be an unwed mother."

"If I give birth to a child and I'm not married, I'm an unwed mother."

He shook his head and grinned. "What a proposal! I'd planned on doing it with, you know, a ring, and the right words, at the right time, in the right place."

"Doing what?" I asked, with a coy smile, raising my hand and brushing his cheek with my fingers.

He paused, his eyes fixed on mine, and said, "Will you marry me?"

I laughed and threw my arms around his neck and cried, "I'll have to think about it." And we kissed and made love again.

Afterward, I lay on my side, my face resting on his chest as it rose and fell, the alarm clock ticking, and my last thought was that he'd have to do a full day's work on about three hours of sleep. It seemed minutes later when the little hammer started pounding the bell on top of the clock. He jumped out of bed, pulled on his clothes, and was ready to leave by the time I'd put on my slip. I offered to make breakfast, but he didn't have time. And then, just before he left, he came up to me and apologized, he was so damn tired, kissed me, turned toward the door, and stopped again and said, "I have to talk with you about something."

"What?"

"Well, ah . . . we'll talk tonight. Okay?"

"You can't say that and then just walk out the door."

"You're right. I shouldn't have brought it up. It's just that it's been on my mind. I have to get to work." He left.

I stared at the door, baffled and irritated. I dressed, made coffee, and sat down at the kitchen table, wondering what was on his mind. Maybe it had something to do with Gerda's recent announcement that she and Hans were getting married over Thanksgiving, at the Methodist church in New Devon, and she wanted us to be there. It would be an inexpensive wedding, no fancy gowns, and Thanksgiving dinner at the house would also serve as the wedding dinner. But John had already talked about having Thanksgiving with his family, and he hadn't given me an answer about attending Gerda's wedding, saying only it would be difficult to do so many things in one day, he'd have to think about it. Whatever thinking he might've done never led to a conversation, and *it* disappeared. So, I thought, if that's what's on his mind, all we need to do is sit down and talk.

I arrived at John's apartment around six that evening and found him lying on his bed, his eyes closed. I sat down, bent over, and kissed him. I undid one of the buttons on his shirt, so I could slip my hand inside and run my fingers through the hair on his chest. He made a humming sound, pulled me toward him, kissed me and murmured, "I bought a couple of steaks on the way home. We can stay in and have dinner."

"Maybe while we're making dinner, we can talk about what was on your mind this morning."

His eyes opened wide. "Let's talk about it now."

He led me to the couch in the living room, we sat down, and I felt, *This is serious*. He looked straight ahead, while I stared at him, tense, wondering what was going on.

"I've already told you my family's Catholic." He paused, appearing to look for words. "The way they think, if I marry a Protestant, I'll go to hell when I die."

"What?"

"Yeah."

"Is that what you think?"

"That's what I was raised to think."

"And you believe that?"

"If we're going to get married, you'll have to convert. I can't marry a Protestant."

A Protestant. I'd never been called that before. I didn't even know what a Protestant was. Mama had taken Gerda and me several times to the Methodist church in New Devon. But Papa, he never went, except to attend weddings and funerals. When I was with him outside, working around the barnyard, I could feel what was important to him from the way he might stop in the middle of what he was doing and listen to a bird sing, or gaze off from the ridge of the hill behind the barn at the pond and the creek and the woods in the distance, or from the same place, watch a flock of birds swirl and swoop and rise and fall in the air like a dancer, the way they often did just before sunset, before settling on the branches of a tree to spend the night. Then his eyes might wander from that tree to the fields, and the dirt paths that bordered them, and a cat walking toward us on its way to the barn for the evening milking and a warm place to curl up and sleep. I always felt that what was important were the things that Papa's eyes, his stillness, and his silence made me feel—his kindness, his gentleness, his compassion for all living things. But, religion?

"What would I have to do to convert?"

"I talked to the priest at the Cathedral. If you've already been baptized, it's not difficult." John went on to explain the steps, like confession of my mortal sins, and the difference between mortal and venal sins, and while he continued talking, I felt angry I would have to convert to satisfy him and his family. And then he said, "The really important thing is that we promise to raise our children Catholic."

"Our children? Not just me, but our children, too?"

"Is there something wrong with that?"

"I feel like I'm being taken over." I closed my fists so hard my nails cut into my palms. "And what if I told you I couldn't marry you unless you converted to Protestantism?" I didn't even know if the word existed.

He looked stunned, and then shook his head.

"You wouldn't marry me then, would you."

"No. I couldn't."

I got up, thought of leaving, but instead walked to the window that looked out on the street and stared at the parked cars and a woman pushing a baby carriage down the sidewalk in the cold. She stopped, fastened the top button of her coat, bent over, and appeared to talk to her baby while tucking in the blankets, and then straightened up and continued walking.

"Do you love me, John?"

"I love you more than anything in the world."

"Except your religion."

I heard him moving. He laid his hands on my shoulders, rested his cheek against my hair, and I leaned into him.

"I love you more than my religion. But if we don't marry in the Church, my parents won't have anything to do with us."

Do I want to marry into that kind of family? I wondered. But I couldn't leave him, I knew that, and there was a chance I was pregnant. "Promise me something."

"Sure."

"When we have children, we'll take them often to see Papa and Mama."

"You don't even have to ask."

The train stopped in New Devon, and John and Bobby and I stepped out onto the platform. I saw Papa, standing in an island of light, looking at me from beneath the eave of the station house, and ran to him. It felt so good to feel him hold me. I pulled back, our eyes met, and he kissed me on the forehead. And then I introduced John and Bobby.

"I invited John to come over tomorrow afternoon and meet the family."

Papa smiled. "We look forward to seeing you. And you're welcome too, Bobby."

"I'd love to, but I've got some things I gotta take care of tomorrow."

As Papa and I drove off, I said, "Guess what. John proposed to me."

Papa nodded. "I saw the way you two looked at one another."

After attending Gerda and Hans's wedding at the church, Papa, Mama, and the boys and I celebrated their marriage with them over Thanksgiving dinner. We were eating Mama's pumpkin pie, when a car appeared in the window in front of me and disappeared. My head snapped toward the window behind Papa's chair that looked out on the dirt driveway and the barn in the distance, and when the car passed that window, I got up and rushed from the dining room to the kitchen and through the mudroom and opened the back door, just as John was walking up the steps. We snatched a kiss and clung to one another before I led him into the house and introduced him. He congratulated Gerda and Hans, who beamed in response. I made room for him between Papa, at the head of the table, and me, and Mama served him a piece of pie. He tried to eat, but Papa and Mama asked him one question after another about his life in St. Paul and how he'd become a baker, and they were amazed to learn he planned on having his own bakery by the time he turned twenty-two. While he answered their questions, Papa and Mama gave me looks that said, *He's a good man*, and the boys stared at him, as if he'd come from another world, or maybe a movie, like *Captain Blood*. Finally, as the questions kept on coming, Gerda shouted, "Mama, Papa, let the man eat his pie," and we all laughed, and John started to eat, looking up to tell Mama the pie was really good. Papa got up and went to the kitchen. I heard the refrigerator door open and close, and he returned with a bottle of schnapps, got some glasses out of the buffet, and soon all the men were drinking. I put ashtrays on the table, John and Hans lit their cigarettes, and Papa, who smoked only on those occasions when he served schnapps, lit a cigar. Mom and Gerda and I cleared the table and moved to the kitchen to do the dishes, and the boys got bored and left. I carried some clean dishes into the dining room to put in the buffet and glanced over at the men, sitting beneath a cloud of smoke and telling stories like old friends, and winked at John when I caught his eye.

After the men had finished talking, John drove me to town in his father's car. We parked in the street in front of a house that looked like the others—white with green trim and an open-air porch. As we walked toward the house in the bright sun, I noticed the windows appeared opaque and assumed, as they faced south, it was just the light reflecting back, or perhaps there were curtains that were closed. And then I thought I saw layers of strange things, and shades of brown and green, and finally, as we walked up the steps, I realized the things in the windows were leaves and flowerpots. John opened the door, I stepped into a room full of smoke and shadows, lit by the few rays of light that weren't blocked by the plants, and a loud voice boomed, "There they are." I started, as if I were guilty of something and had better run for it, and remembered John telling me his father was one of the town's policemen.

Sitting in an armchair set against the wall at one end of the room, he had brown hair thinning on top, a narrow face, and large ears that looked like they might flap in the wind. He wore a brown suit, a white shirt and tie, and held a cigar in his hand. A table stood next to him, and in an identical armchair on the other side sat a little woman in a dress. A few feet above the table, a crucifix with the bone-white figure of Jesus hung on the wall. John said, "Pa, Ma, I want you to meet Ginny." John's father stood, tall and gaunt, took my hand in his big, bony grip, and welcomed me with his booming voice that rattled me and told me to call him George, and the woman with brown hair permed into tight curls appeared at his side and told me in her whispering voice that she was Emma.

And then a wisp of a girl, whose smile and shape reminded me of Olive Oyl, introduced herself as Mildred. Her dark hair, clumped into three mounds of curls—one on top of her head and the other two on either side—and her wire rimmed glasses magnifying her eyes made her look even more cartoonish. When I met her husband, Charlie, a perfectly paired wisp with a deep receding hairline and a low, raspy voice, I remembered John telling me about the older sister who'd lived with him in his apartment in St. Paul and slept in his bed, and he on the couch, until she found a husband. Bobby greeted us and pointed toward the couch he'd been sitting on, and John and I went over and sat next to him, facing Mildred and Charlie on a love seat across the room.

I looked past them at the plants that filled the two windows and blocked much of the sun. Small cactuses in pots stood on a shelf in front of the bottom panes of the two windows, while plants with vine-like stems and taller ones, some with long narrow leaves and others with short broad leaves, stood on two more shelves, one in the middle of the bottom panes and the other just above the bottom of the second panes. The shelves rested on wooden stands on either side of the windows, and a space had been left between the love seat and the stands so the person who cared for the plants could move close to them. The dining room off to the side also had two windows full of plants that also obstructed the light and left us sitting in a gloomy place.

"John told us you grew up on a farm outside of town," Mildred said, startling me.

"Yes, I did." I placed my hand on the couch between John's thigh and mine, seeking his hand, which slipped underneath mine and firmly took hold. "I loved living on the farm, at least until I reached that age when, you know, you start wondering what's out there." I looked at John, and then back at Mildred. "But it's been hard not being with my papa and mama." I smiled, while feeling everyone's eyes fixed on me, and tried to appear as sweet as possible, hoping they'd all accept me.

"And then," Mildred said, "you lived in that hotel while you went to school."

"Yes, I worked at McNally's to earn my keep, because, you know, it just wasn't possible to live at home in the winter months and get to school."

George's eyes remained fixed on me as he puffed on his cigar and blew the smoke into a cloud. He licked his thin lips and spat a piece of tobacco that had stuck to one of them. I had the feeling we were all performing for him, like circus animals that he controlled with his eyes, instead of a whip.

Mildred said, "John told us last night about how the two of you met in the bakery in New Devon, when he worked there, and you were a little girl. And then you two met again in a bakery in St. Paul."

My lips froze in a smile.

"He said you were so beautiful, he had to get to know you."

My face burned from the blush. I looked at John, who smiled back at me and squeezed my hand.

"Yup," Bobby said, taking a puff, exhaling, and leaning forward to stub out his cigarette, while glancing over at me with a grin. "She's a beauty."

"It just seems to me," said Mildred, "like God must've planned all along to bring the two of you together. Don't you think so? Oh, I'm so excited you're getting married."

I continued smiling, until I glanced at John and gave him a look.

"And I want you to know, if there's anything I can do to help with the wedding, or if you would like someone to talk to about what it is to be a Catholic, oh, and I've already told Pa and John I would love to be your bridesmaid."

"Thank you, Mildred. That's very . . . very sweet of you."

I tried to smile, while digging my fingers into John's hand. He was damn lucky I didn't have long nails, because if I had, I would've drawn blood. He leaned forward and put his other hand on top of mine, trying to calm me, or to conceal what was going on. I tried to relax, glancing around at the others, and discovered that while George was still there, Emma had disappeared. Then I noticed her moving silently, like a little mouse, behind the love seat, touching the leaves of the plants, bending close to look them over. I heard Mildred babbling something about Frogtown and wondered, What the hell is Frogtown? Bobby croaked like a frog, and she giggled, and I didn't know what was going on, until Charlie looked at me and said, "Frogtown got its name from the swamps and marshes that used to be in that part of St. Paul. You could hear the frogs from miles away, and one day the archbishop was visiting and laughed and said *Froschburg*." Charlie and Mildred and Bobby laughed, while George watched and smirked.

"We got a real nice house in Frogtown," Charlie said, "close to the railroad shop where I work."

"And," Mildred said, "we've got such a beautiful church—St. Agnes. It has a marble altar, and stained-glass windows, and it's so close to Selby. Maybe you and John would like to go to Mass with us sometime."

I smiled and nodded, not knowing what to say, and leaned toward John and whispered, "How about we get some fresh air?" I stared at him, pleading with my eyes.

"There's so much smoke in here," he said. "We're gonna go for a walk, get some fresh air."

Emma looked away from her plants and said in her little voice, "But it's cold outside."

"We have our coats, Ma. We'll be fine."

The others watched us while I followed John to the closet, where he handed me my coat. As we walked out the front door, he said we would be back soon. I thought I could feel their eyes on me, so I kept my mouth shut, until we'd gotten far enough away, I knew they couldn't see us. I asked, "What's going on?"

John took out his cigarettes and offered me one, took one for himself, and cupped his hands to shelter the flame, while I bent forward to light up.

"What do you mean?" he asked.

I exhaled. "I thought we were going to announce our wedding plan together. But it seems as if your family already knows everything and has planned our wedding for us."

He inhaled with a sharp hiss. "I knew they would have some concerns if we just announced it like that," he said, snapping his fingers at *that*.

"So, what did you tell them?"

"We want to get married, you're a Protestant, you're converting, and everything's fine."

"Yeah? And what did they say?"

"They seemed to accept the idea of us marrying."

"Well, that was nice of them." I gritted my teeth. The click of my heels striking the sidewalk filled the silence. I took a burning drag of my cigarette.

"And they asked questions about your family. I told them what I know."

"Which is?"

"They seem like swell people. And Gerda's a real sweetheart. In fact, they think we should do what Gerda and Hans did, save money by getting married here next Thanksgiving."

"What if we don't want to wait a year?" I snapped and took another puff. He put his arm around my back. "I don't want to get married here."

He nodded. "They also want Bobby to be my best man and Mildred to be your bridesmaid."

I stopped and glared at him. "What!"

"They think everyone in the wedding party should be Catholic."

"Why don't we just ask them to plan everything, right down to the gowns and the suits? Maybe they can pay for it all, and we'll just show up." I took another hissing drag, tossed my cigarette to the sidewalk, and crushed it.

"Let's not put on a show for the neighbors." He looked around at the houses near us on both sides of the street. "Look, my family's Catholic. They're very proud that one boy from every generation enters the priesthood, and this goes back a thousand years. At least, that's what my father and aunts and uncles say. The Church is very important for my family. I don't want a war. Okay?" His eyes pleaded with me.

"I don't want a war, either." I took a deep breath. "Okay. We'll do everything Catholic. But I want some things, too. I want to get married in St. Paul. And I don't want to wait a year."

He nodded and smiled. "Okay."

I shivered and realized I was so angry, my blood pulsing so hard, I hadn't even felt the cold, but was feeling it now. I pulled my coat tight, and John wrapped his arm around me again and said it would be much faster to take the alley. We went partway down the alley, then cut across the yard toward the back door of the house, passing a couple of apple trees and a large garden filled with the vines and stems and leaves of harvested squash and pumpkins, and wood stakes with shriveled tomato plants tied to them, and churned black dirt where root vegetables had been dug up. We entered the enclosed back porch the width of the house, and a musty smell overwhelmed me. Along the row of windows that looked out on the backyard stood two long tables, bearing piles of apples and pumpkins and squash of various sizes, some of them with clumps of dirt still clinging to their skins. From the far end of the second table came a rich, pungent stink, and I suspected the wax paper covering a wooden tray also covered several ripe cheeses. I slowed down and breathed the odors, and while imagining how dank it must be in warmer months, I noticed the gray spider webs clinging to the ceiling and the tops of the windows and the black spots of insects whose lives had ended in the webs.

We entered the kitchen, where John's sisters were carrying bowls and platters of food to the dining room, and little Emma was nosing about, casting sideways glances at her children as they worked, her eyes occasionally glancing at me, her lips spread thin. We all moved to the dining room, and Bobby and John and I sat down across from Mildred and Charlie. The five of us were near the head of the table, where George sat, while John's younger siblings sat closer to the other end of the table, which was vacant. I was wondering where Emma was, when she appeared moving behind George's chair toward one of the dining room windows. She stopped to inspect the plants, culling the loose leaves. I knew she was the one who cultivated the darkness and craved it like a mouse hiding in its hole, and I imagined her on all fours, her brown hair looking like fur, sniffing around the floor, twitching her long whiskers, glancing at me out of the corners of her eyes. She set the dead leaves on one of the plant shelves, walked around the table, and sat down at the other end, not making a sound. George cleared his throat, and everyone bowed their heads and folded their hands at the edge of their plates. I did the same, while sneaking a look around the table and catching sight of Emma folding in upon herself. Then George's voice boomed like a cannon and rattled the room as he recited one prayer after another, striking terror in me. I kept my head bowed and imitated John and his siblings as they mumbled the prayers. When the praying finally ended, the family started passing the Thanksgiving leftovers, and I smiled at everyone and ate.

The next morning, Papa drove slower than usual up and down the slopes of the gravel road and along the highway to town, saying, "I hope like hell we don't have any snowstorms like we had last winter. The damn plows couldn't even get through." He smiled at me. "Mama and me are hoping we'll see you at Christmas." When we arrived at the station, he said, "From what I've seen of him and what you told me, I think you've found yourself a good man." I hugged him, and he kissed me on the forehead, like I was still his little girl. As I got out, I saw John and Bobby on the platform. They waved to Papa, and he waved back. John hugged me and held my hand and gave me the sweetest, happiest look, and then we got on the train and he and Bobby talked, while I looked out the window at the black fields and the stubble of corn stalks and battered grain stems left from the harvest and remembered the day, less than three months before, when I'd taken the train to St. Paul the first time, never dreaming I would find a man like John.

I spent the rest of the day and the night at John's apartment, and after we'd made love and lay in bed smoking, I told him I wanted to get married as soon as possible. We met with the priest at the Cathedral and made the arrangements. When we returned to New Devon for Christmas, we announced to both our families that we'd get married the first Saturday in February. Papa and Mama and Gerda and Hans all got up and threw their arms around us and congratulated us. But in the other house, George just stared at us in the shadowy light, while Emma walked behind the loveseat to inspect the plants—until John mentioned I'd be meeting regularly with the priest. George nodded, and then everything seemed okay, and John's siblings congratulated us. I got Mildred's measurements, and when John and I returned to St. Paul, I bought a sewing machine. After browsing the catalogues of patterns for wedding dresses in some of the stores downtown, I bought two patterns and a lot of satin—white for me and mauve for Mildred—as well as linen and lace. I spent hours at night treadling until my ankles hurt, while my eyes followed the seams I sewed beneath the light above the flashing needle until my vision blurred, and I created gowns that made us look like movie stars, which is what the dresses of brides and bridesmaids were supposed to do back then.

I met with the priest a few times, learned about sins, and confessed my mortal ones to him. And one day, in a special ceremony, he said, "Virginia, **the Lord receives you into the Catholic Church,**" and went on about God's loving kindness leading me to the Holy Spirit and the family of Catholics and gave me holy communion. A few days later, I told John my period was two months late, and he held me and whispered, "You'll be a wed mother," and I kissed him. He and Bobby bought black suits, Mildred and I wore our satin gowns, and John and I had a beautiful winter wedding in the Cathedral, with his family on one side of the aisle and mine on the other.

Following the ceremony, John, Bobby, Mildred, and I posed for pictures in the Cathedral, some of them with John's little brother, Frank, who seemed puzzled by the whole affair. After everyone had left, John and I held hands and looked around at the altar, in front of which we'd said our vows, at the stained-glass windows through which the sun had blessed us with its colorful rays, at the statues that had borne witness in silence to our marriage, and up at the dome that rose as high as our spirits, and I felt my world had changed forever.

We drove down Selby and onto one of the side streets, where we pulled up in front of a big wood-frame house, the home of John's boss, Karl, who had offered to host a reception. John and I walked up the sidewalk, between the snow piled on either side, and met Karl and his wife, waiting for us in the entrance. They congratulated us, took our coats, and led us into the living room, where our family members stood, stiff as mannequins in their suits and dresses, staring at us, drinks in hand, neither clan mixing with the other. Our families approached and congratulated us, someone offered us drinks, and after many toasts, and standing near the fireplace to stay warm, we all sat down at the dining room table—to which several leaves must've been added, it was so long—and feasted on roast pork, red cabbage, and potato salad. And then John and I cut the first piece of the three-tier wedding cake that Karl had made for us, while Gerda took pictures with Mama's Kodak Brownie. As she continued taking photos of me, now alone with some of the guests, I noticed John and Karl in a corner of the living room, standing close to one another, in a conversation that seemed to go on for a long time. Then both men shook hands and walked over to the buffet in the dining room, where a bottle of whiskey stood, and poured themselves a shot, clinked glasses, and drank.

That evening, when John and I were alone in our apartment, he told me Karl was tired of running the bakery and wanted to sell it to him in July, not January as they'd talked about before, and John could make a down payment, and then monthly payments, and I thought, That's the kind of deal a father makes with his son.

John shook his head in disbelief, and his eyes shone with excitement as he said, "I'm still twenty-one and I'm gonna have my own bakery. Twenty-one! And, ah . . ." His eyes twinkled.

"And what?"

"Karl also said that as I planned on naming the bakery The Ginny Ann,

88

and as I thought of you as my partner, maybe you'd like to leave your job downtown and come work for him, so you can get to know the business."

"You're going to name it The Ginny Ann?"

He looked into my eyes. "It's nothing to cry about."

But I did and laughed at the same time.

I gave my notice at Schuneman's and two weeks later left my job.

John and I bundled up for the cold, set out from home around 3:30, walked down Selby under the streetlights and the stars and a sliver moon, and arrived around four. While John started mixing the doughs, I made the coffee, and then wandered around, looking at the oven, the steam box, and the mixer, its beater blending dough in a big steel bowl, and at the work bench and the things he'd left there—a cigarette burning in an ashtray, a pack of Pall Malls, a silver lighter, and a coffee mug. When he finished mixing the first dough, he gripped the bowl and heaved it up and dumped it on the workbench, and the dough rolled out and settled on the table like a big fat belly, on which he sprinkled flour. I sat down at an old roll-top desk in the back of the room and opened a little green wood box and discovered recipes, one on each card, and some of the cards, old and yellowed, contained recipes written in what appeared to be German, with ink that had faded. I wondered about the people who'd written them, if they were John's great-grandmothers and great-great-grandmothers and so on back hundreds of years, or if a boy from every generation had become a baker, just as one from every generation had supposedly become a priest. John called me over to the workbench and showed me how to cut the dough and weigh it, shape the loaves, and then put them in bread pans and the pans in the steam box before going in the oven. I continued working with him, flour covering my hands and arms and sifting into my hair, until it was time to open the bakery, and then I worked in the front, waiting on customers. Over the next few months, every day but Sunday, we'd walk to the bakery, a little slower as time went by, his eyes sometimes looking down at my bulging belly, and I knew he wanted to put his hand on it.

At home he seemed obsessed with the baby inside me. He'd slip his hand under my blouse or nightie and feel the bulge, or rest his head against it, listen, and kiss it. He began talking to it, calling it John junior, then Johnny, and finally

Johnny Boy. While I'd wonder what we'd do if the baby were a girl, he'd talk to Johnny Boy about going fishing, playing ball, and attending Saints baseball games, and he'd teach him everything he knew, give him everything he'd need to succeed and be his own man and do great things—things John never explained, but they'd be great, because Johnny Boy would be special. And when the baby got bigger, began to change positions and poke my stretched skin with his elbows and knees, John's eyes would gleam and he'd shout, "Look, look," as if I hadn't noticed what was going on, and he'd grin like a little kid.

By the time we took ownership of the bakery and renamed it The Ginny Ann, my walk had turned into a waddle, and I often paused and sighed at work, and had to sit down and rest. The last three weeks I stayed home, conserving my energy to go shopping with John in the evenings and on Sundays, and buy the things we needed—a bassinet, so we could have Johnny Boy sleep next to us and bring him into our bed when he woke and needed to be nursed; a rocking chair, so I could rock him while nursing; a baby stroller, so we could take him for walks; baby powder and bundles of diapers; more wash cloths and towels for cleaning him; rattles and pacifiers; and a Leica camera, to take pictures of every day of his life.

We also bought things we wouldn't need for a while, like a crib, and the books I wanted to read to our little one—*The Story of Ferdinand*, *The Story of Babar*, and *The Little Engine that Could*. When John saw that book, he said, "Johnny Boy's going to be an engine that can, you'll see, the whole world will see." Always Johnny Boy. The blankie, with the little bull sniffing flowers, and the baby rompers with images of bunnies and Babar were all one shade of blue or another, and I'd think, What happens if it's a girl? I could tell John that God has his reasons, and we have to listen to him. And maybe I should have a girl's name ready, like Shirley, and John would think of Shirley Temple, that spunky little cherub. Maybe she could make him want to have a daughter, and our Shirley could become his dream child. And then I'd think of the way he talked about Johnny, and I knew it had to be a boy.

I woke up wet, in a puddle, a Sunday morning, close to my due date. John called a taxi and told the person at the other end to hurry, it was an emergency, his wife was having a baby, she's having it now. He got the suitcase we'd prepared, with a baby romper and booties and a quilted blankie with the image of Ferdinand nuzzling flowers, and my things and the Leica, and put everything next to the door. And while he paced, I sat in an armchair, telling myself everything would be okay. He'd stop, squat in front of me, and put his hands on my shoulders, and his eyes would look into mine as he'd tell me the taxi was on its way, we'd be at the hospital in just a few minutes. And then he'd start pacing again. And when the cab finally arrived, he held my arm with one hand and the suitcase with the other as we walked down the stairs. We got in the taxi and drove down Selby, past the places I'd gotten to know so well. I felt scared I was leaving my world behind and might never come back, and with one hand holding John's and the other my belly, I tried to breathe calmly—in, out, in, out—as we passed the Cathedral and the capital. We arrived at the hospital, John walked me in, a nurse had me sit in a wheelchair, and a man dressed in green wheeled me to an elevator and up to a room, and then showed John to a waiting room. I lay in bed as the waves of contractions came, mounting slowly, too slowly, hours passing. I breathed in and out, in and out, hoping the contractions would soon bring the baby into the world. They became more powerful, and I clenched my hands and relaxed, and clenched and relaxed, wondering when this goddamn kid would come. The waves grew stronger and stronger. The doctor was standing between my legs, and the nurse was yelling at me to push, push, push, until the crown of the head appeared, and she yelled at me again to push, and I did, and I could feel the baby moving. And then, everything stopped. Not a sound. Tense voices mumbled words I couldn't understand, and I waited, wondering, panicked by the silence. The doctor did something, a few seconds later the nurse said, "Okay, it's almost over, push!" and I did, and felt the body slide out of me.

When they put the baby in my arms and said it was a boy, I wept and laughed, so relieved it wasn't a girl. Once I'd been returned with my baby to my room and felt the pain of that first nursing, and John came in and bent over and kissed my forehead and Johnny Boy's, I knew we'd be happy. After Johnny had finished suckling and dozed off on my chest, the nurse put him in a bassinet, and John took pictures. The doctor came in and congratulated us on the birth and said our baby looked like he was doing fine, and then explained that the reason for the concern, as he put it, was the umbilical cord had tangled around the baby's neck. But our baby didn't seem to have suffered any harm, he should be fine, they'd monitor him, they'd notify our doctor, nothing to worry about. Little Johnny Boy didn't give us time to worry. He had an appetite, and as soon as he woke up, he wanted to nurse again, and John and I gazed at his open eyes, looking for some sign he recognized us, but he just suckled, his cheeks tightening with each pull, until his eyelids got heavy and closed.

After John had left and Johnny Boy had been wheeled away in his bassinet, I lay in bed, exhausted. The doctor's comments about the umbilical cord came back, and I imagined the little head dark blue, almost gray, and the vacant stare of the open eyes, and not a breath flowing through the parted lips. I rolled over on my side, as if I could just turn away from that image, and closed my eyes so I wouldn't see it, but it was still there. I opened my eyes and got up and shuffled to the window and looked out at the cars parked in the street below and the capital building in the distance and the wood frame houses in between and thought of taking Johnny Boy home to John and the joy of caring for our little boy and forgot about the umbilical cord.

That night in my sleep, I saw a picture of my mother, a black and white photo of my real mother, in a chair, cradling in her arm a tiny infant that was me wrapped in white and asleep. Her eyes looking down at me were closed when the picture was taken. She had brown hair pulled back into a bun and pale skin and wore a white blouse and a long dark skirt and was sitting in what would've been open prairie if not for the wall of a sod hut in the background, outside that little town in North Dakota, where I was born. And where she died. I felt, as I often had, that somehow, she'd died because of me. Because of my birth. I woke, my hands clutching the sheet, and a time returned when I was old enough to remember sitting on Papa's lap. He was telling me how sorry he was I'd never gotten to know my mother; she'd died when I was so young. He turned away from me, and I could see he was trying to hide his tears. I hugged him, and then, when he smiled at me, I asked him how long after my birth had Mother died. He said a year and a half. I asked him if she'd died because of me, and he said she'd died of the flu, like millions of other people. But I never really believed him. I never stopped thinking she'd died because she'd given me birth. And I almost strangled my own baby.

We brought Johnny Boy home five days later and started our new life. John would leave for work around six in the morning, the baker whom he'd hired to work with him being scheduled to arrive at four, and I'd spend the day with Johnny, nursing him in the rocking chair, burping him, singing to him, putting him down for a nap, and nursing him again, my nipples feeling like they were being sucked raw. And while he'd sleep in the bassinet or on our bed, I'd look at his peaceful face and dream of the days when he'd see me and smile at me, and suck on his pacifier and play with his rattle, and begin crawling and toddling, and I'd look around the room, thinking about what I should do to make it safe. I'd page through the books we'd bought him, wondering how long it would be before I could sit him on my lap and read to him, and point at the characters and colors in the pictures. And then I'd get up and do the breakfast dishes, straighten up the apartment and prepare dinner, while waiting for him to wake up, so I could hold him and nurse him again. And when John would come home, he'd rock him, talk baby talk, make funny faces, and try to get him to laugh, and Johnny would stare at him, as if he didn't know what to think of the man, and if he'd start to cry, I'd take him and nurse him. And I'd get up at least twice every night to nurse him, and come back to bed, sometimes bringing Johnny with me, and find John lying there with his eyes open. And we'd sleepwalk through the following day, barely aware of anything or anyone but Johnny Boy.

A Sunday morning, three months later, Johnny woke with a dirty diaper around four. Without turning on a light, I set him writhing and screaming on the changing table, pulled off the bottom of his soaked pajamas, removed the saturated diaper, and wiped his bottom with a warm, wet cloth that John had fetched for me. I dried him, sprinkled powder on him, diapered him, and gave him my breast, his lips searching for my nipple, even though I guided his mouth toward it. I sat on the edge of the bed, looking down at him in the gray dark as he held my breast with both hands and suckled, his eyes gazing up at me as if he were curious about me. I drew my legs up and around on the bed and scooted my bottom back so I could lean against the headboard. I sat there and watched him until his eyes flickered shut and he stopped suckling, and then I laid him between John and me, and while he slept, we lay on our sides, facing one another. John reached across Johnny and ran his hand across my hip and up my side to my cheek, caressing me gently with the back of his fingers, and I smiled and shook my head.

"I just want to touch you." His eyes followed his fingertips as they traced my lips, glided over my chin and down my neck and breast and belly and came to rest on my hip, while his eyes came to rest on mine. "I'm too exhausted to do anything anyhow."

I laid my hand on his and looked down at Johnny, his arms raised and flung as if he'd passed out, and at his little face, his pudgy cheeks, the narrow slits in his puffy eyelids, and his tiny lips pursed into what looked like the beginning of a kiss.

"Is there anything more beautiful, more innocent than a sleeping baby?" I asked.

John yawned. "I envy him. I wish I could sleep."

"Yeah." I chuckled. "How do you like being a father?"

"Hmm. It's like," he looked up at me, "like my life has a real purpose now. Before Johnny Boy, before you, I had something I was determined to accomplish, and that was to build my own business, be my own boss, and not owe anything to anyone."

I thought of what he owed Karl, but I knew who was in the back of his mind.

"After I met you and decided you were the woman for me, I was even more determined to build my own business. But it was no longer just so I could have something of my own and not owe anyone, it was so I could provide for us, so I could give us everything we need to be happy. And then we had Johnny Boy. And ever since, all I can think of is Johnny. I wake up thinking of him, fall asleep thinking of him, and the business, it's just . . ." His hand tightened on my hip, like he wanted to hold onto me. "I'm amazed at how little I wanted out of life, before I met you."

We leaned across Johnny's body, kissed, lay back down, and dozed off. A couple hours later, Johnny woke us with his crying, and I picked him up and sat down in the rocker and nursed him. After he'd fallen asleep, John and I, in our pajamas and bathrobes, went into the kitchen and made fried eggs, bacon, toast and coffee. John nodded at the sun shining in the window as we ate and said, "We should go for a walk."

I said, "Yeah, who knows when we'll get another day like this." We dressed, John put the camera in his coat pocket, in case we should want to take a picture, and carried the baby buggy downstairs, while I bundled up Johnny and grabbed an extra blanket. I laid Johnny in the buggy, tucking him under his blankets, and John pulled the hood forward, so the sun wouldn't shine on Johnny's face, and pushed the buggy as we walked down Grotto Street, through stretches of sunlight that shone toward us from above the roofs and between the houses and apartment buildings. With my hand resting on John's, we watched Johnny's face, his puckered lips. John pulled his hand resting on the push bar out from under mine and wrapped his arm around me, and I leaned into him as we continued walking.

A woman in a beige swagger coat slowed down as she approached us, and we stopped so she could peer into the buggy and admire our baby. I told her he was three months old. As she looked at me, her lips spread, dimpling her cheeks, and she said, "Oh, my youngest is in his thirties. It's so wonderful, being a mother. Enjoy the years ahead, because he'll grow up." I thought I saw a tear in her eye, as she shook her head and sighed. "It's so hard to let go." She said goodbye and continued her walk, and we moved on.

When we returned and reached the front door of our apartment building, I bent over to pick up Johnny and saw his lips spread, and something in his pale blue eyes that suggested he might recognize me. I said, "John, you have to see this."

Bending over next to me, he gazed at our baby's first smile. He removed his glove and extended his hand to trace Johnny's lips with his finger, getting them to spread more, and then pulled the camera out of his pocket and shot one picture after another, each a little closer, until Johnny stopped smiling, and then he shot one more and said, with a grin, "I want a picture of Johnny Boy serious, too."

The following morning, I lay awake, too tired to move, staring at the sliver of sunlight between the curtains, listening to John run water in the bathroom sink as he got ready for work. Johnny Boy had woken us in the middle of the night, crying as if he were starving, crying as I hadn't heard him cry since the day he was born. I'd nursed him while sitting in the rocker, and then, when he'd fallen asleep, I'd put him in the bassinet. He had immediately woken, and after repeating that routine a couple times, I took him to bed with us and nursed him again, and he dozed off. And now John had to go to work on four hours of sleep.

I rolled over and noticed Johnny wasn't lying on his side, as I'd put him, but on his belly. I reached to pull him close to me and touched his hand. Cold. I rolled him on his back, touched his face, and found it cold, too. I shrieked and cried. And then John was next to me, touching Johnny's face and screaming, "No, no." I took Johnny in my arms and held him, and John walked back and forth wailing, "No, oh no." He bent over Johnny and me and touched Johnny's face and fell to his knees, his head resting on Johnny's body in my arms, and cried. He left the room, made a call, returned, and sat next to me. We fell back onto the bed, and John and I lay there with Johnny between us and wept. An ambulance arrived, we rode with Johnny to the hospital, and after they took him away, a doctor talked to us, but I couldn't hear what he said. It was like he was talking to someone else. And then I realized again that Johnny was dead, and I screamed, "I want my baby," and tried to run through the doors, but the doctor stopped me. I threw myself to the floor, sobbing.

At the wake, Johnny Boy lay on a bed of white linen, surrounded by flowers in his coffin, his eyes closed as if he'd found the most peaceful sleep, and his lips slightly pursed, as if he were dreaming of nursing at my breast. I touched his cheek, felt his cold skin, and realized again he was dead. During the funeral, I stared at the casket, and during the burial, I continued staring at it, until it was lowered into the ground. I fell against John. He held me up and walked me to the car.

Sometimes I slept at night, slept like I'd never wake again. Other times, the pain of my engorged breasts would wake me, and I'd go to the kitchen and get fresh cabbage leaves and put them in my bra. Or I'd wake from a dream, stare at the gray ceiling, and see Johnny Boy's smile, his eyes beaming that first look of recognition, and I'd remember the sounds he'd make—the sucking, humming, gurgling, and when he was hungry, that cry of his. And I'd relive that last night, when he wailed, and it took so long for him to go to sleep. And then I'd listen to the silence and wonder, Why?

John worked and worked and worked, trying to wear himself out so he could sleep at night. But sometimes, when I'd wake up, he'd be lying next to me with his eyes open, or sitting on the edge of the bed, or gone. I'd get up, go to the doorway to the living room, and stop and watch him as he stood in front of the window, in his pajamas, staring at the black pane. He'd come back to bed, lie close to me, and sometimes he'd try to see if my eyes were open, and I'd roll over on my side and want to reach for the bassinet that was no longer there.

After several days, I couldn't stand staying home alone, or wandering the neighborhood, like a crazy woman, blind to everyone and everything in front of me, so I started going to work with John, the two of us walking in silence. Each morning it got colder and darker, not a glimmer of sunlight, even by the time we arrived at the bakery, and we'd work until the end of the day and walk back. We returned to New Devon for the wedding of Bobby and Marlene at Thanksgiving, but I don't remember anything. I'd still wake up in the middle of the night, hearing a cry that fell silent when I opened my eyes, looking for the bassinet that was no longer there.

We thought it would help us to get out of our apartment, spend time with family, drive back to New Devon with Bobby and Marlene for Christmas, so we bought a car. And then, a few days before we were supposed to leave, we decided not to go. It was too dangerous, what with the snowstorms we'd had the last few years. But Bobby and Marlene weren't going to let us spend Christmas alone. No, they decided to stay home and celebrate it with us at their place. The day of Christmas Eve, John and I closed the bakery early, went home and changed, loaded presents into the car and drove to their apartment. They greeted us with hugs, and it felt so good to be in their arms. At the last minute, they'd managed to find a tree for sale, a scroungy thing they'd decorated with tinsel, bulbs, and lights. Bobby made a bowl of eggnog and loaded it with rum, and we drank until it was gone. After dinner, and some long silences, we opened our presents, and then fell silent again.

Bobby suggested we drive around town and look at the decorations, and

Marlene thought that would be a great idea. John drove, and Bobby and Marlene, sitting in the back, suggested places to go as we wandered around Cathedral Hill, looking at the decorations—Santa in his sleigh, pulled by reindeer, with Rudolph at the front, and lights strung along the frames of houses and around doors and windows, and inside the windows, trees glowing with decorations, and people talking and laughing. And then Bobby said, "Hey, how about we drive by the Cathedral. I've heard they've got this beautiful manger scene, with baby Jesus, Joseph, and Mary, and the three wise men, and an angel. People have said it's so well lit, you can see it from several blocks away. And maybe we should go to midnight Mass, that'd be fun, with the choir and that huge organ. God, when that organ plays, you don't just hear it, you feel it in your bones."

But John drove the opposite way down Selby. He pulled up across the street from the Rhinelander, one of the few places open, and asked if anyone would like a drink. The lights inside created a warm glow in the frosted windows that beckoned to us. We got out and followed John across the street, his head bent, looking down at the packed snow and the metal tracks that cut through it. I tried to keep up, slipping, almost falling, looking back and forth for a streetcar that might come from either direction. John pushed the door open, and we slid inside, one behind the other, slamming the door shut on the cold that followed us. Christmas lights had been strung around the room, giving a strange red-green glow to the cloud of smoke above the heads of the bartenders and the fellows and girls who lined the bar. I looked at John, wondering how he was feeling, but could only see a small part of the side of his face between the collar of his coat and the brim of his hat. The waitress, who always smiled when she saw him, shook her head, came over, and said something to him that I couldn't hear in the racket of laughter and celebration. John turned toward me, Bobby, and Marlene and said there was room at the other end of the bar. He wedged his way through the crowd, ignoring the people who greeted him, and I followed in his wake, with Bobby and Marlene behind me. We reached the end, where the bar curved and extended to the wall. There was just enough room for the four of us to squeeze in.

A bartender, carrying a couple bottles of whiskey, had Bobby step aside so he could raise the section of the bar that lifted, slid inside, and lowered it.

He told John it was good to see him and hoped he was doing all right, and then asked both fellows what he could get them. John and Bobby ordered their usual, and Marlene her highball. I decided to drink whiskey straight, and ginger beer for a chaser. I took my cigarettes out, offered Marlene one, and we lit up.

The bartender lined up three double-shot glasses and poured, and then served the other drinks. I tried the whiskey. It burned, so I washed it down with my chaser. I took another drink, and this time the whiskey felt good, opened my lungs so I could breathe, and I felt my blood flow through my body and my spirit lift. I took another drink and a puff of my cigarette. John waved the bartender over. He filled three more double shots to the brim. I lit up another cigarette. Bobby, on the other side of John, was leaning on his elbow, facing him, shouting about a recent hockey game he'd seen. I stared off, and my thoughts got lost in the fog, until I heard Bobby's voice again. I dropped my cigarette to the floor and crushed it.

Marlene went on about a film she and Bobby had recently seen, but she couldn't remember the title. It starred . . . and then she remembered—*Heidi*. With that darling little girl, what's her name, oh, Shirley, Shirley Temple. You know, she also starred in *Wee Willie Winkie* and *Poor Little Rich Girl*. As she went on about Shirley's films, I remembered the period leading up to Johnny Boy's birth and how afraid I'd been of having a girl instead of a boy. I'd thought of naming the girl, if that's what we had, I thought of naming her Shirley, because John had seen her films and found her adorable, and I knew he'd come to love having a daughter.

Marlene had fallen silent. I glanced over at her, wondering what was going on, and noticed a man, with a grin on his face, staring at me—a man on the other side of Marlene and the curve of the bar and the couple standing next to it. I turned around, looked past John and behind me to see if there was someone else he could be staring at, but there wasn't. I looked at him. He had a beat-up fedora pushed back off his brow, a cocky look, and a five o'clock shadow two or three days old. His eyes never left me. He took a drag off his cigarette, exhaled, and a bigger grin spread his lips. He raised his glass of beer and nodded at me, as if he were toasting me, and took a drink.

"What's going on?" John asked. "Who's that fellow?"

"Some drunk. He keeps staring at me."

"He'd damned well better stop."

He didn't. John walked around me and Marlene and the others and tapped the fellow on the shoulder, and the guy looked back at him.

Marlene asked, "Have you thought about New Year's Eve?"

"No."

The fellow turned and faced John, and I could almost hear his words as he responded. I glanced at Bobby to see if he was following what was happening, but he was staring down at his drink.

"Well," Marlene said, "Bobby and I were thinking of inviting you, John, Gerda and Hans over to the house. We could have highballs, play cards, listen to records on our new record player, and maybe dance, and then at midnight—"

The man's head snapped back and his fedora flew off. He drew back his arm, knocking over his beer, and took a swing, lunging forward and disappearing in the crowd. A circle formed. John's head appeared, and disappeared. I squeezed between the bodies, forcing my way to the inside of the ring, and saw John hit the man in the face, slamming him against the bar, and hit him again as he slumped to the floor, and swoop down on him and jab his fist into the man's head over and over. Blood ran down the man's face and splattered John's fist, and still he kept hitting him. I screamed, "No, John, no." Someone pushed me aside, and Bobby grabbed John and pulled him off the body. The man's eyes were closed. He didn't move. I thought John had killed him. I kept crying, "No, no," my eyes fixed on the man's bloodied face.

Bobby held on to John as he tried to swing free. He pulled him away and shouted, "We're getting the hell out of here." I followed Bobby as he wrapped his arm around John's shoulder and pulled him toward the door, people recoiling and stepping out of our way. We got outside and crossed the street to the car.

"I need the keys," Bobby said.

Wheezing, trying to catch his breath, John nodded toward the Rhinelander and gasped, "I left my hat in there."

"To hell with your hat. We need to get out of here before the cops show up. That fellow might be dead. What the hell got into you?"

John, still panting, leaned back against the car. Then he bent forward, like he was going to vomit, but didn't. He straightened up, took a few breaths, and said, "I feel better."

"You feel better?" Bobby asked. "After what you did to him?"

John shook his head. "It had nothing to do with him."

"Give me the goddamn keys."

"Don't swear. I'm still your big brother." He started to laugh. "Don't swear, Goddamn it!"

He choked on his laugh and started to cry, and his body slid down the side of the car until he was sitting on the snow-covered street, his legs spread out in front of him. His head dropped forward and shook back and forth as he continued crying. Bobby got down on his knees and took him in his arms and held him as he sobbed.

When John and I got home, we went to bed and held each other, lying in silence, steeping our bodies and our minds in our love for one another, until John seemed to pass out. I couldn't sleep. For the first time, I'd seen violence in him like I'd never seen before. He might've killed that fellow, if Bobby hadn't intervened. But I could forgive him, because I knew he wasn't in his right mind. The loss of Johnny, and of the new life John had already begun living in his head, had made him crazy. He hurt so much, I knew he might never rid himself of the pain.

I felt restless. I got up, went into the living room to the rocker, and sat down and rocked myself, trying to calm my fear, wondering about John and our marriage and my love for him. From my first days in St. Paul, when John and I ate lunch at Bud's Coffee House and dinner at the Rhinelander, I'd seen similarities between him and Papa. When John talked about owning his own bakery, being his own man, his strength and determination made me think of Papa. But I couldn't imagine Papa attacking someone the way John had. Papa got angry sometimes, but John, he had a whirlwind of rage in him. I could hear it in his voice, coming through a crack in the wall, like when he talked about giving the money he earned as a boy to his father, because his father believed children owed their parents for bringing them into the world. Even when John graduated high school and wanted to move to St. Paul, and so be one less mouth for his father to feed, he still had to talk him into letting him keep his money so he could make the move. And then he had to take responsibility for helping his siblings follow in his footsteps. I remembered visiting John's family at Thanksgiving, hearing the father's booming voice as he prayed, seeing his kids bow their heads, and feeling the darkness nurtured by the mother caring for her plants in the windows, and walking through that back porch and breathing the musty smell that made me feel I was in a cave. Whenever I remembered those things, I felt I understood something of the cause of John's anger. If Johnny Boy had lived, if only he'd lived, John would have been such a good father to him. Death had taken our son, and for a moment that fellow in the bar had stepped into Death's shoes, and that's why I couldn't hate John for what he'd done.

The next morning, we went to Mass at the Cathedral. Holding my hand, John pulled me down a side aisle, and we entered a pew in a deep shadow beneath one of the arches about half-way from the front. When it came time for communion, I walked toward the central aisle to join the line of communicants, but stopped when I realized John wasn't following and looked back to see him kneeling, his head bowed. As we were driving home, he said, "I really hurt that guy. Hurt him bad." He shook his head and looked at me. "This'll never happen again. Never. I promise." At work the next day, he called the Rhinelander and talked to the bartender, who told him the fellow was going to be okay, he had some bruises and cuts, maybe a broken nose, but he was able to drink a shot of whiskey before someone took him to a hospital, he didn't remember which one. John dropped me off at home after work and drove to a couple hospitals but gave up after being told they wouldn't release information to him about patients they'd treated.

We talked less about Johnny Boy. Sometimes John would clench his teeth, furrow his brow, and close his eyes, and I'd place my hand on his, or touch his cheek, or pull him toward me, bring him close so he could rest his head on my shoulder and feel my love for him, and he'd do the same with me. Working all day, every day but Sunday, distracted us from our loss. Saturday nights we might go to a movie, or have Bobby and Marlene over to play cards. Sundays, John and I would go to Mass in the morning and to Calvary Cemetery in the afternoon. Our feet buried in snow, we'd stand at the foot of Johnny's grave, looking down at his official name, with JOHNNY BOY beneath it, and the dates of his birth and death, so close, and the statement, AT PEACE IN THE ARMS OF ANGELS, with a cherub hovering on either side. And as the snow whirled around us, I'd pull my coat tight and remember his first smile, his glowing eyes, and my dreams of watching him crawl and toddle as he started exploring the world. As the weeks passed, the snow deepened, burying his headstone, and we stopped going to the cemetery. Instead, we'd go bowling, or to a matinee, and later to Lake Como to watch the dogsled and skating races. We bought us each a pair of skates, real shoe skates, not the kind Gerda and I used to clamp onto our boots, and started skating, arm in arm. Sometimes we'd try to get fancy and do pirouettes like figure skaters and end up in a heap on the ice, laughing. And when the sun shined through the treetops, we'd skate back to the warming house and return home to another night of staring in the dark. In the summer we'd return to the park, rent a boat, and spend an afternoon rowing across the lake, watching the swans glide, listening to the ducks squabble, feeling the rush of air as the geese flew a few feet above our heads. And we'd go for walks through the gardens and find ourselves sooner or later passing through the open gates to the fountain with its jets of splashing water that somehow gave me hope and made me feel better.

One evening after dinner, we were sitting in the living room, John was looking at the newspaper, and I was reading a novel. He lowered his arms, laying the paper across his lap, and stared off for a long time. And then he got up and went over to the buffet and rummaged through the drawers, slamming them shut when he didn't find what he wanted. I asked what he was looking for, and he said, "The camera." I hadn't seen it since Johnny Boy's death. If it wasn't in the buffet, I wondered if it might be in the bedroom. We went in and looked through our chests of drawers and night tables. He found it buried beneath some things, looked at it for a while, and handed it to me.

"Tomorrow, when things slow down, can you get the film developed?"

"But we haven't used all the film yet."

He shook his head. "I'm not interested in taking pictures."

The next day, I took the roll of film to the shop where we'd bought the camera and returned a couple days later to pick up the pictures. When I got in the car, I looked at the photographs of Johnny Boy. The glistening eyes in the slits in his little pudgy face looked up at me almost as if they knew who I was, and the tiny lips seemed to smile as if he already loved us. I looked at the first picture and remembered John running his fingertip across Johnny Boy's lips to try to hold that smile, hold it and never let it go, and continued looking at it until tears blurred my vision. I put the photographs back in the envelope and returned to the bakery. That night, John and I sat on the couch in the living room and looked at them, and I heard his breath tremble and saw tears welling up. He picked out the picture I'd looked at in the car and said, "We should get this one enlarged." We framed it and set it next to our wedding picture on the buffet in the dining room, where we'd see it every day.

We went to the cemetery on Johnny's birthday in August to visit his grave and place sunflowers on it. As we drove down Selby and past the Cathedral and turned north and went past the capital building, I remembered riding in the cab to the hospital to give birth, and the way to both the hospital and the cemetery, each street, each turn, remained engraved in my memory. I couldn't drive down any of those streets without remembering the birth of my baby and his death.

John and I were lying in bed one night, staring at the ceiling in the dark. About a year after Johnny Boy had died. John had tried to initiate sex, but I couldn't respond.

"I want to have a baby," he said.

"We can't replace Johnny with another child. If we had a baby, that's what it would feel like." I looked at John. "How do you live with a dead child?"

His face remained still. And then he looked at me. "We need to move on."

"I can't let go." I waited for him to respond, but he didn't. "I think you want to have another child, because you can't let go."

He didn't give up. When we were in bed, he'd try to seduce me, and I'd turn cold in his hands, stiff and dry, or I'd roll away from him and lie on my side and refuse to respond. And when he'd talk about having another baby, I'd say it was too risky, we both knew there was going to be a war, the Germans had invaded Poland, and then Denmark and Norway, and then France. After we entered the war, I'd remind him he could be drafted, and I didn't want a baby without a father, and he'd remind me of his exemption, because of his place in the food industry, and I'd say that could change, anything could happen, anything, and then where would we be?

And then, about two years into the war, I decided I wanted to have another baby and gave birth again to a boy. As I lay in the hospital bed, nursing our newborn, I told John I wanted to name our son David.

"Why?" John asked.

"Because David slew Goliath."

John gazed at me, as if he were trying to read my mind, and finally he nodded and said, "Okay. David it is."

From the day David was born, I never left him. I nursed him, rocked him, talked baby talk to him, put him down for his naps, changed his diapers when he woke and fed him again. When he slept, I'd clean the house or sew clothes for him or read books about how to care for babies, paying special attention to advice about how to protect them. If he napped a long time, I'd tiptoe into our room and stand above the bassinet and listen until I could hear him breathe, and if I couldn't hear him right away, I'd bend over and hold my ear close to his mouth, and every night I'd wake up and check on him again. Sometimes I'd dream I touched his arm and found it cold, or reached for the bassinet and discovered it empty, or listened for him to breathe and heard nothing, and I'd wake up again and need to hear him breathe.

I'd have dinner ready when John got home from work, so I could be close while he held David, grinned, and traced his lips with his fingertip, whatever it took to get him to smile and giggle. He'd tell him he was the cutest little bug and ask him all kinds of things, simple things, but in a tone that made them sound silly, like, "How are you?" and "What did you do today?" I'd hover nearby, always ready to take David if he started to cry, or looked at me like he wanted me to take him, as he frequently did, or if John, stressed from work, just tired of him and needed a beer. If I was nursing when John came home, I'd tell him dinner was in the oven, he should just help himself, and sometimes he didn't even get to hold David before I'd put him down for the night. As the weeks and months passed, John tried less often to hold him, and instead sat in his armchair, reading the paper, lowering it from time to time to watch me nurse or play with David. John never came up with a nickname for him, nothing like Johnny Boy, and never talked to him about taking him on fishing trips or to baseball games or teaching him everything he knew and giving him everything he had, so he'd be his own man and do great things. No, as the years passed, John hardly talked to him. He just took care of his business.

When I was alone during the day, or at night after John fell asleep, I'd often find myself remembering things I hadn't thought of in years, like the time when I was a little girl, learning to eat at the table, and Grandma, my real grandma, was sitting with me and said, "You have such good table manners, your mother would be proud of you." And Grandma grinned as she looked at the puddle of soup on the table between the bowl and my mouth.

I asked, "Who's my mother." And Grandma's face sagged, and tears filled her eyes. She wiped the tears away, got up, and left the kitchen, and returned a couple minutes later with the photograph of my mother cradling me in her arm as she sat in a chair, the wall of a hut in the background.

As I looked at the picture, Grandma said, "Your mother used to rock you in that chair and sing to you when she wanted to put you to sleep—sing lullabies in Danish, like I did to put her to sleep, when she was a baby. And when she was a little girl, in her own bed, I'd sing them to her. The one she loved most was about Ole, the Sandman, who comes to put little girls and boys to sleep." And then Grandma sang the song to me in Danish and taught me to sing it too.

I told Papa what Grandma had told me, and he said, "Your mother loved you so much, she held you and nursed you and sang to you right up until . . ." And his eyes filled with tears, and he looked away. Another time he remembered the winds blowing dirt across the plains and rattling the planks of the sod hut, and the darkness moving in and covering the land in the middle of the day, and he choked and sobbed, "She died, and all I could do to save her was give her aspirin and whiskey." I panicked and climbed onto his lap and hugged him and cried with him. And yet another time, he told me how fast the flu had taken her. Less than two days after she'd come down with a fever and started to vomit, her lungs filled with fluid and her skin turned blue. The memories seemed to take hold of him and speak through him, and I could see the fear and pain in his eyes, as if he were reliving her death, alone with her and a toddler and a five-year-old girl in a hut, and the wind shrieking and howling and pelting the walls with dirt, and darkness covering everything. He never stopped loving her, and I wasn't surprised to learn the woman whom I would call Mama had the same name as my mother, Anna.

Most children aren't aware of death, I told myself as I gazed at Patty's house, the light in the living room glowing through the dark. David, Patty, and Linda weren't when they were little, growing up in our house in Roseville. Death was something I kept far away from them. Or tried to. I sighed, lit another cigarette, blew the smoke against the car's windshield, and thought about going in and letting my kids know I was alive, they needn't worry. But I didn't. I couldn't move. John's death had seized my mind, and I saw again his grave that I'd visited a few hours before, the plot where he lay beneath the ground, and where I lay above, stretched out on the grass, still wanting to take him in my arms. Everything changed with his death. For David, Patty, Linda, and me. Everything.

John was so strong, so determined . . . How could he die so young? Just fifty. At first the doctors gave us hope with their talk about anticancer drugs, immunological defenses, antitumor curative effects, and the surgeries that were supposed to remove the cancer. Nothing worked. Nothing! John became emaciated, his face, gaunt. We'd look into one another's eyes and see our thoughts, our feelings, but we didn't talk about what was on our minds. We knew. For nearly two years he marched toward the inevitable, like someone condemned to death, walking to his execution. And I walked with him, like it was my death too, because I couldn't see anything beyond it.

The last few hours, I stood near his bed. When his eyes closed, I'd swab oil on his lips that had dried, bleached, and cracked, and stare at his pale face and the black whiskers that covered his cheeks. Sometimes his eyes would open, and I'd see the fear that had seized him, and I'd hold his cold hand, the paper-thin skin covering bones that felt so fragile, and my love would hold his eyes with mine, and I'd kiss his forehead, touch his face, caress his skin. As the hours went by, his breathing changed, and he started to wheeze and opened his eyes less often.

David was standing next to me. I'd called him, and he'd come. I'd always wanted John and David to love one another, and I wanted David to be alone with his father. I sat down in the chair and closed my eyes just to rest but fell asleep. I hadn't slept in days, and with all the pills I'd taken, I couldn't stay awake. I don't know how long I slept, before I sensed people rushing past me to John's bed. I panicked and jumped up. John was gasping for air, his breath rasping, and after each gasp, there'd be a pause, and I'd stop breathing, fearing that gasp might be his last. Then, as if he were waking up, he'd take another gasp, and I'd hold onto every second, hardly noticing the nurses coming to the side of the bed and giving him morphine. And then, after one more gasp, he lay still, his eyes a blank stare, his mouth agape. I collapsed on him.

And I continued collapsing, falling for days, weeks, months. I'd be making dinner for the girls and remember that stare, the mouth agape, the cold hand, and drop whatever I was holding and clutch the counter so I wouldn't fall, my lungs panting, my eyes filling with tears. I'd remember touching his hair and his cheek, and I'd see his green eyes looking at me, and he'd smile, and his eyes would tell me they loved me, he would always love me, always be with me. I'd take one deep breath after another until I stopped trembling, and I'd let go of the counter, and if I didn't fall, I'd take a step, and then another.

I'd rage inside myself at John for dying and abandoning me with our two young girls, and our son, who'd rebelled against him and needed him so much. I'd lash out at the doctors who couldn't do a damn thing to save John. And I'd scream at God, demanding to know how he could will such a thing, and curse him and shout at him to go to hell, and laugh, and then turn on myself and flail away with accusations of having failed John, of not having done more to save him. No one—not Papa, or Mama, or Gerda, or Marlene—no one could reason with me. I'd nod, agree that I'd done everything possible, and close my eyes and wonder why I didn't take him in my arms and hold him and never let him go, never let those people in the hospital take him away. The thought of the hospital would cause me to weep, and I'd wail, "Why? Why?" And I'd wonder how I could go on without him.

I wouldn't. I started talking to him inside myself, as if he were alive and could hear me, and I'd say, "I'll never let you go, never let you go." And when I'd scream, "How could you abandon me? Leave me alone with two little girls?" He'd say, "I haven't abandoned you; I'll always be with you." "But you're dead." "Don't tell me that." He seemed angry. I felt so relieved I was wrong, and he was right. I always trusted him, and when he told me he wasn't dead, I nuzzled my face against his neck and whispered, "Thank you, thank you." He wrapped his arms around me, and I could feel the weight of his body, holding me tight, and then I could sleep. In the morning, he'd be gone, and I'd start to cry. He disappeared over and over again.

But still, I didn't believe he'd never come back. Sometimes I'd feel his presence and think if I were just quick enough, I'd see him before he could disappear. I'd feel him near me as I slept in the morning and snap my eyes open to catch a glimpse of his head on the other pillow, and he'd vanish in a blur. I'd be walking through a store and sense I was seeing him in the corner of my eye and look and he'd be gone. One day I saw a man in a brown overcoat, slacks, and a fedora, just like John used to wear, pushing a grocery cart ahead of me down the produce aisle. I pulled close to him. He stopped to look over some grapes, and I stopped to look at some apples, glancing at him, seeing part of the side of his face. He picked up a bunch of grapes and looked them over, and I picked up an apple and held it to my nose as I looked at him out of the corner of my eye and watched him put the grapes in a bag, and the bag in the cart, and start moving forward. I placed the apple in my cart and followed him. When I was sure it was John, because he had John's gait and his way of looking around, I pulled up next to him and looked over and said, "John, John, I'm so happy—"

He looked at me and said, "What?" And I saw it wasn't John, but I kept on staring, and the man returned my look, his brow furrowed. I couldn't believe it wasn't John, but it wasn't.

I felt so embarrassed, all I could do was mumble, "Sorry, excuse me, I thought you were someone else." I turned my cart and pushed it a few feet and left it and ran out of the store.

I never felt so alone as I did during those first years after John's death. Papa, Mama, family, friends, they'd ask me if I was going to be all right, and I'd nod. "I'll be okay, just need time." I couldn't tell them I wasn't doing fine, wasn't getting better, couldn't sleep at night, and when I did sleep, I didn't want to wake up. I fantasized and dreamt I was falling from tall buildings, walking off cliffs, taking a step and finding my legs were gone and collapse to the floor, pounding it with my fists and screaming, "God damn it, this isn't fair." But I could see things other people couldn't, like John smiling and putting his arms around me—people never saw that. And I had so many prescriptions to make sure I'd do well—Valium, Seconal, and the others, everything I needed to kill myself. Some people didn't really want to know how I was doing. They'd look at me like they were afraid I might tell them, and they'd smile and say they were happy I was doing okay and move on, before I might change my mind and tell them the truth.

When someone would ask me what the kids and I were doing for Christmas, I'd say, "Oh, Santa's coming, same as always." And I'd think, This year he's bringing memories of a dead father and husband, and maybe we should decorate the tree with pictures of John and the girls and David and me, and maybe we could find lights that resemble John's green eyes and turn them on and look at them all night long. And when people would ask how the kids were doing, I'd take a deep breath and say, "They'll be okay," and try not to blurt the truth—that I was a horrible mother, my son had run away, I'd forgotten Patty's birthday, and Linda's too, and my poor kids were lost, and if I were a good mother none of that would've happened. And sometimes, when people would say things to me, I'd stare at them, like there was something wrong with them, or I couldn't hear what they were saying, as if there were a wall between us.

I needed walls. Needed them so my grief wouldn't consume me. The girls always had the radios in the house tuned to a popular-music station called WeeGee, and I'd turn the radio in the kitchen up so loud that "Can't Get No Satisfaction" and "All You Need Is Love" would blast through the house. The girls would come running in and stare at me as if to say, What are you doing? And I'd act surprised. "Is it loud?" Or I wouldn't say anything, and they'd shake their heads and leave. I'd get up in the morning and make breakfast for them and see them off to school, and I was fine until I closed the door and turned around and sensed the emptiness of the house, the silence in which I could feel John's presence, and his voice would whisper, "I'll always be with you."

I'd take a shower, think of him, and begin to cry and lean against the wall, and if one of the girls were home and heard me, she'd come into the bathroom and say, "Mom, Mom, are you all right?"

And I'd say, "Yes, I'm fine, I'll be right out." I'd stay in the shower until the hot water was gone, and then turn off the shower and stand there and weep, too weak to do anything, or lean against the wall and beat it with my fists and sob, "I don't want to live."

Sometimes I was oblivious of everyone. Everything. The kids, the house, the sidewalk I didn't shovel, the grass I didn't mow, the burner on the stove I'd leave on under a frying pan until smoke filled the house and one of the girls would run to the kitchen and turn it off. I'd wake up in the morning and find the lights on in the living room and the front door wide open, like someone had come and gone, and I'd wonder right away if it was John. And I'd tell myself, You have to close the door and lock it, you have to lock it before you go to bed, anyone could walk in. And I'd go to the kitchen to make some coffee and start the day, and I'd think, If I lock the door, John might not be able to get in. And then I'd remember he couldn't come back, and I'd fall, like the ground underneath me had disappeared. I'd fall, and nothing could hold me up. Nothing. Nothing... nothing... nothing.

While I was grocery shopping, I put a large bottle of ginger ale in the cart, without knowing why. That night, after the girls had gone to bed, I went downstairs to the bar in the rec room, brought up a bottle of Four Roses, got the ginger ale out of the refrigerator, and made myself a highball. The first one in years. I took a drink. The whiskey resonated through the sweet tang of the soda, and it tasted so good. I took another. I went into the living room, sat down in the armchair, and picked up a magazine with an article about Jackie Kennedy that I'd left on the table. Ever since JFK's murder, magazines would come out with articles about JFK, Jackie, and the assassination. This one was full of pictures of her—like the one of her dressed in black and standing on the Capitol steps, between Bobby and Teddy, watching the funeral procession go by. I saw the anguish in her face, her furrowed brow and eyes staring at nothing visible through the black veil. She's completely alone, even though she's surrounded by people. With one hand she holds her daughter Caroline's hand, and with the other, John-John's. The children wear matching light blue coats, white socks, and red shoes, and their outfits make them look like they're about

111

to perform in a musical for children—except they're not. They look off, as if lost in another world. They're too young to know what's really happening. And then there was the picture that everyone loved, the one of Jackie and the children, and Bobby and Teddy, standing at the bottom of the steps, and John-John saluting the coffin of his father as it passed. And that was followed by the picture of Jackie walking in the funeral procession between Bobby and Teddy—and again I saw the pain in her face through the veil. In all the pictures, from the one of her in the pink, blood-splattered suit, taken minutes after the assassination, to the one taken at Arlington Cemetery, when a bishop handed her the American flag that had covered JFK's coffin during the procession, I saw a wounded woman standing strong.

I got up, went to the kitchen, made myself another highball, and returned to the living room and continued looking at the pictures. They made me feel the grief of this widow, with two young children, isolated by her loss, vulnerable to all the snooping and gossiping. I admired her; she was a good mother. And then I thought of myself, and for the thousandth time I told myself I was a horrible mother. I wasn't protecting my children. I was numbing myself with Valium and Seconal, and still I'd wake up in the middle of the night expecting to find John—and discover the source of the warmth I'd felt wasn't John, but a heating pad. And then I'd take a sleeping pill and enter the dark, the darkness lit by his presence, and in the morning the girls would try to wake me, whispering, and then shouting, "Mom, Mom, we're late, get up." I'd sit up and shake my head, like I could shake it out of one world and into another, and look at the clock and realize school had already started. I had to get up and drive them. I had to go on living and try to be a good mother for my girls and my son, who was God knows where, but I wasn't strong enough to let go of John. I couldn't live with grief, and I couldn't stop grieving, because I couldn't let him die.

The next night, I made myself another highball. I sat in the armchair and went back over the article and the pictures and nearly drowned in the same swamp as the night before. After taking a deep breath and a drink, I realized I'd been staring at the fireplace, with the wire mesh screen concealing the ashes from the fire I'd made Christmas Eve, the last one with John before he died, over two years ago. As I thought of that Christmas and the ashes, I played with the ring on my left hand, twisting it around one way and the other, back and forth. And then I moved it to my right hand.

The next morning, after the girls had left for school, when I'd usually leave for work, until I'd lost my job, I went to the closet that John and I had shared and slid the hangers on his side back and forth, looking at his clothes, telling myself I needed to take them to Goodwill—and feeling if I did, I'd be abandoning him. And then I took a deep breath and told myself, I have to do this, and went through my side of the closet, pushing hangers out of the way, stopping at one dress after another, until I came to a black sleeveless gown that I'd always liked. I held the dress over my body and looked down at it, and then tossed it on the bed, put on a black slip and the dress, and looked at myself in the mirror on the wall. The dress, which had been a snug fit when I'd bought it a few years before, drooped, and my eyes drooped with it. Then they drifted up my baggy dress and my skinny arms to my scrawny neck, my narrow lips sagging at the corners, my hollow cheeks, and my lifeless eyes. The longer I looked in the mirror, the deeper my eyes seemed to sink, the blacker the rings around them, and the more gaunt my face appeared. I unzipped the dress, let it fall to the floor, and lay down. I probably would've burst into tears if I'd had any left, but my eyes were dry, my mind numb.

I looked for a job until it was time for the girls to come home from school. After we'd had dinner and they'd gone to bed, I put the black dress on, looked at myself in the mirror, decided I didn't care if I looked like a scarecrow, and drove to The Black Lagoon, a bar near one of the bakeries that John had sold before he died. I entered and stopped just inside the door. On one side, people sat in black cushioned booths along the wall, and on the other, a few men and a couple women sat at a black Formica bar, facing glass shelves with bottles and a mirror that rose to the ceiling. Recessed lights along the base of the bar and the counter beneath the mirror and in the ceiling created a warm glow that welcomed me into this dark space, and as I walked past the people at the bar and headed for a black-cushioned stool with an empty seat on either side, a juke box played "Eleanor Rigby." I felt as if I'd found the answer to the question, "All the lonely people, where do they all belong?" No one seemed to notice me when I sat down and put my purse on the bar. I looked up and down the black surface, with specks of gold and silver, at the people leaning against it or hunched over it, and at the martini glasses and whiskey tumblers and beer bottles and ashtrays and smoke from the cigarettes rising toward the ceiling. And then, while I was looking at the rows of bottles behind the bar and at my image in the mirror, a man stopped in front of me, blocking my view, and laid his hand on the bar.

"What'll you have?"

"A highball."

"Okay. And what would you like in it?"

"Ginger ale and whiskey."

He smiled. "Any particular whiskey?"

I knew the name of just one. "Four Roses."

He nodded and moved off to make my drink.

I stayed for over an hour. The bar was a place where I could be alone, with other people, and not feel lonely. Not be some Eleanor Rigby. I enjoyed the noise, the voices talking over one another, the occasional bursts of laughter and loud exclamations about things that meant nothing to me, and the music—the Beatles, and Simon and Garfunkel, and the Supremes—never played so loud that it irritated me or prevented my mind from wandering. I remembered the Rhinelander and the feeling of being part of a small, intimate world, where everyone seemed happy. I sat there relaxed, alone, and content.

I returned frequently. The bartenders would see me walking toward the bar and make my highball and serve it to me within seconds after I sat down. I loved the soft light, the glow, and the shadows. And I noticed more of the bar's details over time—like the poster of *Creature from the Black Lagoon*, in which the green monster, with gills on his neck and big red lips, sinks deep into the blue water, holding in his arms the heroine, in a white bathing suit with breasts like cones, her red lips open in a scream.

I was sitting at the bar, smoking, drinking, staring at the gold glow of the whiskey in the bottles and at a fragment of my face in the mirror, when someone sat down next to me.

A man's voice said, "You come here a lot."

I took a puff and blew smoke at my fragmented image and tapped my cigarette against the edge of the ashtray.

"You're always alone."

Again, I didn't say anything.

"I'm alone too." He took a drink of something. "My wife died a few years ago."

I looked to my side and saw a man with brown hair cut in a buzz, a thin face, and brown eyes gazing at me with a kind of sad sympathy that held my eyes. I took another puff and blew the smoke past him, while looking him over. He was wearing a plaid shirt and a sport jacket, and looked to be about forty, maybe a little older, but definitely younger than me. His arms were resting on the bar, one hand holding a cigarette, the other a tumbler.

I stubbed my cigarette out, and he took a puff and stubbed his out too.

"My husband died. Over two years ago."

He nodded. "I kind of thought you'd experienced some sort of loss. You want to be alone, but not all alone. I know that feeling."

"That's why I come here."

"I know what you're going through. People always ask how you're doing and if you're getting out much, and they tell you, you need to get out, you need to have a life of your own."

"Yeah, so I can get over the loss of my husband. Like that's what I want."

He sneered. "Like getting over the flu, right? I mean, the way they talk about it." He nodded. "I remember that kind of stuff."

"You do?"

"Yeah."

"Is that why you come here?"

"That's one reason. I also like to have a drink now and then." He looked over at me and chuckled. "I'm not perfect." He saw my glass was nearly empty. "You want another? I'm buyin'."

"Okay."

He caught the bartender's eye and pointed at my glass and his. And then he said, "You wanna talk about what it's been like the last couple years?"

I shook my head. "For now, I just want silence."

"Yeah."

He gently laid his hand on mine. At first, I was going to pull my hand out from underneath his. I thought of looking at him and saying, Your hand is on top of mine. But I didn't say anything, just left my hand beneath his. I liked the feeling of his large hand covering mine, sending its warmth into me, and for the first time since I'd understood that John would die, I felt I could have a life.

The bartender returned and set our drinks down—a tumbler of whiskey on the rocks and my highball. Ken let go of my hand, reached for his whiskey, and looked like he was about to take a drink, when he paused, with the glass a few inches from his lips. He looked at me and said, "Maybe we should, you know, clink glasses, the way they do in the movies, to celebrate."

I found that amusing and said, "Okay."

We clinked our glasses, he grinned and nodded at me, and we drank, our eyes glowing at one another.

I took a puff of my cigarette and stared into the dark, tears blurring my vision, remembering how good I'd felt that night twenty years ago, and how I felt a few months later when I learned Ken's wife was alive. You're such a fool, I thought, shaking my head. How stupid! Some people never learn. I stubbed the cigarette in the ashtray, started the motor, lurched forward and swung into Patty's driveway, almost slamming into the rear end of Linda's car, backed out and nearly hit David's, and floored the accelerator, peeling out of there like a teenager. A dumb teenager.

David

In the dark space of a deep sleep, a hand grabbed my neck, and I felt myself pinned against a wall. My eyes popped open, and I saw my father's face red with rage, his piercing eyes, his teeth bared, and his fist pulled back. Mom threw herself between us and screamed, "Stop, John. STOP!"

I sat up, gasping, looking for his fist, but didn't see it. He wasn't going to hit me, because what I'd seen was a dream. He was dead, this had happened long ago, and I was safe. Scared, shaking, but safe. I looked around the room, saw the heap off to the side, and after a few seconds, recognized the rocker piled high with cushions and my clothes on top. I sat up on the edge of the bed and leaned forward, my head collapsing into my hands, my elbows resting on my knees. Sleep opens the door to dreams, dreams open the door of time, and anything can come back, anything can happen again.

Still trying to catch my breath, I turned on the lamp, saw my pants on the rocker, put them on, stepped into the dining room, and let my eyes adjust to the dark beyond the light in which I stood. The night outside the living-room window was dimly lit by the stars and the moon. In the shadow next to the window, I detected the shapes of the end table and the armchair. I walked to the chair, collapsed, and took deep breaths while hearing Mom scream, "Stop!" I couldn't remember how old I was, probably twelve or thirteen, or what I'd done wrong, but I'd never forget the fear I'd felt so frequently when I was young, the fear that lived inside me and generated anger and hatred that fermented and distilled into an inner rage that he would tap one night.

Maybe he'd had reason to hate me. I wasn't an easy kid to manage. That's probably why he and Mom sent me to that Catholic military academy on Summit Avenue, where I became one of the cadets who wore military-like uniforms—blue shirts, black ties, gray wool pants with a black stripe down the side, and black shoes that we were supposed to polish and buff until they shined like mirrors. The upper classmen were officers, we were privates, and they bossed us around. They had us line up in formation so they could inspect us, march us back and forth, and bark their orders at us, and we were supposed to salute them and respond, "Yes, sir," anytime they addressed us. By the end of my first semester, I'd salute them and say, "Yes sir, no sir, anything you say, sir," and wear my hat at an angle, with the black visor pushed back, my tie loosened, the top buttons of my shirt undone, and my shoes and fake gold buttons and brass badges unpolished.

The academy was a prep school, too, but Dad and Mom didn't send me there to be prepped for college. They'd never talked to me about going to college, probably because they'd never gone and had done well for themselves. I assumed after high school I'd get whatever job I could and move off on my own, and that was fine with me. But then why was I studying Latin? And taking a course on religion? And did I really need to know anything about algebra for what lay ahead? And as for history and English, I loved to read, but had no interest in learning grammar or memorizing dates. So, some of my teachers weren't terribly fond of me. Like my religion teacher. The day I informed him for the hundredth time I'd forgotten to do my homework, he got up from his desk, came over, stood in front of mine, and looked down at me. I was scared, because he was thick chested and broad shouldered and rumored to have been a boxer before becoming a priest, and I could imagine the huge biceps under the sleeves of his cassock. But as he lectured me about my responsibility to do my homework, I started to relax and wondered how long he'd drone on before he'd go back to his desk. Then his hand came flying out of nowhere and whacked my face so hard my head snapped one way and then the other. That was the one thing he did that left an impression. The course was a joke. We'd study passages from a missal, and the tests would include the same passages, with key words removed, and we'd fill in the blanks. My lousy grades didn't bother me at all.

At a meeting the headmaster called with Dad, Mom, and me, he informed them my academic performance was unacceptable, I had more demerits than any other student, frequently talked back to the officers, and had become such a disruptive force that the school was expelling me. When Mom tried to defend me by arguing I was a smart boy, loved to read, and could certainly do much better next year if allowed to return, the headmaster leaned forward, his eyes bore into her, and he said, "Mrs. Habermann, permit me to give you two examples of your son's unacceptable behavior. He learned somehow that the first name of our Latin teacher, Father Dooley, is Thomas, and he and some of his friends would enter and leave the class singing a song called, 'Hang down your head Tom Dooley,' a song about a murderer. And the other example. One morning, Father Dooley discovered a chalk drawing of him on the wall outside his classroom that made his cassock look like a dress and gave him a belly that resembled a pregnant woman's. And next to the image, someone had written, 'Mother Dooley.' That someone was your son."

Mom didn't have a response, and Dad sat rigid, saying nothing. Once we were outside the office, I got a look at Dad's face and could tell from the way his jaw was set and his eyes smoldered that I'd get the crap beat out of me when we got home. That didn't happen. Sometimes he surprised me. I never knew when he'd explode. I did talk to Mom, though, and told her I had nothing to do with the Tom Dooley song or the drawing of Mother Dooley on the wall, but I knew about them.

She studied my face, waiting, and when I didn't grin and blush, which I always did when I tried to lie to her, she asked, "Why didn't you say something?"

"I don't wanna go back to that school."

"You should tell your father."

"Why? I'm still expelled."

She gazed at me for a while, and then nodded. "I'll talk to him. I want him to know the truth."

"Mom."

"Yeah."

"Father Dooley, in his cassock, he does kind of look like a pregnant woman."

She laughed and shook her head. "But you didn't do the drawing."

"I didn't."

I always suspected the military academy was Dad's idea, because he was all about discipline. He disciplined me to be a worker and started working me once a week in one of his bakeries, the Ginny Ann, when I was eight, having me clean the basement where he stored the sacks of flour and buckets of fruit puree. And by the time I was twelve, I was working Saturdays as a baker. We'd say nothing to one another when he drove us to work at six in the morning or as we worked through the day. Sometimes he'd set down a doughnut or a Danish next to my cup of coffee, about the closest thing to an affectionate gesture that I ever saw from him, and I'd thank him and eat it while continuing to work.

He never said, I love you, and never complimented me when I did something well. But when I screwed up . . . One Friday night, I stayed out late, snuck in the house, tiptoed to my room, and slipped into bed. I was supposed to get up early the next morning and go to work with him. He shook my shoulder, and when I didn't wake up, he slapped me, and that slap stung like a belt across my face and penetrated my consciousness with an edge a hundred times sharper than a baby's shriek. I leapt out of bed, threw on my clothes, and showed up in the kitchen to find him drinking his coffee, smoking his cigarette, and glaring at me. "Out bummin' again?" *Out bummin*—that was one of his favorite expressions. If I hung out with friends, did what other kids did, I was out bummin', up to no good, and he'd glare at me with disgust that could morph into rage in a second, and when it did, I'd freeze, because a slap was coming. And if he whipped off his belt, I'd cower, because in seconds I'd feel its sting. But sometimes the disgust passed, and nothing happened. Not only were his outbursts of violence unpredictable, I often didn't know what I'd done wrong, if anything. I learned early on the best thing to do was avoid him. When he entered a room, I'd try to leave without him noticing.

I wanted to leave for good and looked for every way to get out. I took a job working in a supermarket, stocking shelves, and packing groceries, so I didn't have to work with him. With my money, I could buy my own clothes and look cool, like James Dean or Elvis Presley, a look that provoked a disdainful stare from the old man when he'd see me. But on Saturday nights, if I wanted a car to go out with friends or with a girl and maintain my cool image, I had to borrow his brand-new white Buick convertible, with a red leather interior, or else take Mom's car, a tiny Morris Minor that he'd given her for her birthday and that sounded like it was farting when I drove it. Fridays and Saturdays, he'd get home from work after Mom and my two sisters and I'd finished eating, go downstairs to the rec room, sit in his armchair with a small table in front of it, and watch Perry Mason as he ate dinner. I'd come down, stand nearby, and ask, "Dad, can I borrow your car tonight?" No answer. A few minutes later, "Dad, would it be okay if I used your car?" Still no answer. I'd lean against the bar, just a few feet from his chair, and continue asking, when there was a commercial or a pause in the action.

This might go on for ten minutes, until Mom, sitting on the couch, with Patty and Linda close to her, would say, "John, would you please just give him an answer."

Either he'd ignore her or say, "Goin' out bummin'?"

I saved my money that summer and bought a black 1950 Ford, just like the one Robert Mitchum's character drove in *Thunder Road*, and thought, Fuck you, old man.

The first day of my junior year at the public high school, I was sitting in English, trying as always to look cool—my shirt unbuttoned to my chest, the back of my collar turned up, my Brylcreemed hair combed so a lock would fall across my brow and the corner of my eye, and that look, that look of contempt and disdain that the rebel always has for his surroundings and for what other people call the real world. Yeah, I had all that when I was sitting there, waiting for the teacher to enter. A couple minutes after the bell rang, she walked in on her high heels, clicking across the front of the room, wearing a tight skirt, a blouse, and a colorful scarf around her neck. She had brown hair swept back and falling to within an inch of her shoulders, and a face that looked sculpted, with a strong jaw and chin and high cheek bones. When she got to her desk, she turned, leaned against it, introduced herself as Miss Mueller, and asked us

121

to introduce ourselves and say something about our interests. The students did what she asked, but when my turn came, I said my name and nothing else. Everyone looked at me, waiting, while I stared off, like I hadn't done anything unusual. And then Miss Mueller said, "You got caught smoking and got kicked off the football team." I looked at her. She was waiting for me to say something. When I didn't, she said, in a stern voice, "I want to see you after class." I would've skipped the meeting if she hadn't been the most beautiful woman I'd ever seen. The bell rang, the students left, and she stood near her desk responding with a smile to those who said goodbye on their way out. When they were gone, I approached her. Her eyes locked onto mine, and her lips spread just enough to suggest she might be amused by the cool guy.

"How did you know I got kicked off the team?"

"Everyone knows. You think that's cool?"

I smiled.

"I don't have time to talk now, but I'd like to see you at the end of the day."

"Why? What did I do?"

"I imagine you've done all kinds of things."

"Yeah, so you've probably heard a lot of negative stories about me."

"I've heard negative and positive."

"Positive? Really?"

"I'll be waiting for you."

At the end of the day, I stood in front of my locker, thinking about leaving, but went to her room and found her sitting at her desk, looking at some papers. She got up and pointed in the direction of the front desks of two rows and said we could sit there. We turned the desks to face one another and sat down, and I looked at her radiant eyes and red lips. Maybe I was already fantasizing something.

As we talked, it became obvious she knew all about my sophomore year— getting kicked out of Latin, nearly flunking second-year Algebra, and never being prepared for class. After a pause, she asked, "David, what do you plan on doing after you graduate?"

The question surprised me. No one had ever asked. I wondered for a minute if I should trust her, and decided I would. "I want to be a drifter and keep a journal."

She grinned and bit her lip at the same time. "Do you like to write?"

"I don't know. I've never tried." I reflected. "I kind of dream about it."

"And how would you earn a living, if you're a drifter, keeping a journal?"

"I'd find a way."

"Ever thought about going to college?"

"No."

"Anyone ever *talk* to you about going to college?"

I shook my head.

"You like to read?"

"Yeah."

"What do you read?"

"Novels."

"What's your favorite novel?"

"*War and Peace*." Her eyes bulged. I explained, "I didn't get to see the movie when it came out, so I read the book."

"What do you like about reading?"

"Escaping into another world. If I really like the novel I'm reading, I feel sad when I come to the last page. I don't want the story to end."

She smiled and nodded. "I think we can work together."

We continued to meet and talk, often about me, my interests, and my future. I started preparing for and participating in the discussions about nineteenth century writers, like Thoreau, whose *Walden Pond* I loved, and about the expatriate writers, Fitzgerald and Hemingway, whom I admired because they'd done exactly what I wanted to do—be my own man and leave and let my curiosity and my dreams be my guide. Other teachers began to treat me differently. My psychology teacher got into a conversation with me about Freud, and soon I was checking out books like *The Interpretation of Dreams*. The speech teacher asked if I'd be interested in auditioning for the school play, and I got the role of the hero in a comic melodrama, *A Fate Worse Than Death; Or, Adrift on Life's Sea*. At night, I'd sometimes have trouble sleeping and would get up, go to the living room, and sit in this armchair. Once in a while, I'd find Mom already there, reading one of the books we were discussing in class. I'd sit in the other chair and tell her about my meetings with Miss Mueller, and all the positive things she was telling me, like maybe I should go to college, because—according to her—I was smart and talented, and she was afraid I'd waste my gifts if I didn't go. Mom nodded in agreement and told me how happy she was I had Miss Mueller for a teacher.

I'm sure Mom knew I had a crush on Maria, as I called Miss Mueller in my dreams, after I'd learned her first name through the grapevine, but she might not have guessed I fantasized making love with her. To realize that fantasy, I had to get closer, more intimate. One day, Maria and I were talking about what we liked to do on the weekends, now that winter was gone. She mentioned that sometimes she'd take a lawn chair to Lake Calhoun and recline on it and read next to the lake, it was so relaxing. I said, "What a coincidence, I like going to that lake, too." She was surprised we'd never met.

I'd never been there before, but I found it that Sunday, on the west side of south Minneapolis, and drove around it looking for her, wishing I had Dad's convertible. The wish turned into a fantasy in which I saw myself driving around the lake with the top down, my right arm stretched out across the back of the passenger seat, like I was already positioned for her to get in, a breeze sifting through my hair, and a cigarette hanging out of the corner of my mouth. She'd see me looking so cool and wave and get up from her chair and come running toward me in her bathing suit, a grin on her face, because she'd been hoping for the same thing. And as soon as she got in the car, my dream would come true. I completed my tour of the lake but didn't see her.

The following Saturday, I got off work early and tried again. This time I spotted her, in a bathing suit, her legs extended on a lawn chair, talking with four men, in slacks and short-sleeve shirts, who were sitting on the grass and looking up at her, like she was a goddess—wearing sunglasses. I stopped the car. As I watched her admirers, my heart sank. I decided to hell with it, I'd come this far, I might as well find out who my competition was. Maria removed her glasses as I walked toward her, and the men's eyes followed hers and looked up at me. She said, "David, what a wonderful surprise! I'm so happy to see you." She introduced me to the men as one of her students, and introduced them to me as her friends, musicians who were scheduled to perform that night at The Padded Cell, a club over on Lake Street. I sat down near a couple of them and gazed up at Maria, who put on her dark glasses and smiled down upon us. The conversation picked up, and the men talked about Miles Davis, John Coltrane, Charlie Mingus, and other jazz musicians, as they vied for her attention. I couldn't find anything to say. After what felt like an hour of sitting in silence, ignored by everyone, I stood and said, "Well, it was good to see you Ms. Mueller. Thanks for introducing me to your friends. And, ah, I really enjoyed listening to everything you guys had to say about jazz. I, ah, don't really know anything. I mean, I know some things, but, ah, well, I need to get going. Good to meet you. Goodbye." I tried to smile at Maria, who stared at me through the lenses that concealed her eyes, and at the men, and turned around and walked away, feeling like shit, imagining the men looking at one another, sneering, and shaking their heads. As I drove off, I realized my fantasies of making love to Ms. Mueller would never come true. I felt depressed for days, as I mourned the loss of my dream.

Two things helped me get over my loss. I came onstage and swooped the heroine off her feet as I performed my lines with heroic gusto to cheers and applause.

And I met Sandy. Thanks to my best friend, Buddy, who brought me to a graduation party, even though my graduation was still a year off. He'd already been to the house on White Bear Lake, beyond the suburbs of St. Paul, so he drove us to the party. The sun was low on the horizon when we reached the lake and cruised down a narrow blacktop street. Buddy leaning forward, looking past me at the vacation houses along the shore, until he found the right one. We got out and walked up the edge of the driveway, past some parked cars, toward the front door. Halos glowed in the windows, and couples, their arms wrapped around one another, moved in and out of the glow, dancing to the muted music.

Buddy opened the door to the sound of Bobby Darin singing "Dream Lover," and we stepped inside the living room and stopped to look at the couples dancing in the glow of candles and the murky haze of cigarette smoke. The kid throwing the party came up and said, "Hey, man, good to see you." While he and Buddy talked, I tried to see if I could recognize anyone, and did, but none of them were kids I hung out with. A door off to the side opened, a girl walked out of a dimly lit room, a smirk on her face, and a kid with a beer in his hand followed, leaving behind a double bed with a rumpled quilt. I followed Buddy and his pal through the living room to the dining room, weaving our way among the dancers, getting bumped and elbowed. We passed another bedroom, with two girls and a guy lolling on the bed and veered around couples toward the other side of the room where a table stood covered with stacks of records, a portable hi-fi, and wine bottles corked with lit candles. Next to the table, a kid in jeans and a T-shirt, with one sleeve rolled up over a pack of cigs, was going through the singles, picking out the next one. We continued on to the kitchen, where a metal tub full of ice sat on a table. Buddy's pal grabbed a couple of beers out of the ice, snapped the caps off, and handed them to us. Buddy and I took a swig. While he and the kid talked, I scanned the porch onto which the kitchen opened and the row of windows that looked out on the last rays of the sun shimmering like red liquid copper on the surface of the lake.

That view drew me to the porch and out the screen door to the backyard, where kids sat around a picnic table and on lawn chairs and blankets spread out on the grass. I walked past them to the dock, stopped at the end, and looked out at the shimmering copper and around at the shore, and at the weeping willows, the neighboring docks, and the large lots that distanced the houses from one another. I took a swig and watched some ducks flying low, skimming across the surface of the water, and nestling together in a little inlet. Footsteps caught my attention, and I turned around to see a girl in a blue-jean jacket and jeans, with the bottoms rolled up above her penny loafers and white bobbysocks. She pulled a red candle globe out of a bag, smiled, and said she wanted to put a couple of them where I was standing, so people could see where the dock ended. I stepped aside and walked back toward the house, hearing Bobby Vee singing "Take Good Care of My Baby," and thought, I'd love to find a babe I could take care of. I looked around at the kids sitting together, but didn't notice anyone alone, and went into the house and got another beer.

I couldn't see Buddy anywhere. He might've been one of the kids dancing in that obscure space beyond the glow of the candles. I headed outside, looked around, and saw a girl sitting alone, next to a couple of empty lawn chairs, a beer in one hand and a cigarette in the other. She had her brown hair pulled back in a loose coil and wore a blouse and a skirt that ended just above her knees. I walked toward her, gazing at her raised chin, the clear line of her jaw, and the strands of hair that had escaped the sweep backward and fell across her thin neck. I stopped in front of the first of the three chairs and said, "Hi. Can I join you?"

She looked up, her head cocked to one side. "Who are you?"

"David."

She snickered. "David who?"

I chuckled. "Yeah. Really. David Habermann. I'm a friend of Buddy."

"I know Buddy, but—"

"So now you can get to know me."

She looked me in the eye and finally said, "Sit down, if you want."

She took a drink and a drag of her cigarette and watched me, as I settled into the chair next to her and looked out at the red sunlight disappearing along the horizon and then at her to find she was now gazing at the lake.

"You haven't told me *your* name," I said.

She took another drag, looked at me, as if wondering whether she wanted to tell me, and said, "Sandy. I don't remember seeing you at graduation."

"I didn't graduate."

"So, when do you?"

"I've got a year to go. What are you gonna do, now that you've graduated?"

"I've got a job for the summer, and then I'm going to Minneapolis School of Art."

"You're an artist?"

"An artist? I don't know. I liked the art courses I took, and wanna take more. How about you? You know what you wanna do?"

"Someone asked me that last fall, and I said I wanted to be a drifter and keep a journal."

She laughed, while repeating what I'd said. "So, what would you write?"

"I have no idea." I looked at her, and our eyes met. "I've changed my mind, though. I'm gonna go to college."

"Like everyone else." Her voice fell, as if she were disappointed.

She turned her attention toward the lake, and I gazed at the profile of her face before looking out at the globes glowing at the end of the dock. The sound of the voices of the kids talking and laughing in the yard and of Buddy Holly singing inside filled part of our night, while the other part was an invisible cocoon of silence, in which I felt Sandy's presence, the warmth of her forearm and her hand on the armrest of her chair almost touching mine. I moved my hand a little closer.

"Are you here with anyone?" I asked.

"A friend. She's dancing with someone."

Still gazing at the dock, I moved my hand again until it touched hers. She glanced at me, looked back out at the lake, and left her hand in place. I wanted to hold her, feel her body close to mine, and the only way I could do that was by dancing with her. I was building up my courage to ask, when Bobby Freeman started singing, "Do You Wanna Dance?" I looked at her, her eyes fixed on mine, and said, "You wanna?"

And she said, "Yeah." We got up, went inside, and found an opening among the couples and started dancing.

When the song ended, there was a pause, and another guy, whom I couldn't see, took over the role of DJ. He played a very different kind of music—songs that created a melancholic and euphoric mood, like in a dream of being carried off by a love so intense it hurt and felt like a premonition of loneliness. Songs like "Only the Lonely," "Blue Angel," "I'm Hurtin'," and "Crying" by Roy Orbison; "I Fall to Pieces" and "Crazy" by Patsy Cline; and "You Send Me" and "Summertime" by Sam Cooke. We danced, and kept on dancing, even when the music stopped, and drew closer until our bodies pressed against one another, and her head rested on my shoulder, and my cheek against her hair.

Someone tapped my arm, and I saw Buddy grinning and shaking his head. "That's the third time I've tried to get your attention, pal. It's late, I gotta work in the morning."

I said, "Shit, so do I." I looked at Sandy and asked how I could get ahold of her.

She gasped and said, "My purse, where did I leave it?" She ran outside, and I followed her in the dark. She groped around the chair where she'd been

128

sitting, found her purse and sighed, and we returned to the kitchen. She tore out a page from her address book, handed the book to me, and I wrote my name and phone number in it, while she did the same for me on the torn page. She looked up at me, her eyes holding onto mine, her lips parted, as if she'd suddenly stopped breathing, and seeing how my eyes responded to hers, she smiled, and I brushed a long strand of hair off her cheek and bent over and kissed her, until Buddy said, "Come on, lover boy, we gotta go." As I turned to leave, a couple guys raised their bottles and cheered us, and I gazed at her, like my eyes could bring her with me, and then I let go and followed Buddy out the door.

I was useless in helping him find our way home, because my mind was still with Sandy. Buddy missed a turn somewhere in the dark, and we ended up driving around the lake until we came to a bend in the road that brought us close to the shore. I saw something and shouted, "Stop!"

Gazing at two lights glowing on the other side of the lake, I recognized the globes at the end of the dock and felt they were there to guide me back. I told Buddy about them. He said, "Shit, we missed our turn." He swung the car around, floored it, and we careened around the curve and sped down the straightaway. We got home, and I gently closed the door as I got out of the car, snuck into the house and into bed without waking the old man, and relived the night as I lay there in the dark, feeling Sandy's body pressed against mine.

The next day at work, when I was tossing cases of canned goods onto the conveyor belt and stocking shelves, I'd hear in my mind the songs Sandy and I'd danced to, and I would pause as I held her close and we danced under the moonlight. In the late morning, when I was on break, I called her, and we decided to go to the Rose Drive-In Theater that night. I turned off one of the county roads onto her street, curving back and forth, passing ramblers and two-story houses on large lots, with perfect lawns and young trees, and a few old-growth trees that stood like giants above the others, and parked in front of her house. I rang the bell, and Sandy opened, pulled me in, and kissed me, pressing herself against me like we were still dancing, and then took my hand and led me into the living room.

A painting on the wall above the couch seized my attention, and I stopped to gaze at the inlet surrounded by trees in the foreground, the opening between the trees in the center middle ground, where a short channel connected the inlet to a lake evoked by the open space in the background, and the miniscule woods near the vanishing point. The sun was hidden by the trees, but its light penetrated the inlet and illuminated the autumnal reds and golds of the leaves mirrored by the still water. In the areas of the inlet off to either side, where the sun couldn't reach, the surface of the water was murky, and the limb of a fallen tree rose out of the dark water like a skeletal hand. I gazed at the sunlight, the glow of the leaves, and the luminous reflections in the dark mirror and felt that the stillness of the woods and the water and the darkness concealed something. Somehow, I knew this scene.

"It's called *Autumn Woods*," Sandy whispered.

I nodded, mesmerized. I'd never seen a painting in a house before. My friends' parents hung framed photographs on the walls, and maybe a reproduction, like *The Last Supper*—everyone had that. Ours hung in the dining room. But real paintings, I'd only seen pictures of them, and none of them had captivated me the way *Autumn Woods* did.

Sandy took my hand and led me toward two portraits at the other end of the living room—one of a woman, with waves of white hair, gazing down at us with a benevolent smile, her hands folded on her lap, and the other of a man, in a suit and tie, with white hair, tight lips, and dark eyes devoid of warmth.

"They're my grandparents. The landscape you were looking at, they gave that to us. They collect art, and so does my mother."

I nodded again. My eyes wandered from the portraits to the dining room off to our right, and to the still lifes hanging on the walls on either side of a dark wood table that glistened in sunlight. That light flowed past the French doors, at the other end of the dining room, which opened onto another room, with three walls of windows that looked out on gardens and a lawn. Sandy said, "That's the sunroom." At the sound of her voice, a woman in an armchair looked up from whatever she was reading and rose and approached us. She was wearing a dress of woven gold and silver threads. Sandy introduced me to her mother, we shook hands, and her mother asked what we were planning on doing.

"Just going to the drive-in," Sandy said. Her mother wished us a good time, and we left. The casualness with which she sent us off made me feel I was just one of many guys who'd come to take Sandy out.

We drove down Snelling Avenue until we saw the white back of the theater's screen, decorated with a neon rose about forty feet tall and the words, ROSE DRIVE-IN / THEATRE, in pink letters above the flower. A long green neon stem, with the bottom end lying flat, curved one way and then the other as it rose to the bright red blossom that seemed to bow to its audience. The blossom and stem made me think of a girl acting coy, like Betty Boop, bending one way and then the other, while bowing her head and batting her lashes — the perfect image for a passion pit.

We headed for a row in the back, off to the side, where people would be less likely to pass us on their way to the concession stand, and parked next to one of the posts, with speakers attached on either side. Sandy slipped off her flats, pulled her feet up on the seat, and leaned into me. I laid my arm around her and placed my other hand on her cheek and kissed her, and we continued kissing, my hand moving from her cheek to her neck to the buttons on her blouse, but her hand grasped mine when I started unbuttoning one. I ran my fingers across her head and undid the coil that held her hair pulled back and felt it fall across my fingers, and she whispered, breathing deeply, "We'd better stop."

We pulled back, exhaled some of our excitement, and looked around. Still too much light. Wheels crunched the crushed rocks outside my window, a car pulled up next to ours, and a girl glanced at us. Sandy and I lit up, took deep drags, and listened to the music, while voices erupted as kids walked by her side of the car on their way to the concession stand. My eyes lingered on Sandy's hair flowing down to her shoulders. I couldn't resist touching it, running my fingers through it.

"Why do you always wear your hair pulled back?"

"I can't stand it getting in my way. I was doing a painting in class and brushed my hair back, with the hand I was holding the brush, and got paint all over my hair." She smiled. "But it's okay down when I'm with you."

"Hmm," I hummed, as I started winding a long strand around my finger. "I'm curious. There were a lot o' guys at the party last night. Why did you stick with me?"

131

"I don't know. Maybe because of what you said about wanting to be a drifter and keep a journal. I'd never heard anyone say anything like that before. Does that mean you wanna be a writer?"

"No, I think it means I wanna get the hell out of here and see the world, and write what I see, that's all."

"Now you'll have to wait until you finish college."

"Yeah, but I'm still leaving."

"My parents travel a lot. They go visit family and friends in Chicago. Visit museums and see musicals."

"And you?"

"I'd like to travel on my own. But I could never be a drifter." She shook her head. "I can just imagine the look on my parents' faces. Hey, Mom, Dad, I've decided I wanna be a drifter, and draw what I see. They'd have a fit."

We laughed so hard we snorted like pigs.

Light flashed through the dark to the screen, projecting a commercial for the concession stand and previews of upcoming films. I hung the speaker on my window, rolled the window shut, and the two of us started making out again. I ran my fingers through her hair, she rested her hand on my thigh, and we kept on kissing, as our hands wandered and undid buttons and zippers and hooks so we could explore and caress. I slid out from behind the steering wheel to the other end of the seat and stretched out, the back of my head resting against the door, and she lay on top of me. We continued kissing and caressing, until my pants and her skirt ended up on the floor, and we both gasped and panted as I penetrated her. I pulled out just in time and laughed like a hyena as I came all over us, and she laid her fingers across my mouth and whispered, "Shh," and kissed me.

Our bodies didn't separate until we could no longer ignore the puddle of love juice. She found some tissues in her purse, and we looked around to make sure no one was watching and wiped ourselves and lay back down. We watched The Savage Innocents, joking about Anthony Quinn and the Asian actresses with their Hollywood makeup playing Inuit characters, and laughed when one of the women danced like she was on American Bandstand. I said, "We're the real savage innocents," and we rubbed noses, did a tongue tango, and started licking and sucking. We would've made love again, if the film hadn't ended, and people hadn't started their cars and flipped on their headlights and made us feel like we were on stage.

While buttoning her blouse and pulling her hair back in a coil, Sandy grinned at me and said, "You know, I talked to my parents about me staying home when they go on their trips this summer. I told them I'm eighteen, I've graduated high school, and need to work. And they said, 'Okay.'" Sandy and I kissed, as if sealing a pact.

We made love nearly every night in my car at one or another drive-in, where we'd steam up the windows so we couldn't even see the film, and in the little parking lots along Mississippi River Boulevard or next to one of the lakes, where other couples would steam up theirs. We eventually found our own place, just off a vacant road, on the side of a lake, with tall reeds and cattails on the shore, where no one else ever parked. An office building stood on the other side, in an area of Roseville that had yet to be developed. But when Sandy's parents would go away, I'd concoct a story for mine about sleeping over at a friend's house, and Sandy and I would open up the couch in the sunroom, nestle down together, and make love all night long. She checked out a book from the library about the pleasures of sex, and we tried all the positions.

She was very open about her love of sex, unlike one of her friends, who got married that summer. While Sandy and I were driving to the church, she told me that when the girls would talk about sex in the bathroom at school, her friend would say, "'Oh, if my boyfriend ever tried doing it with me, I'd scream.'" Sandy laughed. "She must not've screamed too loud, because she's about five months pregnant." Luckily, the friend didn't start showing until after graduation. Sandy and I took no precautions, but she never seemed to worry about getting pregnant. She used to say, and always with a grin, "The Great Northern always pulls out on time, and if it feels like it might not, you give it a hand." She had a kind of fuck-you attitude that I loved, and maybe that was part of what attracted her to art, the attitude of some of the artists she talked about, like Salvador Dali and his weird paintings, with pocket watches lying as if they'd melted across tree limbs and dead things, and Magritte and the painting of the pipe with the words, *Ceci n'est pas une pipe.*

She'd also studied French and taught me to say, *"Veux-tu coucher avec moi?"*

133

And she'd respond, *"Oui, mon amour."*

One weekend afternoon, she picked me up in the Plymouth Valiant her parents had given her for graduation and drove us to Walker Art Center to see work by some of the rebels she'd talked about, but when we entered the building, I saw ahead of us, on a pedestal about four feet tall, a bronze bust that looked strangely familiar. As we got closer, I could see it was a bust of Maria Mueller. Stunned, I stopped to look at it, touch it. Sandy said it reminded her of Nefertiti. I'd seen pictures of that sculpture. I nodded, also seeing a resemblance, and said, "This is Maria Mueller, my English teacher."

Sandy exclaimed, "What!" and looked at it closely. She asked if Maria's cheekbones, jaw, and chin were really so pronounced.

I said, "Yes."

She said, "She's beautiful."

I smiled. The sculptor had proven me right about my infatuation with Maria. I looked at his name and realized he was one of the artists she'd invited to school to talk to her classes. Maybe the whole world was infatuated with her. The woman who'd helped me see myself in a new way wasn't a nobody. People respected her, and if she was worthy of such respect, then her respect for me was even more meaningful. It felt good to know she would always be here, and I could come and see her any time, any time I might feel down, might feel worthless, she'd be here.

Toward the end of the summer, I turned seventeen, and Sandy and I began talking about getting married. She started classes at the art school, I began my senior year of high school, and we could no longer see one another every evening. But we talked on the phone at night and spent weekend evenings together, and the weekends when her parents left, I'd find an excuse to spend the nights with her. The beautiful nights. We spent them together our second summer, too, when she did all the driving, because I blew out the motor of my Ford. But I'd no longer need a car, because at last I was leaving home.

Leaving for that little liberal arts college in Dubuque, Iowa. I'd applied to Dartmouth and Amherst, but with the grades I'd had the first two years of high school, that college was the best I could do. My father paid my tuition, room, and board, without complaining, and I wondered if he was happy to get rid of me. Mom drove me to the college and helped me move into the dorm—an old redbrick building, like most of the buildings on campus. When she left, she said she was so happy for me that I got to go to college, and she had tears in her eyes as she turned away and got in her car.

I wrote often to Mom and to Sandy, and at Christmas I came home, taking a train that followed the Mississippi up along the eastern borders of Iowa and Minnesota and over to St. Paul. As I sat at a table in the club car, drinking a beer and looking out at the cold dark river flowing south, I thought of Thomas Wolfe's long descriptions of train rides and the excitement of exploring the world I'd always felt when I'd read them, and I wanted the train to continue running on the tracks of my dreams to New York and Paris and other cities I knew from novels—until I realized we'd arrived in St. Paul. I thought of Sandy, grabbed my suitcase, and jumped off as soon as the train lurched to a stop. I weaved through the crowd on the platform, found her waiting for me, and dropped my suitcase and kissed her. We walked through the station with the tall ceilings and huge skylights and marble floors, and she took me to our place by the lake across from the office building. We made love, and afterward, as we held one another, she gazed into my eyes and whispered, "I love you. I love you so much."

She brought me home, and Mom hugged me like I'd been gone for years, and my sisters hugged me, too. We sat in the living room, on that couch over there in the dark, and I talked about how boring the little town in Iowa was and of wanting to transfer to the University of Minnesota. After Sandy left, we had dinner, and that night, or the next day, I did something to irritate the old man, he got angry, jutted his face into mine, his green eyes riveting me, and seethed, "It cost me a twenty-dollar bill for you to come home. A twenty-dollar bill." And I felt I wasn't worth the money. I spent the days leading up to Christmas making pfeffernüsse cookies in one of his bakeries. That might've made me worth something.

The vacation came to an end, Sandy drove me back to the station, the train pulled away, and we waved a slow, sad farewell, my forehead pressed against the window. But during her spring break, she drove down on a Friday to visit me and stayed in a motel. We spent the first night making love, and the morning, too. When she went to the bathroom, she screamed, "Oh, my God!"

and laughed. I ran in to find a horse staring in the window, its big brown eyes just a couple feet away. When it lowered its head to graze, we saw a field and more horses standing a ways off, staring at us.

We drove to a diner and had breakfast, and she talked about how St. Paul was changing and becoming more hip. She and a girlfriend had discovered a coffee shop on some narrow dark street downtown, where poets would go to read their tragic poems about love and loss, and each poem would be followed by a long silence, and people talking in hushed voices, like they were in church. She took my hands in hers, looked into my eyes, and bit her lip. When I asked her if something was wrong, she shook her head, smiled, and said no, and then looked away.

I felt anxious, wanted to talk to her, bring her back to me, so I told her about my friends to whom I was going to introduce her that afternoon—like the kid from New York, whose parents were dead, and whose older brother, a banker, had sent him to school here because he wanted to get him out of the city. The kid hated the Midwest, just as much as I did, because there was nothing here. He liked to repeat the line, "Go west, young man, go west," to which he would add, "Just don't stop in the middle," and we'd crack up laughing. He was going to go west and not stop until he got to San Francisco, where he planned on finishing his degree. And I talked about my friends who'd come to my room at night, and we'd discuss books until two in the morning. And I told her about Dostoyevsky, whom I'd discovered the previous summer. I asked her if she remembered McCosh's bookstore in Dinkytown, and at first, she seemed to draw a blank. I said he's the guy who looks like some patriarch from the Bible, or a Russian, with a huge black beard, and has a reputation for being an anarchist plotting to undermine the government. He'd noticed me sitting on the floor in front of one of the shelves, reading *Crime and Punishment*, and came over and talked to me about what a great writer Dostoyevsky was, possibly the greatest, and I bought every book by Dostoyevsky in the store and read all of his work translated into English.

She listened and nodded, with a fading smile that made me feel uneasy, and I asked, "What's the matter?"

She shook her head, as if she were shaking something off, and said, "Oh, I've just been feeling a little . . . strange lately." I gently squeezed her hands, and she looked into my eyes and gave me a firm smile that assured me everything was okay.

I showed her around the campus, introduced her to my friends, with whom we talked for a while, and then we ate dinner and saw a movie. The next morning, I looked out the bathroom window, and the horses were grazing at the other end of the field. We walked around town, down by the river, and had a pizza. Back at the motel, we were lying on the bed talking, when she asked, "Do you still want to marry me?"

"Of course I do."

"How would we live?"

"I don't know. I mean, you know, we'll find a way."

"What do you wanna do?"

"I don't know yet."

"Do you wanna be a writer?"

"I . . . I think that's kind of a dream." I had a queasy feeling in my stomach. She placed her hand on mine. Her eyes looked down.

I stayed the night, but we didn't make love. We just held one another, until we fell asleep. In the morning, I looked out the window, and the horses were gone. She drove me to my dorm, we kissed, just a quick kiss, and hugged. When I pulled back, I saw a mournful look through a mist of tears in her eyes and asked, "What's the matter?" She shook her head. "Write to me," I said. She nodded, and I opened the door and got out.

I wrote to her, wrote three or four times, and checked my mailbox every day. Nothing. And then I finally received a letter. I opened it and felt sick. All of her previous letters had been handwritten; this one was typed. She'd started seeing someone else. I caught a bus that took me to the street that became a highway out of town and hitchhiked home. I shocked my parents when I walked in and explained why I was there. I called Sandy, asked if I could come over, borrowed my mother's car and drove to her house. She opened the door and invited me in, keeping her distance, and as I followed her toward the stairs I saw her mother, standing in the living room, a pained smile on her lips and a furrowed brow that seemed to say, Poor you. I followed Sandy upstairs to her room. She pointed toward her bed, I sat down, and she pulled the chair over from her vanity and sat in front of me.

"I thought you loved me," I said.

"You mean a lot to me."

"We were going to get married."

"I'm sorry. I've met someone."

"Who?"

"No one you know."

I bowed my head, and then looked up at her. "Who?"

She sighed. "Someone at MSA. He's graduating in design."

"Design? Design what?"

"He designs ads. Like in a magazine." She stared at me, as if she were waiting for the words to sink in. "He knows what he wants to do and how to earn a living."

My mind went numb, and during the days and months and years that followed, I could only remember one thing from all she'd said during the rest of the time I was in her room—"Make me proud of you." I clung to that wish for years, because it made me feel I would somehow continue being part of her life if I did make her proud. I couldn't let her go. I tried to put a wall between us, but almost anything could knock it down. If I heard on the radio one of the songs to which we'd danced, like "Dream Lover," I'd hold her, and we'd dance, and it would feel again like the dance would never end. And sometimes in the night, when sleep would open the door to dreams, I'd see the two lights in the dark, at the end of the dock, and she'd come back to me, and we'd fall in love all over again.

The only docks I saw after our breakup were loading docks. The previous summer, following my high school graduation, I got a job in the Heinz warehouse down on University Avenue, in an area of warehouses and railroad tracks, about a mile west of Frogtown. I'd spend my eight-hour shifts loading and unloading semis that backed up to docks on the side of the building and railroad cars that stopped at docks in the back. The other men, who'd worked there for years, had to tell me to slow down, I was working too hard, it was a long day and I had to pace myself. I got along well with them, listened like a kid to their jokes and stories, and would chuckle when they'd kid me about becoming one of those uppity educated people. When I left at the end of the summer to go to college in Iowa, the manager told me I was welcome back the next summer. But when I did come back, after the break-up with Sandy, I wasn't the same person. I'd work in silence with my partner, and often the rage generated by my pain would grab hold of me, and I'd hurl fifty-pound cases one after another to my partner at the top of a stack, or down below as he stood next to a platform truck, fling the cases as if he personified the separation I wanted to obliterate, and he'd shout, "Whoa, slow down, take it easy," and I'd stop, panting, realizing my mind had been somewhere else.

I talked to the manager after a few weeks and said I was moving to New York, wanted to start over. He asked if I knew anyone there. I told him I had a friend who'd said I could stay with him until I found my own place. The manager nodded and said if things didn't work out, I could always come back. I flew to New York and stayed with that friend, whom I'd met through Sandy, until I found a tiny basement efficiency apartment in midtown Manhattan. It had a window that opened onto a courtyard, which was nothing but a patch of dirt and a tree that looked like it belonged in a Beckett play, a scrawny thing with a branch that might tempt someone to hang himself but wouldn't hold up long enough for the suicide to finish kicking. I walked all over the city, trying to get a job as a waiter, found nothing, and after a few weeks moved back to the Twin Cities, this time to Minneapolis. I rented an apartment in an old building, a couple blocks from the MSA, and got my job back at the warehouse. Every weekday I'd go to bed as soon as I got home from work, get up around eleven at night, and read until it was time to go to work. I'd obtained a list of the great books of the Western World and read everything from Homer and the Greek playwrights to Plato and Aristotle and onward. I read so I could wall Sandy out of my mind, but there was no wall when I slept, and she'd come back, and I'd lose her all over again.

In September, I moved to a rooming house closer to the University's campus, and at the end of fall quarter, desperate for money, moved home, where I could live for free and complete another quarter. To ease the tension when Dad was home, I'd study in my room, coming out only for meals. I'd sit at the opposite end of the table from him, avoiding his eyes and not talking, unless he spoke to me, and then I'd still avoid looking at his eyes. Winter quarter started out the same way. After a few weeks of silence, of the tension level rising every night and weekend when the two of us were in the house, I decided to leave again. When I learned the University of Virginia had an undergraduate creative writing program, and Faulkner had been a writer in residence there, I sat Mom down in the living room and told her I wanted to apply but couldn't pay for tuition and room and board by working part-time jobs. I'd need help from Dad. I'd never tried to have a conversation with him. There was always the possibility I might say something that would flip his switch and he'd go ballistic.

"What is creative writing?" Mom asked. "What do they teach you?"

"You learn how to be a writer. It's for people who want to write short stories, or novels, or poetry."

"You want to be a writer?"

"It's been a dream. I've written a play and some poems, but nothing . . ." I shook my head. "I never thought of myself as being good enough."

"Why not?"

I shrugged.

Mom studied my face, while biting her lower lip. "Maybe you and your dad and I should sit down together after dinner tonight, when he's had some time to relax, and talk about what you want to do."

"Okay."

"You know, your father's a smart man, and he has a lot of respect for education." She smiled, trying to reassure me. "He's even talked about retiring when he's fifty and going to law school. He has dreams, too."

I nodded. I felt like telling her he'd have to get an undergraduate degree before he could go to law school but decided to leave that alone. She might feel that was an attack, and she didn't like me attacking him anymore than she liked him attacking me.

That night, after we finished eating, Mom suggested the girls go downstairs and watch TV. While I helped her clear the table, Dad smoked a cigarette and watched us. When Mom and I finished, I sat down at my place, and she at hers. She took her cigarettes out of her apron pocket and lit up, exhaling a stream of smoke that flowed into his.

"I feel like someone's planned something," Dad said, as he stared at me.

"David wants to talk to you about his education. What he wants to do."

"Okay." Dad looked at me and smirked. "Well, David, fire away."

I felt as nervous as I had the first time I'd stood on stage in front of an audience, and it took me a second to find the words I'd rehearsed. "I've decided I want to be a writer. And there's a program—"

"Wait. You wanna be a writer? Like someone who writes for a newspaper?"

"No. Like someone who writes novels."

"Oh. Well, if you wanna write novels, go do it. No one's stopping you."

"I also want to finish college, and I need to earn a living, and, ah, I'm not really sure about . . ." My mind went blank.

"About what?" His eyes burned into me. "Come on, about what?"

"John, let him explain."

"For the last three years or so, I've kind of dreamed of being a writer, but I never believed I could. Writers always seemed to come from somewhere else—New York or Paris or London. But when I was a junior, in Miss Mueller's class, I learned that F. Scott Fitzgerald—"

"Who's he?"

"A writer. He grew up over on Summit Avenue, just a few blocks from St. Clair."

"Summit and St. Clair are two different worlds."

"I know, I know. St. Clair's middle-class working people and streetcars and Summit is mansions and Cadillacs. But just the fact he lived that close to where we once lived. Until I learned about him, it seemed like everything important that happened in the world, happened somewhere else. But Fitzgerald came from here."

I realized what I was saying didn't make any sense. I looked at Mom, and she nodded her head, like I should continue.

"My desire to write sort of comes from my love of reading novels. It's an adventure, it's exciting, I explore other worlds, I live in those worlds, in the novels of writers like Fitzgerald, and Hemingway, and Wolfe, and lately I've really gotten into the Russian writers, like Dostoyevsky and—"

"Russians? They're so ignorant. They don't know anything."

I clenched my jaw, so I wouldn't say what was going through my mind. I looked at Mom. She nodded and smiled.

"I want to create other lives that readers can live and worlds they can explore. That's why I want to be a writer. But I don't know how to get from here to there." I ran out of steam. His eyes remained fixed on me. I felt he was running out of patience. "The University of Virginia has an undergraduate creative writing program, and I could earn my degree and at the same time learn how to become a writer. They have famous writers who teach there, and—"

"I see. Now it's clear." He stared at me, nodding, pursing his lips. "You're going to ask me to pay for you to go to this university. Pay tuition and room and board and all that. Sounds to me like this writer profession is for people who grew up on Summit, not St. Clair, and not in Roseville. You know," he leaned forward and glared at me, "no one's going to pave your road for you. You're gonna have to learn how to do it yourself."

"What if you lent me the money, and I paid you back after I finished school?"

He shook his head.

"Why not?"

"Because."

"I'm not asking you to give me the money. I'm asking for a loan."

"No."

"Why?"

"Because."

"Because why?"

"Because."

I stood up and said, "Because it's me?"

"Yeah."

"Well, I'm going to find a way. I'm going to find a way to become a writer."

He sneered. "Lots of luck finding a patron."

I looked at his sneer, clenched my fist, wanted to scream, but instead I took a deep breath and thought, Fuck you! I turned and rushed through the house and out the front door and into the cold and the night and down the block to the dark field at the end of the street. I turned and kept on walking in the street, reliving the meeting, the humiliation, the sneer, cursing him over and over, the goddamn piece of shit. I felt cold and buttoned the coat I'd grabbed on my way out of the house, each one of my breaths clouding in front of me. By the time I got back to the street I lived on, it had been dark for hours, and the only light came from the moon behind the clouds.

I stopped in front of my house and looked around at the neighborhood that I'd called home for the last ten years. Lights glowed here and there in the windows of the dark forms that were ramblers and two-story houses, much smaller than those on Sandy's street. The black skeletal trees, planted along the street not long before my family had arrived, looked like forlorn creatures in the cold night. I gazed at my house at the top of the slope and remembered standing in the living room, in my rented tuxedo, next to Sandy in her prom dress, my arm around her back, and Mom taking pictures, telling us what a lovely couple we were. I gritted my teeth. The house next door reminded me of the young woman who'd lived there, had left for college somewhere on the East Coast, and almost never returned. I looked down the street at the house where Buddy had grown up. He'd moved off to St. Cloud, where he was going to a state college. I'd seen him the previous summer and knew he wouldn't be moving back. And I thought of my friend from New York, the one who liked to say, "Go west, young man, go west, just don't stop in the middle," and who now lived in San Francisco. He'd told me in a letter to let him know if I ever wanted to come and stay with him.

I kept my distance from Dad, attended classes, did my homework, and worked whatever part-time job I had at the time. I planned on finishing the academic year and renting a room by the U and moving out. A few weeks into spring quarter, I got home from classes one day, and Mom said I'd received a letter from the U. I opened the envelope. It was my grades for winter quarter. Nearly all *As*. She said she wanted to show them to my father when he got home from work. That evening, after dinner, he was reading the newspaper, sitting in one of the armchairs in the living room, and I was sitting in the other, reading a book. Mom had set the ironing board up in the living room, where it merged with the dining room, just a few feet from Dad, and set the clothes to be ironed on the table.

She walked over to him and said, "Look, David received his grades today." She handed the grade report to him and returned to her ironing, watching for his response.

He looked at it, set it on the table, and continued reading.

"What do you think of David's grades?"

His head remained in the newspaper.

"John, aren't they good?"

He didn't answer.

"John, what do you . . ."

"Yeah, they're good!"

I waited a couple minutes, got up, and went to my room.

I wrote to my friend in San Francisco and bought an airline ticket. A couple weeks later, I left, without telling Dad. I'd paid the tuition with my money and owed him nothing. I spent a few days getting to know the city, and then started looking for work. I came across an ad for jobs at Yosemite National Park, applied, and got one, as a busboy in a cafeteria at a place called the Glacier Point Hotel, at the summit of a mountain. A series of bus rides got me there.

A couple days after my arrival, a snowstorm closed the only road up the mountain, and with a half-dozen guests and twice as many employees, I had time to strap on a pair of snowshoes and head out onto trails buried deep beneath the snow. I entered a dazzling white haze, with no separation between land and sky. I walked for about twenty minutes and stopped, peered into the haze, hearing nothing but the sound of my lungs panting, and tried to determine if what lay ahead of me was land, or a void. Would the next step be on solid ground, or would I plunge a thousand feet to my death? I turned around and followed the prints of my snowshoes back to the hotel.

The mountain made me feel the frightening enticement of self-annihilation. When summer arrived, a guy would build a bonfire every night at the edge of a cliff, a space a couple hundred feet from the cafeteria and surrounded by a railing, and when the fire had burned down to glowing embers, he'd push them over the edge, and the people in the valley would watch the spectacle of what they called the firefall—the steady stream of falling embers that looked like liquid fire. Once, when no one was around, I climbed over the railing, edged as close to the drop-off as I dared, and peered at the valley four thousand feet below. I felt that if I let myself go, just spread my arms and lunged, I'd soar. The feeling I was on the verge of an ecstatic experience terrified me. I inched my way back, realizing how easy it would be to dive and plummet.

Living and working at the hotel opened the world to me, and me to the world. At the beginning of summer, a lot of college kids moved in to take jobs. They'd join those of us who were already there at night in a large rec room in the basement, where one of the guys would play guitar and perform songs by Bob Dylan, Joan Baez, and Peter, Paul, and Mary, and we'd sit around him on the floor and on couches and chairs and sing along. I spent a lot of time with an Englishman, a student from Oxford, talking about Greek and Roman literature, and a philosophy major from the University of Michigan, talking about Kant, and a woman who studied literature at Barnard College. The first time I saw her, she was standing in the viewing porch at the back of the hotel, a tall woman with long brown hair, gazing out at the mountaintops that extended for miles. I stopped next to her and said, "It's beautiful."

She looked at me, with an easy smile and a warm gaze, and said, "It's gorgeous." She asked me my name, where I was from, and why I'd come, and I said I just needed to get away from home and see the world. We started going on walks together on hiking paths that provided magnificent views of Half Dome and other mountaintops, sometimes with clouds hovering just above them. We liked one path in particular that followed a dip in the mountain from Glacier Point down to huge flat rocks at the side of a waterfall, where we'd sit close to one another and watch the river gush toward the edge and plummet over a thousand feet and talk about our favorite poets. She'd recite lines from Emily Dickinson and Anne Sexton, and I from John Berryman, James Wright, and Dylan Thomas. Sometimes we'd lie on our backs, hold hands, and listen to the steady roar of the water falling, feel the mist drifting across us, and stare up at the evening sky. But as soon as the sun touched the top of one of the mountains, we'd begin walking back up the trail. Once, as it started to get dark, we heard an animal that must've been a bear crashing through the brush off to the side, and panicked, ready to run if the animal appeared. The last couple weeks she was there, I'd walk her to her room at night, and we'd kiss before she'd go in. She only stayed a few weeks before returning home, and I never saw her again, but I wasn't sad to see her leave. She'd helped me come back to the world, and I knew there would be other women.

I'd planned on staying in California for a year, so I could become a resident, get free tuition, and transfer to the University of California and finish my degree. But I decided not to wait to go back to college and returned home in time for the second summer session. I got a job at the University's library, in the reserve room, and with money I'd earned in California, enrolled for a couple of the courses I'd dropped in the spring. I could feel the tension between Dad and me at the kitchen table every night and did everything to avoid him. I'd never again try to borrow money from him or think he might compliment me if I did something well or expect any kindness. I finished the summer session and celebrated my twentieth birthday alone, by simply buying some clothes with money Mom gave me, supposedly from Dad.

One night, when I couldn't sleep, I sat up and turned on the light attached to the head of my bed and began reading a book. I'd read a few pages, when Dad's voice snarled, "Turn off that light and get to sleep."

My whole body started. I saw his silhouette and phantom face in the dark doorway, tossed the book onto my night table, turned off the light, slid down into my bed and lay still, watching him until he disappeared, listening, hearing nothing. I wondered why in the hell he should care whether or not I read in bed, it was none of his damn business. After a long silence, I sat up, turned the light back on, and started reading again.

"Turn off that goddamned light."

I flinched, saw his silhouette, and felt his eyes glaring at me. I dropped the book on the table, snapped off the light, collapsed and pulled the covers up, and stared at him lurking in the dark, until he was gone.

I wondered what was the worst he could do to me. He could beat me. But I wasn't a little boy anymore. And I'd learned how to defend myself. I sat up and turned on the light and opened my book. After a few minutes, I heard feet padding down the hall toward my room.

"I thought I told you to turn that goddamn light off."

He bore down on me, like he intended to kill me, knowing I wouldn't have the guts to stand up to him. In the past, I would've cowered and waited for the cuffing that would've left my ears ringing. But this time, I threw the covers aside and stood up, and he stopped. And then the rage that had been accumulating in me for years exploded in a torrent of words, and I hissed, "I hate you, I hate you for all the times you hit me and beat me, hate you for ridiculing me, for belittling me, for refusing to recognize anything good I've ever done. I'm not afraid of you anymore. I'm not afraid." And then I paused, panting, and looked into his eyes as I never had before and said, "If I wanted to be perfect, all I'd have to do is be the opposite of *you.*"

I waited for the blow that would knock me to the floor, but it never came. He stared at me, a strange mixture of rage and sadness in his eyes.

"In the morning, I want you to pack your things, call a cab, and leave. And don't ever come back."

He walked away. I heard his door close, and then silence.

My hands were shaking, my whole being was trembling. I collapsed onto my bed, staring at the empty doorway, blood rushing through my head, amazed at what I'd done. When my breathing calmed, I stood up, took another deep breath, and closed the door. I got dressed and packed whatever clothes I could, along with my books and notebooks, and lay down on the bed and stared at the ceiling, thinking about my mother and my sisters, the people I loved and was leaving behind. I wondered what Mom and Dad would say to the girls about why I wasn't there for dinner. Why I would never come back.

A few hours later, the sound of running water in the bathroom startled me. Daylight reached across the ceiling, and the objects in the room stood out in the gray light of dawn. A cupboard door slammed shut in the kitchen, and after a while, the motor that opened the garage door downstairs whined, the wheels creaking along the tracks as the door rose, the car started and pulled out, and the wheels creaked again. When I was sure he was gone, I got up, took my suitcase, and stopped in the doorway to look around the room at the bed in which I'd slept for so many years and the desk where I'd spent hours studying and writing papers. Across the hall, the door to my sisters' room was closed. I cracked it open, peered at them sleeping in their beds, and wondered if I'd ever see them again. I walked down the hall toward the closed door to Mom's room, stopped and stared at it, wondering if she knew, and then carried my suitcase to the kitchen and called a cab.

147

I had the driver drop me off at the University, walked to the library, and headed for the reserve room. When I found my supervisor, she looked down at my suitcase and up at me and asked, "What's this?"

"I have to find a place to live before dark. Can I leave my suitcase here?"

Her brows furrowed, and her mouth opened, like she wanted to say something, but couldn't find the words.

"I'm hoping it'll just be for a few hours."

"Are you okay?"

"I'm fine."

She studied my face and said, "Do you want to talk?"

"I just need to find a place to live."

She nodded. "All right."

She led me to the back of the room, behind the rows of bookshelves, and pointed to a space between the wall and the side of her desk where I could leave my suitcase. I thanked her and set it down and headed for Dinkytown.

I spent hours walking the streets, looking for RENT signs, and found one in a side window near the back of a house on a corner. I opened the fence gate and walked toward the closer of two back doors, finding it bizarre a house would have two of them. I rang, and a lady with gray hair opened and greeted me with an accent I didn't recognize. I told her I was looking for a room and had seen the sign. She asked if I was a student at the University, and when I said yes, she invited me in. She led me past the entrance to the kitchen and up the stairs to a room with a single bed and a desk and a chest of drawers, and a bathroom down the hall that I would share with another renter.

We returned to the first floor and sat down at the kitchen table. She asked me to tell her about myself. I said I was entering my third year at the University, was majoring in English, and was going to begin a minor in classical languages. When I mentioned Latin and Greek, her eyes warmed, and she said in Lithuania, where she was from, people respected the educated. She told me she and her sister had fled the Soviet occupation, and her sister also lived in this house, on the other side of a partition that divided the building in half, and she, too, rented out rooms. I was taking refuge in the house of a woman who'd also fled a dictator. I paid the rent, picked up my suitcase at the library, and unpacked and set the book I'd been reading on the night table.

I never spoke to my father again.

Mom called a few months later, in early January. "David." She breathed into the phone. "Your father's in the hospital." Her breath caught. "He's dying." Her voice trembled. "The doctors say he could go at any time." She paused. "Are you coming?" I couldn't answer. "David, are you going to come?"

"I'll be there."

I took a cab to St. Paul and ran into the hospital and found his room, and Mom standing at the side of his bed. I stood next to her and looked down at Dad, his eyes sunk into dark cavities in his gaunt, pale face, his cheeks covered with several days' growth of stubble. He seemed to look at me, but I couldn't tell from his eyes what he saw or felt. She took my hand in hers, squeezed, and slowly released it. After his eyes closed, she whispered, "Let's go to the waiting room."

We walked down the hall to a large room, sat down far enough from the other people so we could talk in private, and lit up. She took a drag, and then another, while her eyes stared off, and her lips remained separated.

"A year ago," she said, "he had that operation done to remove part of his colon, and we thought he'd be fine."

I nodded. I knew about that.

"The cancer came back toward the end of the summer, and in the fall, they removed his rectum. It was too late." She shook her head, her eyes full of tears. "He's gone downhill so fast. By Christmas . . ." Her voice broke, she took deep, trembling breaths to try to get control and grabbed some tissues from a box on a table and wiped her eyes. I placed my hand on her arm. "By Christmas, he couldn't walk by himself. He'd lost so much weight; I could almost pick him up and carry him."

"I should've been there."

"You didn't know. And I didn't know how to get ahold of you. This morning, I called the University and got the phone number of your boss and called her and explained everything, and she gave me your number."

"I'm sorry, Mom."

Tears flowed down her cheeks, and she sniffled and shook her head and wiped her eyes. "I feel so . . ." She took a couple of deep breaths. "I wanted the two of you to . . ."

And then she closed her eyes and started sobbing, and her face collapsed in her hands, and her body trembled. I knelt before her, tried to hold her, and repeated, "Mom, Mom." She eventually stopped crying, leaned back, gazed upward and sighed, "I haven't slept in days." She looked at me and shook her head and wiped her eyes. "Let's go back. I don't want him to be alone."

I put my arm around her shoulders, and we returned to his room and stood by his side. His eyes were closed. She laid her hand on his, her fingers curling around his, and he tightened his grasp to hold onto her. And then his hand relaxed, and she removed hers. She sat down in an armchair, leaned her head back, and fell asleep.

For the first time in my life, I was able to look directly at his face, look as long as I wanted. I felt sad his life was coming to an end and he was leaving the people he loved behind to become nothing. I wondered what it was to live with that thought for the short time he had left. I watched and listened to him breathe, the air rasping through his lungs, a long pause between each breath, and I wanted him to live. I remembered when I was little, he'd hold me on his lap, and I'd feel his whiskers rubbing against my cheek and smell the cigarettes on his breath. I felt the memory was real. And those times that Mom told me about, when she and Dad would work at the bakery at night and take me along, and Dad would show me how to make a little pie, just for myself, and he'd bake it for me. And the other time Mom mentioned, when Dad told her he felt sorry for me because of the break-up with Sandy.

I knew he was capable of love. I could see it in the affection between him and Mom—like that evening, when I was about fourteen, and I walked through the living room and the edge of the dining room and stopped just before I reached the kitchen, because I saw Dad standing behind Mom, who was leaning back in her chair at the table and raising her lips toward his, and he was bending over her, and as they kissed, he slipped his hand beneath her dress and bra and held her breast. I stepped back and disappeared around the corner. I thought of Christmas, when I'd pick out records from the collection in the hi-fi cabinet, and we'd listen to the Andrews Sisters and Bing Crosby and Frank Sinatra sing "Santa Claus Is Comin' to Town," "White Christmas," and "Winter

Wonderland." And Dad would make eggnog for the family, and he and Mom might waltz around the kitchen, and then they'd take the girls for a ride, so I could play Santa and put the presents under the tree. I remembered, too, the evening I went down to the rec room and found him dancing with my sisters to the music of Lawrence Welk on TV, and the girls would take turns standing on his feet as he held their hands and twirled them around, and they'd throw their heads back and laugh.

As I looked at him, I realized how much I wanted a father, wanted his love, and wanted to hold onto him, because somewhere deep inside him, I knew he loved me, he cared about me, and I loved him. And if he died, that love would be lost forever.

He died. And the love? I can't recall who had brought the girls to the hospital, or how long they were there, but I remember, after we'd all gone home, walking down the hall to my old room and hearing one of my sisters crying in the dark, in the room across from mine. I left the light off and moved slowly around her bed, her sobs guiding me toward her. I sat down next to where she lay and placed my hand on her shoulder and gently rubbed, until she stopped crying and sat up. I took her in my arms, she laid her head on my chest, and I held her with one hand and caressed her head with the other, feeling her tears when my fingers glided across the side of her face, and she said, "He was so mean." My hand froze, while her words echoed in my mind. I held her and rocked her, and when her body went limp, laid her down on the bed and covered her with her blanket. I went to my room, undressed, lay down, and remembered her dancing with our father and laughing, and the words, *He was so mean*, echoed through my mind.

Love will never be simple in this family, I thought, as I looked around Patty's living room at the dark forms of the furniture she'd dragged from one home to another. I wondered about the burden of memories that had come with those things, which were more than just reminders of the happy life she'd had with Mom and Dad. And I wondered if Mom had been doing more than just helping her daughter with a gift of furniture, if she'd been unburdening herself of memories she could no longer bear, memories of a dead husband she could never bring back to life. All of us, Mom, Patty, Linda, and I, we have that in common—we bear the burden of memories. And if love isn't simple, life isn't either.

A couple days after Dad's death, classes started at the University. I felt relieved to escape the house in which I'd grown up and all its reminders of the past, but discovered there was no escape. The first few days of the quarter, students, faculty, the newspapers—everyone was talking about the death of T.S. Eliot, who'd died about the same time as Dad, and every comment about Eliot's death made me think of Dad's, and I'd find myself back in the hospital room, looking down at the closed eyes in their deep sockets, listening to each rasping breath and the long pauses, and grieving for him as I tried to believe he loved me.

I was constantly moving during the months that followed his death, from one rooming house to another, and then to the basement apartment behind that dive, the Viking Bar, on the West Bank, the west bank of the Mississippi, with all those bars where musicians, hipsters, drunks, and students hung out. I studied hard for my classes, trying not to think, not to feel the sadness that never left, the feeling that everything in my life had failed, I'd failed, and if Dad didn't love me, it was because I wasn't worthy of his love, I wasn't good enough. And I'd wonder again, What was wrong with me? Why was I unworthy? Trying to believe he loved me, I'd remember those brief moments when he seemed to, like that summer night he came home from work and found Sandy and me kissing in my car, just before we pulled away, and tapped on the window on the passenger's side and waved at us with a grin. And that day up north at the resort, when I was a little kid, and I was swimming in the lake and stepped on a tin can partially buried on the lake floor and came running out of the water, crying, blood streaming from my foot, and he and Mom applied a tourniquet and rushed me to the hospital in town. And then I'd feel the love I'd lost when he died. For years, I'd fled my father, but there was nothing I wanted more than a father—a father who loved me.

I'd go home for a day or two, and Mom and I would talk. She told me once she'd felt such a relief when I moved out, because the tension between the two of us, seated at either end of the dinner table, left her stomach twisted in knots, and she felt sick by the end of every meal. I wondered if I should've just died,

152

so they could've been happy. She also told me he was proud of me and boasted to his friends about his bright son who earned such good grades. I believed her, wanted to believe her, and then, later, as I lay in bed, feeling that house closing in on me, I remembered Dad and I reading in the living room, and Mom showing Dad my grade report and saying, "Look at David's grades, aren't they good? John, didn't David do well? . . . John . . . John . . ." No, love was never simple in this family.

One summer day, after the girls had gone off with some friends, Mom and I were sitting in the living room. She was telling me how happy she'd be in the fall, when they'd go back to school, and she'd get a job, and they'd all have to get up in the morning, get dressed, eat breakfast, and be someplace at a certain time. And then she fell silent and stared at the fireplace, her face looking dead. She became aware of me gazing at her and looked back at me, and then looked away and stared again at the fireplace. "I still have all of his things." She bit her lip, pulled her forearms together and pressed them against her stomach, as if she were trying to hold herself together. "Why don't you go in our room. . . in my room. . . and look through them. See if there's anything you want."

I was going to say I didn't want anything of his, but then wondered, What would it be like to walk into that space with him gone? I tensed up when I entered the room, expecting his voice to snarl, What do you want? But was relieved to find silence. The large bed, standing against the wall facing me, between the windows looking out on the driveway, was unmade on Mom's side, the side furthest from where I stood, and her pajamas lay on a heap of clothes piled on the chair in front of her vanity. My eyes drifted toward the two folding doors of the closet in the wall opposite the head of the bed. I went over, opened a door, and glanced at Mom's clothes, and opened the other, revealing Dad's. I pushed the hangers back and forth, looking over the sport jackets and suit coats and shirts, and fingered some of the ties on the rack attached to the wall just inside the door. I turned away, and noticed his alarm clock on the night table, next to where he slept, and thought of him getting up every morning to go to work and build the life that was now gone.

I was about to leave, when I noticed the four framed pictures of infants arranged on the wall, next to his chest of drawers. I walked around the bed, past the chest, and stopped in front of the photographs of Patty, Linda, and me, each taken when we were a few months old, and the one of the baby Mom called Johnny Boy. His cupid lips smiled, and his eyes shone as they peered at the camera between puffy eyelids. He looked as if he were just beginning to see the world around him and felt excited by what he saw, a moment of awakening caught by Mom or Dad.

"I thought you were going to go through your father's things." Mom was standing inside the doorway.

"I remember, when I was a kid, playing in the apartment we used to live in, before the girls were born, the one over on that cobblestone street."

"On Summit Lane."

"This picture used to stand on a shelf in the living room. I'd stare at it and wonder, Who is that baby?"

Mom walked toward me, while gazing at the picture. I sat down on the edge of the bed, and she sat down next to me.

I said, "You remember the little round red table that used to be in my bedroom, with the black square painted on top, and the three chairs?"

"Yeah."

"I'd put my dolls—my soldier doll, Timothy, and my rag doll, Shirley—I'd set them at the table, put plastic cups and plates in front of them, and set a place for myself, too, and pretend to serve us things to eat. Well, one day, I took that picture off the shelf, brought it in my room, and propped it up on the empty chair, so that the baby seemed to be looking across the table. I said to the baby, Timothy wants to know why you're called Johnny Boy. And your voice said, Your dad and I wanted to name our baby after him. And I looked and saw you standing in the doorway. You said, Johnny is just another way of saying John. And we call him Johnny Boy, because we love him so much. You smiled, like you were really happy to talk about him. But then I asked, Where is he? Your smile faded. And then you perked up, like you'd resolved to be strong, and you said, He's here. He'll always be with us. And I looked around and asked, Where? And you closed your eyes, shook your head, and turned around and left. Another time, I asked you if Johnny Boy was big enough to play with me, and you said, Johnny Boy will always be a baby."

Mom nodded, while gazing at the picture.

"And then one August, you and Dad took me to a cemetery. You gave me a bouquet of sunflowers and told me to put them on Johnny Boy's grave, because that's how we showed him we loved him. I put the flowers on the tombstone, under his name, and that phrase, AT PEACE IN THE ARMS OF ANGELS, and looked up at you, wondering what I should do next. Dad had tears in his eyes. I'd never seen him cry before."

"Your father loved him so much. He's the one who started calling him Johnny Boy. He'd talk all the time about the things they'd do together, and he'd imagine Johnny Boy taking over his business, or becoming a lawyer, becoming whatever he wanted to be. He'd get so carried away about his life with Johnny Boy, and that was before he was even born. I think what your father wanted more than anything else was that his son would have the life he didn't have when he was growing up."

Her eyes teared, she wiped them with the back of her hand, gazed at the picture, and rested her hand on mine.

"Did Dad ever love me?"

"Of course he did."

"Then what happened?"

She took a deep breath and sighed. "I don't know." She shook her head. "I don't know. I'm sorry, David. I really am."

The voice of one of the girls shouted from the kitchen, "Mom, we're home." She let go of my hand and left the room.

I'd gotten through winter and spring quarters and the summer following Dad's death by never taking time off from work or study except to binge drink on Friday and Saturday nights, driving myself as hard as I could, so I wouldn't have time to think. In the fall, I registered for as many courses as possible. But the barricade I'd constructed so I wouldn't see the faces, hear the voices and the words, and remember the things that haunted me, caved. Instead of sleeping, I'd lie in bed at night and relive everything. I'd see his eyes, sunk in their black sockets, looking at me as he lay on his deathbed. I'd hear his rasping breath, and his last words to me—"Don't ever come back." And my sister's words, "He was so mean." And I'd remember cowering, my heart speeding, as his hand or his belt was about to strike me. And wondering, Why? Why?

The place where my roommate and I lived, the basement apartment behind the Viking Bar, made my insomnia and depression worse. As I lay in bed, footsteps would pass next to the window two feet above me, at the same level as the sidewalk, and at midnight, or one or two in the morning, voices would shout, fights would break out, and bottles would smash against the sidewalk or the wall of the building. I'd lie there, anxious, afraid someone or something would come flying through the window. I'd set off in the morning a little after eight, with an hour or two of sleep, enter the bar through the back door near the cigarette machine, buy a pack, and walk past the men, hunched over their boilermakers, or leaning against the bar and staring at me, and I'd glance at their faces covered with stubble and ignore the who-the-fuck-are-you look they'd give me. By the end of the quarter, I'd dropped half my courses and got lousy grades in the other half. After the term ended, I went to the student health clinic, saw a psychiatrist, and got a prescription for Librium, which helped me sleep and put my life back together.

I moved again, joining another roommate in the upper duplex of the house just off Seven Corners, on the West Bank, and across a pot-holed street from the tire company that owned the house. If I were standing in the front bedroom or the living room, the screech of electric wrenches loosening and torquing lug nuts would pierce my nerves like a dentist's drill, so I was lucky to have chosen the back bedroom, a quiet space where I lived and studied and made love with the women I brought home. The apartment was a dump, its ceiling and floors sagged, and its rickety external staircase in the back swayed as I descended on my way to the yard, which served as the company's storage area for used tires, piled six or seven high. I'd sometimes spread out a towel on the top of one of those piles, lie down in the sun, read a book, and drink a beer. One of my girlfriends, learning from my roommate I was in the back, started walking down the steps and stopped, a look of terror on her face, and shook her head, so I got up and bounced across the piles and walked up the stairs to the girl and my bedroom.

Toward the end of the summer, the second one after Dad's death, Mom invited me home for dinner. I was sitting on the edge of the weathered planks of the front porch, when a red Dodge Dart convertible with the top up creeped along the empty street, the driver peering at the IOGT Hall next door, and stopping in front of my place. Mom honked her horn and waved. Amazed to see her driving something so cool, I flipped my cigarette and got in. Her eyes stared past me at the house, her mouth agape, like she'd just gasped.

"What's the matter?" I asked.

"That house, the whole thing sags. It looks like it's rotting."

"Yeah, the next gust of wind and it could come down. But, you know, you gotta think of the positive. It provides a home for students and bats. Above all, bats. The attic is full of them, and the floor is covered with bat shit. It's so thick, you could grow crops in it. I wouldn't be surprised to see corn growing there someday."

She laughed and shook her head, and we hugged. A whiff of perfume startled me.

As she turned the car around, and we headed for the bridge across the river, I looked at her gold earring and black sleeveless dress and wondered what was going on.

"What do you think of my new car?" She grinned.

"It's cool. Very cool. When did you get it?"

"I sold the Morris Minor. I never liked that car. Your dad thought it was cute, but . . ." She fell silent, as if her thought had been derailed. And then she said, "And I sold his car, too, and got enough money to buy my own convertible."

"That's great. How are the girls doing?"

Her eyes remained fixed on the road. She didn't answer.

"Mom, how are the girls?"

"Oh, they're fine. Fine."

About a half-hour later, she turned down our street, and as we approached our house she said, "I want you to meet the man I'm dating."

"You're dating?"

She looked at me. "Is there something wrong with that?"

"Dad died just a few months ago."

"Twenty months ago."

"But, still—"

She glared at me, and I fell silent. She pulled to a stop in the driveway, turned off the ignition, and looked at me. "I have needs, David."

I nodded. "I know."

We got out of the car, and I followed her up the front walk to the door, amazed at how thin she was, how fragile she seemed, as I thought about her needs.

We entered the house, I asked where the girls were, she said downstairs, and I went down to the rec room, where they were watching cartoons. They welcomed me with a grin, and I sat down between them on the couch, put my arms around their shoulders, and they leaned into me, and we watched the roadrunner, his legs spinning in an orange blur, going beep beep as he fled Wile E. Coyote, whose legs spun in a brown blur as he pursued. We laughed as Wile E.'s tricks backfired, and he'd get caught in a giant mousetrap or crushed by a boulder that fell from the sky, and most often he'd end up plummeting off a cliff to a valley with a stream flowing through it far, far below, and sometimes his falls would be accompanied by music that seemed absurdly sweet, like a waltz. A few seconds later, he'd be at it again, setting his next trap. The cartoons came to an end, Patty turned the TV off, and Linda said, "We've been watching a lot of cartoons lately."

Patty asked, "Did Mom invite you home for dinner so you could meet her date?"

I shook my head at her mischievous grin and then glanced at Linda, who rolled her eyes and sighed.

"You guys don't seem impressed."

Linda said, "His jokes are *so bad!*"

"No one laughs. Ever. Really. And his stories go on and on and put everyone to sleep."

"Even Mom fell asleep once."

The doorbell rang, and the girls cried, "That's him."

A few minutes later, Mom called us up for dinner, and I met her date.

He must've been boring, because I have almost no memory of him. I do remember he was a little shorter than Mom, had begun to go bald, and had a bit of a paunch that stretched his sport jacket to the point a button might pop. During dinner, he smiled and nodded a lot and talked about taking her dancing that evening. After dinner, he and I went into the living room and sat down to talk, while Mom cleared the table. Within minutes of folding his hands over his belly, he nodded off. I picked up a newspaper and looked through it, until

Mom came walking around the corner from the kitchen and froze when she saw him. She shook his shoulder, he started, and his eyes snapped open. "Oh," he said, "shall we go dancing?"

She said, "No, my son's visiting, and I'm tired. I think I'd like to go to bed." When he reached the front door, he gave me another big smile, said it was good to meet me, and hoped to see me again soon, and I responded in kind. Then he stood on his tiptoes and leaned toward Mom with his lips pursed. She turned her cheek toward his kiss, ushered him out the door, and shook her head and sighed. She said she needed to lie down, apologized for not being good company, hugged me goodnight, and headed for her room.

Later, as I lay in bed, I thought again of Mom's comment about having needs, and remembered some of the intimate moments I'd glimpsed between her and Dad. I'd always found it reassuring that my parents had had that kind of a relationship, but oddly I hadn't seen what they were doing as sexual. I had a hard time imagining the love she felt for him, including a craving to have him inside her, and the two of them going at it in bed. I'd had sex with several women, and I knew they needed it just as much as I did, but now I was seeing Mom as a sexual being, too. She was forty-nine, a lot of men would find her attractive, and she'd find some of them attractive. She had to start a new life, and as a mom, probably felt awkward and frustrated, and maybe guilty, and the last thing she needed was her son hovering around her.

But I didn't hover. I moved on. I had to drop out of school that fall and find full-time work, because the financial-aid employee at the University, who thought I could get money from the Federal government to help with expenses for the academic year, was wrong. I borrowed a pair of black slacks and dress shoes from my roommate, so I could present myself for interviews, and got a job waiting on tables at a restaurant called The Gaslight, located a block away, on Washington Avenue. The restaurant was in a brick building, painted white, constructed as a theater in the early twentieth century by Scandinavians, who screened silent movies and staged vaudeville shows and Strindberg's plays that they performed in Swedish. Snoose Boulevard, as the neighborhood was called, had changed, and drunks staggered the streets, curled up in doorways, and sometimes were found dead in the morning. Two months later, I got a job at Charlie's Café Exceptional, in downtown Minneapolis, a restaurant where male waiters wore tuxedos, did flambé dishes, and made big tips. I moved from my duplex in the old house to another duplex I shared with a classics professor at the University, until he discovered my thirty-five-year-old waitress-girlfriend in the kitchen one morning and gave me the choice of not bringing her home at night or moving out. So, I got an apartment near Loring Park, from which I could walk to work, and continued with the girlfriend, the last one in the United States, before I bought a one-way-ticket on a cargo ship from New York to Southampton and sailed to England.

I didn't just pack a suitcase, like I was going on vacation, I took a trunk as well, because I didn't know if I'd ever return to the United States. And I brought an attitude, too. I liked to think I was a fearless explorer and tried to project that image to everyone I met. When a guy in a pub or a woman in bed would ask, If you don't know anyone in Europe, and you're all alone, what made you decide to come? or, How could you leave everything behind? I'd lie and say I was an adventurous spirit, motivated solely by curiosity, never telling them the truth, that I didn't leave everything behind, I couldn't, even if I wanted to, because there was no getting rid of what was inside me. After six weeks, I tired of England, left my trunk with the English woman I'd met on the ship, and headed for Paris. I spent most of the next ten months wandering through the different *quartiers*, parks, and museums; past the book stands of the *bouquinistes* on either side of the Seine; visiting the bookstores and hanging out in cafés and *brasseries*; and living in a youth hostel, cheap hotels, and with the women with whom I slept. And then, one day, I decided to go to Spain.

I got a ride to the Costa Brava with those two guys I'd met at a French-language program, and for three nights, we slept on the beach with kids from other countries, sprawled out on towels and in sleeping bags, and spent our days swimming in the Mediterranean and going to cafes and drinking beer. Then we drove to Barcelona, where we split up. I carried a French translation of Garcia Lorca's poetry with me that I'd bought in Paris, and the first time I went into one of the bars by the waterfront and set it on the counter, the man standing next to me looked at it and back at me, his eyes wide open. He nodded at the book and said something in Spanish about a great writer, and something else I didn't understand, and seeing I didn't, he pointed at his glass of wine and asked me again, and I nodded and said, *Sí*, and he ordered me a wine, and then talked a little more about Lorca, until there was nothing more to say to someone who couldn't understand.

We clinked glasses, I said, "Salut!" and we drank. During that week in Barcelona, I carried the book with me constantly, and every time I entered a bar someone would buy me a drink and praise Lorca, the people's poet murdered by Franco's forces. After a week in Madrid, visiting the Prado and spending days gazing at Goya's paintings, like "The Colossus," I took a train to Granada, where I brought Lorca to the bars and got the same kind of reception as in Barcelona.

After ten days in Granada, and running low on money, I bought a ticket on what Americans called a fourth-class train to Madrid and boarded a car. I found most of the seats already taken by men in berets, wearing suit coats and pants that didn't match, and women in dresses, shawls, and scarves, and their clothes looked just as faded and worn as the men's. I swung my suitcase up on a rack, found room to sit down between a couple guys, and looked around at my neighbors, with their wicker baskets and sacks arranged by their feet or on the seats next to them. A blind man, unshaven, in a shabby dark coat and pants, sat across from me, his gray-black hair tousled and matted, his mouth open, his head sometimes swaying as if he were lightheaded, and other times pausing at a strange tilt, as if he were trying to see the sources of sounds and movements he sensed. I could tell from his mutterings he was drunk.

The train lurched forward and picked up speed. After we got out of the city, I was surprised to see some of the passengers pull up their sacks and baskets, take out loaves of bread and hunks of cheese and sausage that they cut up with pocketknives and shared with one another, and then wash the food down with wine in bottles that reminded me of the French *vins ordinaires*. I wondered why they didn't wait to eat until they arrived at their destination. We hadn't traveled for long before stopping at a little village, and a few more people boarded the train. It started moving forward again and picked up speed, but then it stopped at another village, and another. Sometimes, as the hours passed and the sun faded, the train would stop in the middle of nowhere, and I'd look out the window and see nothing but plains and some large hills in the distance. We'd sit there for fifteen or twenty minutes, no one appearing surprised or curious, and then move on.

Meanwhile, the blind man, who'd occasionally pull a bottle out of a wicker sack and take a swig, had continued his mutterings, but they'd gotten louder, more emphatic, and apparently more offensive, because some of the passengers would look at him and shake their heads and frown in disgust and look away. I had no idea what he was saying and watched his behavior and the responses as an outsider. The train stopped again, and I looked out the window and saw darkness. And then two *guardia civil* appeared, in their green uniforms and black tricornio hats that shined like they were made of plastic, and grabbed the blind man by his arms, lifted him, and hauled him out the door. I looked around at the passengers, but no one looked back at me, and they all appeared determined to avoid one another's eyes. After what seemed like a long time, I heard boots stomping on metal, a door banging, and the sound of feet scraping across the floor, and the *guardia civil* reappeared dragging the man. They flung him back in his seat and looked around, and everyone looked away, except me.

For a second, my eyes connected with those of one of the *guardia civil*, and his brows furrowed, as if he were wondering who in the hell was this guy who had the gall to look back at him. I dropped my eyes and stared at his black boots until he and his partner walked off. I looked up at the blind man, who'd sunk back into his seat and was crying, blood leaking from his nose and mouth, red smears on his chin and cheeks, and I could only imagine the beating he'd suffered and the pain he felt. He seemed to continue to sink into himself, his body still shaking from barely audible sobs that morphed into whimpers, until he fell asleep, his breath occasionally catching on a snore. I reached Madrid and gave him a last look, hoping he was okay as he continued sleeping in a heap.

The memory of that *guardia civil's* eyes staring at me lingered, and I thought about the fear that all of us in that car had felt, the fear that had made us look the other way. The fear I'd sensed all over Spain during the weeks I'd wandered, when a conversation with a Spaniard in my French and limited Spanish might end the second I evoked something political, and the person would fall silent and refuse to look at me. The fear I'd felt the time I was hitchhiking through Basque country on my way home to France and got stranded near sunset on a narrow country highway. Two *guardia civil* walked up to me, one of them carrying a machine gun, as they frequently did in the countryside. They studied me with suspicion, and one of them, as he looked up from my passport, asked what I was doing there. I tried to explain in French and Spanish, gave up, and said, *"No habla espanol,"* while staring at the barrel of the gun pointed at me from four feet away, the man's finger on the trigger. I knew, if he squeezed it, I'd be just another nobody who disappeared.

As I stared at the furniture from the house in which I'd been raised, I felt the presence of the dictator I'd grown up with and remembered the terror I'd felt the day he'd pinned me by my neck to his bedroom wall. A few years later, I had the courage, or the gall, or had been sufficiently fed up and enraged to look him in the eye and hiss that if I wanted to be perfect, all I had to do was be the opposite of him. Maybe that was some kind of victory . . . it was a victory, because I am the opposite of him. I tell Alan every time I talk to him, every day I see him, I tell him I love him. But Dad, he left his mark. He's been dead for twenty-three years, but I still feel fear, feel worthless and empty—empty of love—and know I'll feel that until the day I die. And I want a bottle of whiskey, wanna drown myself in the emotions I've never been able to live with.

There's a black hole inside me, drawing me back to the cavern I've done everything to escape. When I remember traveling to Spain, I sometimes forget the beautiful things I saw and relive the fear, and those memories awaken others from my adolescence and pull me back into the cavern, where winds cry and howl and echo through the passages of time. There's no end to this. No end. And yet I'm returning home. I want Alan and Barbara to know Mom, the woman who loved and protected me. I want to be close to her. Her love draws me back with every bit as much power as the emptiness, the absence of love that Dad left me.

Virginia (Ginny) Ann

I can't stop thinking about what Ellen said last night, after I got back from sitting in my car near Patty's house. This is *not* the time to leave Ken. You have to stay focused on everything positive in the prognosis, you have to think of your children and grandchildren and treasure the life that lies before you, you have to stay focused on that life. I was so overwhelmed by depression, thinking of the possibility I'd never waken from the operation, but now I can see what I have to do.

I got up from the couch and went to the kitchen, wrote Ellen a note, thanking her for everything, placed it on the table, got in my car, and headed down the street, the same one on which John and I'd lived. Each time over the last two days, when I'd drive by our old house on the hill, I'd slow down, because I'd see David glancing at me as he gets out of his black Ford that he's just parked in the street, and the girls jumping rope and singing in the driveway, the windows of our bedroom above the garage looking out upon them, and I'd remember living inside those walls and preparing dinner for John and the kids and making love with him at night, and the two of us falling asleep side by side behind those dark windows. And then I'd realize David wasn't getting out of his car, the girls weren't jumping rope, and I was looking at something that was gone, and neighbors were staring at me because I was a stranger who'd stopped in the middle of the street, beneath the shade of the maple trees that had been no taller than I was when John and I'd moved into

164

our house. But today, I didn't look, didn't slow down. I drove by, my mind focused on what I had to do.

I arrived at Patty's house, parked behind David's car, went up the walk toward the front door, and saw him in the window. Before I could reach the door, he opened it and greeted me, standing in his bare feet, wearing jeans and a T-shirt, and looking as if he'd been up all night. We hugged, and he asked, "Mom, Mom, where have you been?" his voice trembling with emotion. Before I could say anything, Patty, in her pajamas, came rushing down the stairs, and Linda, in slacks and a blouse, came running down behind her. I felt the girls' tears as we held one another, and saw David shake his head, as if he couldn't believe I was there.

"Come on in, Mom, come on," they pleaded, while crying and laughing.

I sat down on the couch, with Patty on one side, Linda on the other, and David on the edge of the armchair. I nodded, determined to get this done, took a deep breath, and said, "I saw an oncologist Thursday. I have pancreatic cancer." They stared at me, their mouths hanging open. "If I do nothing, I can live for . . . maybe a year. Maybe more." I paused, thinking about the person I'd heard of who'd died within a month of being diagnosed. "However, the doctor thinks he discovered the cancer early enough so he can operate, and there's a chance"—I paused and smiled—"a good chance, he can get it before it spreads."

"And you'll live a full life?" David asked.

"I'll live a full life."

They laughed and shook their heads and repeated, "Mom, oh, Mom." When they stopped laughing, Patty asked, "Why didn't you just call and tell us? Instead of worrying us sick for two days?"

"Yeah," Linda said, her voice trembling. "This brought back horrible memories." She wiped tears from her eyes.

I took Linda's hand in mine, and Patty's. "I'm sorry. I really am. But I needed to be alone and think things over. I can't do that at home. Not with Ken. He'd panic."

"Is there something you're not telling us, Mom?" David asked.

"What do you mean?"

"You could've told us, and asked us not to say anything to Ken."

I shook my head. "I couldn't think straight."

"Where did you stay last night?" Patty asked. "And the night before?"

"At Ellen's."

"Ellen's?" Patty asked.

"You gotta be kidding," Linda said.

"I had to think this through. Everything's clear now. I'm going to have the operation, live a full life, and be a good mother and grandmother." I smiled at them. "That's what I need to do."

"Is there any risk involved?" David asked.

"There's risk, as there is with any operation. The doctors were very clear about that. But it's frequently performed. And as I said, if they get the cancer soon enough . . ." I explained the operation, telling them everything I could remember—the removal of part of my pancreas and of my stomach, and my bile duct and gallbladder, and lymph nodes near the pancreas—and the more I talked, the less anxious they appeared. When they no longer seemed worried about me or why I'd disappeared for two days, I left.

Driving home, I wondered if I'd done the right thing. I made what the doctor said sound so positive. There's a chance they can't get all the cancer, or that I won't survive the operation. And how can I allow someone to put me under, if I know I might never wake up? I tried to imagine that moment and panicked. I need my children, need to be close to the people I love. And so help me God, if Ken does anything to prevent them from being with me . . . Does he really love me? Our life together started with a lie, about which I didn't learn the truth until his wife knocked at our door. She didn't want him back. Just wanted a divorce. He told me I was the one he loved, and not the other woman, who used to belittle him, above all when he was drinking. She reminded him of his father, who'd ridicule him every time he failed, and that seemed to be all the time. I paid for the divorce, got him out of trouble, and we married again. Every time I think of the lie about the dead wife, I remember that night in the Black Lagoon, when his hand covered mine and took hold of it. It was like his hand closed an open wound that nothing had been able to heal before. I can still feel the warmth, the calm, the peace I felt when his hand took hold of me. Is that love? If he really loves me, wouldn't he love my children, too? They're part of who I am. But he just needs me. Maybe that's what love is for him. I know he feels for me. He'd be lost without me. When I told him to quit drinking or leave, he quit. But he made me pay. We've rarely made love since he went through AA. That's his revenge. And maybe, now that he's sober, he thinks of me as . . . as a mother. Is that why I love him—because he's another child for me to care for? A child who had to struggle to find happiness. I need him, he needs me, we need one another. Maybe love is nothing more than that.

I pulled up next to our trailer house and parked behind Ken's pickup and went in, expecting him to cry, "Where have you been?" but found silence. The door to the bedroom was open. He was lying on his belly, his face turned toward me, his breathing slow, a pause between each snore. He's not the most handsome man I've ever met, with that buzz cut and big nose and skin that's both ashen and ruddy. I sat down on the bed and ran my hand across his forehead and the buzz, petting him like a cat, until he opened his eyes enough to peer up at me. When I was certain he was awake, I told him what I'd told the kids, and then said, while looking into his bloodshot eyes, "I need you. And I need my kids and my grandkids. Don't try to come between us."

He stared at me as he seemed to reflect on what I'd said, and then he laid his hand on mine, and I felt again the warmth that always made me feel whole and at peace, until he tightened his grip, threw my hand away, sat up and leaned into me. "Were you thinking of leaving me?" His eyes pierced mine, trying to find the answer. "You were, weren't you. All because of our argument the other night. I had the nerve to get angry when David told you over the phone that he and Barbara and Alan were moving here this summer. Your kids and grandkids constantly invade our lives, but that's nothing compared to the way things'll go when David and Alan get here. Where the hell am I in all of this? What's my place? Whatever's left when the kids and grandkids aren't around? You were thinking of leaving me, but then you learned about the cancer and, oh, maybe now's not a good time to start a new life."

"You have your place in my life, and you know it."

"Your kids aren't my family."

"Alan and his cousins call you Grandpa Ken. They're the closest thing to a family you've got. Your family threw . . ."

"Go ahead, say it. My ex and my father threw me away, because of my

167

drinking, and now he's dead. And I was gone in my drunk world when my mother died."

I took a deep breath. "I won't throw my family away. I won't let you come between us. If you try to separate me from my kids . . ." I glared at him.

He glared back. He stood up, walked out, and didn't return until late. I knew he'd spit venom in my face if I asked where he'd been, so I said nothing. When we went to bed, he slept on his side, and I on mine.

Ken lingered, looking around the dimly lit room, asking me how I felt, telling me everything would be okay, and making me more anxious. Before he left, he held my hand, smiled down at me, told me again he'd be here when I came out of the operation, and bent over and kissed me. I couldn't sleep, not with the thought this might be my last night alive, and that thought brought up another, and another, about John and David and the girls and the life we'd once had, and the life I now had with Ken. A nurse came in with a little paper cup containing pills—just sleeping pills.

The next morning, I was hardly aware that I was being put under.

When I opened my eyes again, I was freezing cold, but alive. The only sound was the beeping of a monitor. A nurse appeared above me, holding my wrist, looking up at a hanger and the liquid in a plastic sack, and then down at me. She left, and I wondered where Ken and the kids were. My mind wandered . . . I woke to sharp pain in my hand and saw a nurse standing above me, adjusting the tube in my IV, and behind her, David and Barbara. As soon as the nurse left, I reached toward them with my free hand, David took it, Barbara rested her hand on ours, and I said, "There are two reasons I want you to hold my hand. I love you. And I'm cold." We laughed. And when Ken and the girls came in, I looked at all of them and said, "I'm alive, because you've given me so much to live for."

Sitting on the couch, muffled in my head, oblivious to whatever Ken was watching on TV as I looked down at the scarf I was knitting, lost in my thoughts about David. From the time he was a young boy, I'd felt the tension between him and John, and that tension increased until the two of them could no longer be in the same house. And then John's death shattered the family, and I lived in a haze with my drugs and whiskey. But after I got past all that, I tried to bring my kids back together and make the family whole, make myself whole. It took years to help Patty and Linda recover from the trauma, but David, he's still out there. But now, he and Barbara have moved into their new home in Minneapolis, and tomorrow I'm having lunch with them.

I have to get this scarf done for Alan. He'll arrive any day and stay for a month with his dad and stepmom, before Chantal takes him to France, where they'll stay with her parents until just before school starts and then fly back to Tulsa. Alan gets to go to France every year with his wonderful mother, my wonderful daughter-in-law. I thought for a while she'd turned David around. He finished those two doctorates when he was with her. They should've had a good life. She was so happy about being pregnant with Alan and about David's job prospects and told me on the phone he was one of two finalists for a job teaching at Harvard. And what does he do the night before his interviews? Goes out and gets drunk. And then he takes that job at the University of Texas, but doesn't like the way the chairman treats him, so he moves to the University of Tulsa, and then he's really miserable and hits the bottle and starts an affair with Barbara, and when Chantal finds out, he tells her he isn't going to stop, and then he marries Barbara and leaves Chantal and Alan in Tulsa and moves to Iowa, and now he's here. He hadn't even thought of going to college until he was a junior in high school, when Miss Mueller talked to him, and then he gets two doctorates and almost becomes a Harvard professor and look where he is now.

He has something in common with his dad, of all people. When John and I first started seeing one another, I thought he was so strong, the way he'd talk about owning his own business and being his own man, and I felt he'd be able to offer me and the children I hoped we'd have a good life. He made me think of Papa, and the way Papa had started out with nothing and ended up owning a farm, and the life he and Mama had provided for Gerda and me and the boys, and I thought both men were like tempered steel. Papa had talked about his father, a blacksmith in a little town in southern Minnesota, who'd made plow blades, heating the steel until it glowed red and pounding it and quenching it in water. John had been tempered by everything he'd gone through growing up, those years that had provided the fire and the beating, and the plunging and the hissing of the hot steel in cold water, but what I didn't see at first was that that experience had fractured him inside—the steel was flawed, and though he appeared strong, at any time the anger, the rage might break through, and God help whoever was near. David has a lot seething inside him, too. And some kind of fracture in the steel, but worse than what John had, because it's destroying David.

"Did you hear that?"

Ken's voice startled me, and I looked at him in the armchair off to the side, my mind still caught up in my thoughts.

"Are you here?" he asked.

"Just daydreaming." I grinned and shook my head, as if I were a poor old lady, for whom the world was just too much. An ad in support of Jesse Jackson for President started, with Jackson shouting, "Keep hope alive," and his supporters shouting the slogan back at him. I looked at the TV, using my hand as a visor to block out the sun coming in through the two windows.

"I bet David's been out campaigning for this guy," Ken said, getting up to close the curtains and plopping back down in his chair. "Well, what they said on the news, while your mind was wandering, is that Bush has the nomination locked up, and Dole and Robertson have dropped out. And on the Democrats' side, Dukakis has got it, and the others have quit, except Jackson. That lefty's staying in, right up to the convention. You think David supports him?"

I continued knitting. "David hasn't talked to me about politics lately."

"I'll have to ask, next time I see him."

"Won't that start the kind of conversation you don't like? Remember, when David and Chantal were students at the U, you used to get upset when he'd criticize Nixon and Agnew. So, if you start a conversation about Jackson, isn't he going to say something about Reagan or Bush you don't like?"

"He just wants to get my goat." Ken picked up the coffee mug on the table and took a sip. "That's the only reason he used to talk all the time about the war and Nixon being impeached and that stuff, just to get under my skin."

"You're the one who keeps on talking about politics. I asked him years ago not to, and he stopped, but you keep on."

Ken stared at me, and I smiled, to let him know I wasn't being critical.

"He doesn't need to say anything. I can tell, just from the look in his eyes."

The Gravity of Love

"You don't know." I returned to my knitting.

After the news, Ken prepared dinner, as he'd been doing ever since I'd come home from the hospital. We sat down in the dining area, just off the living room and next to the kitchen, and he dug into his broiled steak and peas and baked potato loaded with butter, washing it down with coffee, while I sat at his side and ate my mashed potatoes and peas and hard-boiled egg and sipped my apple juice.

Ken was lying next to me, reading one of his detective novels, while I was reading the novel David sent me as a Mother's Day gift, about a Black woman living with the ghost of her beloved daughter. He often sends me novels with women characters for my birthday and Christmas and Mother's Day, and the stories make me wonder if he's sending me messages through them, like this one, about living with the ghost of someone you love. Ken leaned toward me and interrupted my thoughts to wish me goodnight with a kiss and rolled over on his side, his back turned toward me, and turned off his light. I listened to his breathing, and within minutes knew he was asleep. I laid my novel down on my lap. Tomorrow, I'm going to see David and Barbara. It's hard, letting go of one daughter-in-law and embracing another, as if nothing has happened, as if I haven't lost someone I love. How does Barbara feel about that? And what does she know?

It's been about eight years since David, Chantal, and Alan moved to Austin. I thought they'd be together forever. Chantal, such a wonderful wife and mother. David seemed happier than I could remember him being anytime since . . . since high school. Even Ken loved Chantal and was more accepting of David when she was with him. She and David would write and send us pictures of little Alan in Austin, New York, and France, and I'd write back and send pictures of us, the girls, and their families. And just two years after the move to Texas, they moved to Tulsa, and then drove up and stayed in a motel and spent time with us and Patty and Linda, and I got to see my little grandson, hold him on my lap, and look at picture books with him. And they sent us photos of them at Christmas in Tulsa. And then I didn't hear from them for months. I called several times before David answered and told me he and Chantal had divorced, it was an amicable divorce, like that made it less of a

171

divorce. I asked, Why? He gave vague answers, like, things just weren't working, he needed a change, needed to move on. Always needing to move on, from everyone who loved him, from everything that could bring him happiness. He came home alone the next Christmas, and I wondered, If the divorce was so amicable, why are you so reluctant to talk, why do you seem to be in such pain?

The next Christmas, Ken and I received a picture of Alan in front of the Christmas tree, playing with the yellow truck we'd sent him, and of a lovely woman with long brown hair, in a skirt and blouse, sitting on her folded legs next to him. A few weeks later, David called to tell me he and Barbara had gotten married, and he'd sent pictures of him and his bride. And then a year and a half later, after they'd moved into an old farmhouse in Iowa, they drove up and spent a few days in St. Paul, visited Ken and me at the trailer, and Patty and Linda and their kids came over. I could tell from the way David and Barbara looked into each other's eyes that they loved one another, and the way the three of them often stood close to one another, Alan in front of his dad, but also close to her, that they could be a family.

I was supposed to join David and Barbara at their place for lunch. I must've taken a wrong turn somewhere, but after having checked the directions, I was confident I was in their neighborhood and on the right street. The houses and trees looked familiar. Was this the same area where David lived before, when he was an undergraduate? I turned onto a side street and saw two rows of brick townhouses facing one another. I parked and walked toward them, while glancing at two more rows of identical townhouses behind them, remarking that the large space between the rows on one side and those on the other form a common backyard, with an oak tree in the center and huge limbs that extend above the lawn. On the sides of the townhouses, a pair of large board-on-board fences ensure privacy, and the cement walkway that I followed between the fences leads to a quiet space, with the front doors of the houses on both sides and trees planted down the center. I found the address, knocked on the door, and Barbara opened and greeted me with a hug. Seeing her black skirt and red silk blouse, I said, "You don't need to get all dressed up for me."

172

"I didn't. I have two job interviews this afternoon. Otherwise, I'd be wearing jeans and flip-flops. But while I'm gone, you two can get caught up. I'm sure you have a lot to talk about."

She led me past the kitchen to the living room directly ahead, and we sat down on a couch facing a big armchair and matching ottoman covered with a tan fabric, a table and lamp on one side, and a pile of books on the floor on the other. I could imagine David sitting in that chair and reading for hours. At the other end of the room, a plate glass window and sliding door looked out on a patio surrounded by more board-on-board walls. Footsteps behind us mounted a set of stairs from the basement, and David, in blue jeans and a T-shirt, appeared from around the corner and walked toward me, smiling, "Hey, Mom," and took me in his arms and hugged me.

He asked how his sisters and Ken were doing, and Barbara asked if I'd like a tour of the house. They led me upstairs and showed me the master bedroom, with their bed, chests of drawers, an old writing table with a computer on it, bookshelves, framed pictures of paintings, and windows that looked out on the backyard and the oak tree, and then Alan's room across the hall, with a bed, a night table, a chest of drawers, a set of bookshelves, and a kite attached to the ceiling, as well as stars that David said "glow in the dark." I lingered in the room, looking at the kite, the stars, the Bambi quilt on the bed, and the books on the shelves, and felt the love of David and Barbara for Alan. We went downstairs to the dining area, David slid open the glass door, and we stepped out onto a concrete patio, with lawn chairs, a grill, the fences on either side, and an opening through which we walked into the backyard. David stopped, shook his head, and smiled as he stared at a play area in the center, where kids on swings reached with their legs to see how high they could fly, while others screeched as they hurtled down a slide next to a sandbox where toddlers played.

"This is kid heaven," he said. "Practically everyone here has a kid, and some people have two or three. Alan's going to love it."

"He's so lucky! And only professors live here?"

"Faculty and spouses. And their kids."

Over lunch at the kitchen table, I got Barbara to talk about herself. Her parents divorced when she was little, and her father had always lived in a different part of the country and didn't have much of a relationship with her. I sensed pain beneath her statements, but she always managed to smile. She thanked me for joining them for lunch and left for her interviews, David seeing her off at the door. As I helped him clear the table, he asked if I'd like some coffee, and I reminded him I couldn't drink anything with caffeine. I sat down, and he filled a teakettle, set it on the stove, and ground some coffee beans.

"Barbara seems to have had kind of a rough childhood."

He turned toward me and leaned back against the counter. "Yeah, she hasn't had it easy. Both of her parents are drinkers. Her mother, who raised her and her siblings, would often come home drunk at night, and they were always moving from one place to another." He reflected. "She said one of the things she wanted most growing up was to be able to go to sleep at night without having to worry about cockroaches crawling on her."

While David continued talking about Barbara and her mother, I thought about the kind of mother I'd been and wondered if her mother also felt alone and overwhelmed by the responsibility of raising her children—and helpless, desperate, depressed, and . . . and I remembered that feeling of trembling inside, of dizziness, of falling.

"Her mother must've had a really hard time."

"I think she did."

"I like Barbara."

"She likes you, too. She's really happy we moved here. You know, if you want to, you can have lunch with us any day of the week, at least until I start teaching."

"When's that?"

"Second summer session, around the middle of July. I'll be able to spend all my time with Alan while he's here. The only thing I have to do before I start teaching is prepare my courses for the summer and the fall. And one of them is a course I taught at the University of Iowa last spring—a survey of the French novel." He came over and sat down, brushed his long hair off the side of his forehead, and looked at me with his hazel eyes, his face still young in spite of his forty-three years. "I think I use an interesting approach for teaching the course. In every novel, I have the students study the way characters fall in love. For example, do they really see the person with whom they fall in love, or is there something mediating their perception that causes them to desire that person? In one of the novels, there's this wealthy guy, who collects art and hangs out with aristocrats, but he falls madly in love with a prostitute, in part because of her resemblance to a woman in a famous Renaissance painting. She uses him, he sees this, and still loves her. How could he?" David chuckled. "That question comes up often, doesn't it." His eyes fixed on mine. "We see a woman fall in love with a guy who's violent, or a con artist, and we wonder, How can she love him? Does she not see him for what he is? Or does she just not care?"

I felt he was accusing me of something.

The teapot whistled like it was going to explode, and he leaped up and poured water over the grounds while continuing to talk, his voice calm again.

"The students seem to think falling in love happens magically—you know, lightning strikes—or it's a rational process, and they tend not to reflect on the question, Why do people fall in love? Even though they're at a point in their lives where there's a good chance they'll fall in love. And have to live with the consequences."

"How old are they?"

He pours more water. "Twenty, twenty-one."

"So young."

"Yeah. How old were you when you fell in love with Dad?"

"Eighteen." I could feel David's eyes on me, and my stomach started to whine, like it was upset with what I'd had for lunch, but the lunch I brought couldn't have caused this churning in my gut.

"A couple years older than I was when I fell in love with Sandy, and I thought we were going to get married. And eight years younger than I was when I fell in love with Chantal."

"She was a good wife."

He poured himself some coffee and sat down. "A very good wife."

"You're fortunate. You had a good wife, you divorced, and you got another good wife."

"Yup."

"I hope you hang onto this one."

He nodded. "I intend to."

175

I heard pain seep through the determination in his voice. He had a lot on his mind, and so did I. "When I was driving over here, I thought this area looked familiar. Is this the same neighborhood you lived in when you were an undergraduate?"

"You mean, after Dad told me to leave and never come back?" He stared at me, chuckled, and nodded. "Yeah. The house I moved into is just a few blocks from here."

"How does it feel to be back?"

"How does it feel?"

"Are you happy?"

"What are you getting at, Mom?"

"I'm concerned about you."

He shook his head. "You just had an operation for cancer, and you're concerned about me? Don't you think it should be the other way around?"

"I think it's strange, you living in Paris with Chantal for over two years, and then you move back here, and then you go to the University of Texas, and you quit that job, and go to the University of Tulsa, and quit that one, too, and then the University of Iowa, and now you're at the University of Minnesota. Why are you moving all the time?"

"For your information, most of the faculty in my department at Tulsa resigned, because the chairman changed the requirements for tenure. At Texas, they'd promised to make my job a tenure-track position, and never did. And Iowa was just a one-year gig, as is Minnesota. So, there's nothing to understand about me moving back here."

"Why did you divorce Chantal?"

He clenched his jaw.

"She always stuck by you, even with all your problems."

"My problems?"

"Drinking. Throwing away opportunities, like Harvard, when you got drunk the night before your interviews. She put up with that. And with the affairs—I'm sure Barbara wasn't the first. And then she tried to save your marriage and pleaded with you to see a counselor with her."

"Have you been talking to her?"

"She's my daughter-in-law. My relationship with her doesn't end, just

176

because you get a divorce. And yes, I've talked to her a few times since you split up. You were lucky to find someone like her, and you were lucky to find someone like Barbara, but when it comes to women, you've always been lucky."

"Wasn't lucky with Sandy."

"Women love you, and you deserve to be loved. But for years you've been moving, always moving, like you're trying to run away from something. Something inside you. And I can't help but wonder, Did you make Chantal pay the price for whatever that something is? Did you take it out on her?"

"With a father like the one I had, is there any wonder I always wanted to leave?"

"There's a lot you don't know. You don't understand."

"Oh, I know." He glared at me. "Believe me, I know. If I'd understood, maybe I wouldn't have had to see a psychiatrist when I was an undergraduate, and another one when I was a graduate student. And I wouldn't have undergone psychoanalysis when Chantal and I were living in Paris. Every time I was lying on that analyst's couch and memories brought me back to the house with Dad, I'd start crying. Every. Fucking. Time." Tears glazed his eyes.

"David, I'm—"

"Any kid who grew up in our family needed all the help he could get."

I bowed my head and closed my eyes and tears seeped onto my cheeks. I'd failed him. I should've . . . should've done more.

He took my hands and held them. "I'm sorry, Mom. I'm sorry."

"I think it's time I go home."

"You're crying. You can't drive."

I slipped my hands away from his and wiped my tears with my napkin. "I'll sit in the car until I can." I took a deep breath.

"I'll drive you home."

"No!" I stood up. "I can take care of myself. Where's my purse?"

"It's probably in the living room. I'll get it."

I closed my eyes, took a deep breath, and tried to get control of myself. He came back and handed me my purse, and we walked to the front door.

"I'm sorry," he said.

I shook my head. "I'm the one who should be sorry." I looked into his

177

eyes. "For a lot of things."

He gave me a hug, the hug my children and I always give one another, even when it feels like everything's falling apart.

"Come over anytime, Mom. Just give us a call. We'd both like to spend more time with you."

I thanked him and left. I sat in the car, gripping the steering wheel, until the emotions churning inside me had settled enough so could I drive home.

Over the next couple days, my thoughts returned again and again to our conversation. And then he called.

"Mom, I've got some great news."

"What?"

"Chantal called. Alan's flying here a week from Saturday."

"Oh, that's wonderful! I'm so happy for you. Maybe you and Barbara could bring him to the house for dinner."

"Of course."

"How about Sunday, around five, so we can spend time together. I wonder, should I get a soccer ball? A kite? I should probably always have those things handy."

"I've got that stuff here, Mom. But I want him to spend time with us. I'll bring the *Karate Kid* tape, in case he gets bored."

"With his ol' grandma?" I laughed.

He laughed with me. "No, Mom, not with his ol' grandma. With all of us. Oh, I've gotta tell you this. Last summer, when Barbara and I were living in that farm house outside Iowa City, we took Alan to see *The Karate Kid* at a drive-in, and the next morning, I was walking from the garage to the house, and I saw Alan in the backyard, wearing Barbara's black silk kimono top and a pair of shorts, with his hands raised karate style in front of his face, jabbing with one foot and then the other, doing karate chops with his hands and shouting *huh* with each chop and jab, providing his own soundtrack. And then he saw me and grinned and looked away and wandered back and forth, looking off at the tall grass and the woods, as if he weren't up to anything, and I went into the house, looked out a window, and there was the Karate Kid jabbing his foot at an invisible opponent, this time without a soundtrack."

I was so moved by the story, I almost forgot to remind David to please not say anything political around Ken.

Sunday came, and I hummed and sang to myself while cooking. I was doing all the cooking now. The operation was weeks behind me, and I felt better, just some back pain that I treated with over-the-counter painkillers.

I sat down in the living room with Ken, who was watching a baseball game, his reading glasses perched on the end of his nose, the *Pioneer Press* sports section spread out on his lap. A commercial appeared, and before he had a chance to look at the paper, I said, "You know, David and Barbara and Alan are going to be here in a little while."

"I know."

"I want us all to have a good time. So, could you please, please, not talk politics?"

He yanked both sides of the newspaper, making it snap, as if it were coming to attention, looked down at it, and then, feeling my eyes on him, looked up and said, "Okay. But, if he says anything like what he said last summer, about the Teflon President—"

"He wouldn't have said that, if you hadn't started talking about the Iran-Contra affair."

"Reagan did nothing wrong. He's the only president we've ever had with the guts to stand up to those Russian commies and tell them to tear down that goddamn wall. Sometimes I think David's a little bit of a commie himself."

"I don't want any arguments. Just want us all to have a good time. So, please, I've already talked to David about not bringing up anything political, and—"

"All right. If he doesn't say anything political, I won't either."

"Thanks."

The commercials ended, a batter walked to the plate, Ken fixed his eyes on the television, and I hoped he'd remember our agreement. I'd just finished setting the table, when I heard feet running up the stairs outside and a knock at the door. I rushed to open, and there stood David and Barbara, and Alan in front of them, looking up at me with his beautiful dark eyes, Chantal's eyes. We hugged, and I gave Alan an extra big hug. It felt so good to hold him close. Ken said hello to everyone, ran the palm of his hand back and forth across

Alan's short hair, and asked, "How ya doin', buster?" Alan grinned up at him.

A cheer erupted, and Ken turned to look at the TV. I invited David and Barbara and Alan to sit on the couch, Ken sat in his chair, I turned off the TV and sat in mine, and we looked at one another in silence. Alan was wearing a red T-shirt over his cargo shorts with the question *HOW DID I GET HERE?* on it, each word printed below the preceding word on one side, and little male figures in black suits walking in a row from a word toward the other side, their bodies looking as if they were responding to a musical beat.

"Alan," I said, "that's a strange T-shirt."

"Dad gave it to me."

"Barbara and I gave it to him. It's a line from a Talking Heads song."

"That's Dad's favorite band."

I picked up the package on the end table next to me and held it like bait toward Alan. "Well, I have a present for you, too."

His eyes latched onto the package. I said, "If you want it, you gotta come and get it." He sprang up and hopped over, and I made room for him so he could sit next to me on the armchair and gave him his present. He looked at the wrapping paper, with the images of boys dribbling soccer balls and kicking them into nets and tore it open and discovered the scarf I'd knitted for him. He stood up, letting it unfurl, revealing the red and white Santa and brown sleigh and reindeer on a green background.

"That's for when you come at Christmas. The winters here are very cold, and I want to make sure you stay warm."

"You'll need that scarf, kiddo, so hang onto it," David said, watching Alan wrap it around his neck. "You gonna thank Grandma?"

He looked at me and said, "Thank you, Grandma," and gave me a hug.

"You're welcome. And while I've got you here, I want to show you some pictures. Come on, sit back down with me." I patted the cushion, he sat down, and we scooted back so we'd be comfortable. I picked up two pictures on the table and showed him the top one of him sitting on my lap in the same chair and looking at a picture book when he was about two, his eyes open wide beneath his blond bangs. "Do you remember this?" I asked. He shook his head. I smiled, because of course he wouldn't. Then I showed him the second picture of me reading to him as he sat on my lap, only this time he was about three-

and-a-half, his hair was a little darker, and he no longer had bangs. I was probably reading *The Story of Babar*, or *The Little Engine that Could*, one of the books, worn and falling apart, that I'd read to David when he was little and would've read to Johnny Boy if he'd lived. Alan's eyes in the picture were wide open, and his lips parted, as if he were living the story. "Do you remember this?" I asked, but didn't hear his answer, because I noticed a woman's hand on one side of the picture, a left hand reaching in from outside the frame and resting on Alan's shoulder. The hand had a ring composed of gold bands woven together on the ring finger, and I knew that hand still reached into my heart, and into the hearts of David and Alan. David asked to see the pictures, and Alan brought them over to him.

When I no longer felt Chantal's hand, I announced dinner was ready. Barbara and David offered to help and followed me to the kitchen, while Ken sat down at his end of the table, and had Alan sit to his side, next to the place where Barbara would sit. I took the roast out of the crock pot, put it on a platter, and started making the gravy, but found the sight and the smell of the meat and the juice repulsive. I'd lost my taste for meat since the operation, and had a dull, vague pain in my belly the last few days. I asked David to finish making the gravy and slice the roast, and I mashed the potatoes. While Barbara carried things to the table, I went to the bathroom and took a couple pain killers.

During dinner, Ken asked Barbara how she liked her new home and her job, and smiled at her frequently, as if charmed by what she said. And from time to time, he looked down at Alan and asked him questions—Do you want to become a professional soccer player when you grow up? Do you like to fish?

"I've fished a few times with Dad."

"Maybe someday, when you're bigger, you can go up north fishing with your grandma and me. Would you like that?"

Alan looked at David and back at Ken and nodded, all excited. "Uh-huh."

"You know what, when we get done eating, I'm going to show some pictures of the last trip your grandma and I took, and then maybe you can come out to the shed and help me get my gear ready. Me and Grandma are leaving tomorrow for up north."

"A trip up north?" David eyed me.

"Yeah. I'm feeling good."

David glared at Ken, and I felt the kind of tension between the two of them that I'd felt between David and his father, when they'd sit at either end of the table and hardly ever talk to one another.

We made it through dinner without any spats, and Barbara and I cleared the table, while Alan and the two men went into the living room. By the time Barbara and I joined them, Ken had set up the screen in front of the TV, positioned the slide projector on an end table, and closed the curtains. I sat down in my chair, Barbara rejoined Alan and David on the couch, and Ken began the show. Light flashed, the carousel made a clicking sound as it turned, and the machine projected one picture after another of the cabin we'd rented, the lake and the dock, the beautiful sunsets, and the clouds, some of them tinted by the sun, others casting dark shadows across the lake. And there were pictures I'd taken of Ken in his boat, his hand grasping the handle of the motor, or posing with a string of fish, a proud grin on his face. I watched the slides go by, looking from time to time at David, Barbara, and Alan on the couch to see if they were getting bored, when a totally different kind of picture appeared—a photo of Chantal sitting on the same couch, her dark blond hair pulled back in a coil and a gold earring hanging from her ear. She was leaning toward her side, smiling at someone off-camera with whom she was talking, probably David or me, and she looked so happy, unaware of the separation and divorce that lay ahead.

Alan shouted, "Mom! Hey, Dad, there's Mom!"

"That's right, there's Mom," David said, glaring at Ken.

"Sorry," Ken mumbled, "I have no idea how that slide got in there." He pressed the remote, and another picture of the vacation appeared on the screen.

A few slides later, Ken finished his show. David stared off, and Barbara looked down, while Alan bounced on the couch.

"Okay, buster," Ken said, avoiding everyone's eyes but Alan's, "you wanna come and help Grandpa with his fishing gear?"

Alan grinned and shouted "Yeah!" and ran over to the door to meet Ken, who looked down at him and said, "We got a lotta gear to go through." They stepped outside.

David sighed and leaned back, while holding Barbara's hand in his. "I wonder how the hell that picture got in there."

"It was probably an accident," I said.

He shook his head. "This kind of thing happened once before, when Chantal and I were sitting right here, and he accidentally"—David snorted a laugh—"*accidentally* put a slide in the carousel that shouldn't have been there, a picture taken of you about twenty years ago. You remember that? You were wearing a black dress, and you looked stunned, like you'd been ambushed by the camera."

I nodded. How could I ever forget the humiliation of seeing that picture of me, with the black rings around my eyes, and knowing that David and Chantal were staring at it. Ken said that was an accident. And I believed him. Then.

"Last April," David said, "when you didn't come home from work, and Patty called me at my office at the University, that picture flashed through my mind, as clear as that time I'd seen it. I'd like to know what's behind it. It was taken while I was gone, and a lot happened that I don't know about."

"I doubt Barbara wants to hear all this."

"Barbara and I don't keep things secret from one another."

I glanced at her, our eyes met, and she looked at David and back at me and said, "I'll go see how Ken and Alan are doing."

"It's all right, Barbara. You can stay." I looked off, and then back at David. "After your dad died, I fell apart. I hardly ate or slept, almost became addicted to Valium. I was a horrible mother. And then I started drinking, and I was worse than horrible. You disappeared, and I had no idea where you were. I felt so alone, and everyone treated me as if I should be fine. So, I just avoided . . ." I shook my head, took a deep breath, sighed, and told myself I had to get through this. "I avoided everyone. I couldn't stand being with people who wanted me to act normal, when nothing was normal for me. At night, after the girls would fall asleep, I started going out to a bar, where I could be with other people and be alone at the same time, and feel it was all right to be alone. And that's when I met Ken. A few months later, we were going to go somewhere. I put on make-up and that dress and got a glimpse of myself in a mirror. I looked dead. My eyes were just black holes. Everything had collapsed inside me." I took another deep breath and continued. "That night, I set something down on the coffee table and was standing up and turning toward Ken, and he snapped my picture. It was like he'd shot me, and I was afraid he'd shoot me again and screamed at him to stop." I remembered bursting into tears, and Ken taking me in his arms. "We'd been drinking. So, that's the story behind the picture."

"Were you ever angry at me for not being there with you, when you—"

"You were twenty when your father died. The only thing I was angry about, angry and scared, was that for a year I didn't know where you were, or even if you were alive. No one did. And then one day, out of the blue, I got a postcard. You were in Paris." I started laughing, shaking my head, tears welling up. "Unbelievable. You were alive, and in Paris, and I was so relieved, I forgot how worried I'd been. And then, when I remembered, I wanted to wring your neck." I chuckled, shaking my head.

"Oh, Virginia," Barbara said, her warm eyes on me.

David leaned forward. "So, Mom, why do you think Ken put that picture of you in the carousel and projected it?"

"He said he didn't know how it happened. The pictures were all jumbled together in boxes. Things just got mixed up."

"And now that it's happened a second time, do you still believe him?"

David was right to suspect that both times Ken had wanted, for whatever reason, to project something we didn't want to see, something that might hurt one or more of us, but I knew Ken would never admit to that, and I wanted to keep peace in the family, so I said, "The second time in ten years? That doesn't seem hard to believe."

Feet pummeled the stairs, the door flew open, and Alan burst in, shouting, "Grandpa showed me his lures. They're really cool. And he caught a Northern Pike once that weighed thirty pounds."

Alan plopped onto the couch next to David, while Ken headed for his chair.

"I'm sure Ken has a really good collection of lures," David said, "and I've no doubt he's caught some whoppers."

Ken sank into his chair, looked at his watch, and sighed. Alan leaned into David and whispered something. David looked at me and asked, "Would it be okay if Alan watched *The Karate Kid*?"

I said, "Sure." Barbara took the cassette out of her purse, I put it in the VCR, and we watched the opening of the film. Ken put on his glasses and picked up his newspaper.

"Would you like some coffee?" I asked David, Barbara, and Ken. "We can sit at the table and talk, unless you'd rather watch the film."

Ken yawned, shook his head, and lit a cigarette.

David chuckled. "We don't need to see the film again. But it's a little late for coffee." He looked at Barbara, she whispered something, and back at me and asked, "Do you have some herbal tea?"

I put water on to boil, we sat at the table, and as the soundtrack for *The Karate Kid* played in the background, David talked about wanting to take Alan to a nearby park the next day, so they could fly a kite, and Barbara talked about the English family that lived across from them. They had a son a year younger than Alan, and the boys had already spent time swinging in the backyard and hanging out together. "See," David said, "I told you, the place is kid heaven." The water boiled, and I made ginger tea for us.

Ken appeared, scratching his belly and yawning, said he was tired and going to bed, entered our room and slammed the door. I got the message: it was time for people to leave. I wondered how long it would take for the movie to end. And then I got angry with myself for feeling anxious and decided if he wanted to go to bed before sunset, that was his decision, but it wasn't going to affect my life.

"Are you looking forward to going up north tomorrow?" Barbara asked.

"Oh . . . I'm okay with it. I hate going out in boats, and I have *no* interest in fishing. But Ken loves to fish. So, when he goes, I usually stay in the cabin, or sit outside and read. If there's another couple nearby, and a wife who also doesn't like to go fishing, I try to make friends, and we sit around and talk. I enjoy that. It's beautiful up north. So relaxing. When John was alive—David's father—we'd take the kids up to a cabin at a resort, and they'd make friends with other kids and spend every day in the lake, swimming and playing. And then another couple from our neighborhood, with girls the same age as Patty and Linda, started going to the same resort, so our daughters had their friends with them. The men would go fishing sometimes, but often we'd just sit outside our cabins and look out at the lake and watch the kids and talk, and spend our evenings playing cards or Monopoly, drinking beer or Kool-Aid. We all have wonderful memories of those days."

"What did David do when you were there?"

I looked at him, arched my eyebrows, and said, "David?"

He chuckled and shook his head. "I had my summer girlfriend. Her parents always rented a cabin the same weeks we did. We'd hang out on the beach and swim and go for walks."

"That's all?" Barbara grinned.

David smirked. "That's all."

The soundtrack went silent, and we found Alan curled up on the couch. David waked him and helped him to his feet, and Alan rubbed his eyes and leaned into him. When they were about to leave, I said, "Any time the two of you want to do something, I'd be very happy to take care of Alan for you." And then I leaned toward Alan and said, "Do I get another hug?" He gave it to me, and they left.

I put everything away, brushed my teeth, and took a couple more pain killers. I found the lights turned off in the bedroom. I undressed and crawled into bed next to Ken, who snorted and rolled over on his side, away from me. As I lay in the dark, I thought of the picture that Ken had projected and wondered what might have motivated him to do that. He'd always liked Chantal, probably more than he liked any of my kids, and maybe he was angry with David for ending that relationship and wanted to hurt him and Barbara or embarrass them.

In the morning, while Ken was eating his eggs and bacon and hash browns, I stared at him and asked, "Why did you project that picture?"

"Huh?" He looked surprised, and then glared back. "It was an accident."

"I don't believe you. I don't want you to ever do anything like that again."

"I said it was an accident."

"And I said don't do it again."

We glared at one another, until he looked down at his plate.

Ken and I pulled up in front of Patty's house. Patty and David had decided to celebrate the birthdays of Julie and Alan, as they're just a few days apart, so I'd get to see all of my grandchildren. I saw smoke drifting from behind the house as we walked up the driveway, past two motorcycles near the side door. When we reached the end of the house, we saw David, Linda's husband, Tom, and his brother standing on the deck, not far from the grill, each man holding a drink in his hand; and Barbara, Linda, and Patty sitting at the table in front of their glasses of wine; and Alan dribbling a soccer ball around his older cousins, Chris and Scott, in what was left of the yard after the deck had been added to the back of the house.

We joined the women at the table, the men gathered around, and everyone asked about our trip up North. Ken told them about the fish he'd caught, and how one was so big it had taken forever to reel it in, and he'd nearly lost it. I talked about the couple who'd also rented a cabin, and the wife with whom I'd spent every day, while her husband and Ken went fishing, and about the sunsets, with all the beautiful colors, and the way the darkness moved in, and the feeling of night, of dark forms in that black space that always scared me, because I knew there were animals lurking out there, I could hear them, and I loved being inside the cabin by the furnace, with the lights on and the door locked. And everyone laughed and joked about being sure to lock your doors up North, because you never know, those animals, they're smart, they know how to walk on their hind legs and push down latches and turn handles, and you don't wanna wake up in the middle of the night facing a bear, or a moose, or a wolf, or finding a raccoon in bed with you. Lots of jokes, lots of laughs, lots of happiness.

And then everyone except me lined up in front of the table laden with food, picked up their paper plates and plastic forks, and served themselves brats, hamburgers, beans, potato salad, and coleslaw, while I had the lunch I'd prepared, along with a couple pills for the pain in my belly. We ate in the heat of the sun, Ken and I with the women at the picnic table, while the other men and the boys sat on lawn chairs. And then it came time for the two birthday cakes that Patty and Linda carried out and set on the table, one with white frosting and twenty candles for Julie, and the other with chocolate frosting and nine candles for Alan. The birthday kids blew out their candles, everyone but me had cake and ice cream, and Alan and Julie opened their presents. And then Alan and his cousins headed for a nearby field to play catch, Julie and a girlfriend left with Ashley in a stroller, and Tom and his brother kick-started their cycles, the roar of the engines reverberating against the side wall of the house and took off. The heat from the late-afternoon sun beating down on the deck from above the trees in the backyard became unbearable, so David, Barbara, Patty, Linda, and I decided to go inside. As I was about to enter the house, Ken took my arm and said he was going to go wait for me in his pickup.

I stared at his sagging face and told him I wasn't ready to go.

"When will you be?"

"When I'm ready."

"I'll wait out front."

He turned and walked down the driveway.

I entered the kitchen and found David sitting at the head of the table, his back to me, Barbara and Patty seated on one side, and Linda on the other. They each had a glass of wine in front of them and were talking and laughing, and it felt good to see my kids and Barbara happy.

Linda said, "Here, Mom, I saved a place for you."

I sat down between her and David and set my glass of ginger ale on the table. Linda saw the glass was nearly empty and got me another can.

David asked, "Where's Ken?"

Patty said, with a grin, "I bet he's waiting in his truck, huh Mom."

"Yeah," said Linda, snapping the can of ginger ale open and setting it down next to my glass, "you're supposed to leave now."

I didn't want my relationship with Ken to become the topic of conversation, so I didn't say anything, just poured the ginger ale and took a drink.

"You're going to make him wait?" Patty asked, as if she couldn't believe what she was seeing.

"I told Ken I'd come when I'm ready. He's okay with waiting in the truck."

There were grins and nods and comments like, Oh, we get to keep you for a while.

"So, how does it feel to be retired, Mom?" Linda asked, with a big smile.

"Yeah," Patty said, "finally, at the age of seventy-one."

"Don't ever let anyone say you're not strong," David said. "If it weren't for the cancer and the operation, you'd probably work another twenty years."

"You've kept this family together," Linda said.

"You're the reason we're still a family," Patty added.

"That's so nice of you to say those things, but I can never forget . . ." I had to bite my lip to keep from crying. I took a few breaths and closed my eyes, and Linda pressed a paper napkin against my hand, and after a long sigh I opened my eyes and wiped the tears away. "I'm sorry. That took me by surprise. I'm getting to be a silly old lady." I laughed sheepishly. "You know, those first few years after your dad died, it seemed as if I was constantly coming across articles about Jackie Kennedy—how strong she was, what a good mother she was." I shook my head and looked at Patty and Linda. "Remember those Roadrunner cartoons you two used to watch on TV?" They nodded and smiled at the memory. "Sometimes I'd go downstairs, looking for something, and you'd be watching one, and I'd stop and stare at that crazy coyote, trying to catch that weird bird, thinking he was going to get it, and then he runs off the edge of a cliff and looks down, and there's that second of recognition, when he knows he's going to fall. It was like a cartoon version of what I was living every day, when I'd realize again my husband was gone, I couldn't run fast enough to catch him, I could only run fast enough to fall."

Linda placed her hand on my forearm. "You can't continue beating yourself up, because of what happened twenty years ago."

"Mom," David said, as he looked into my eyes, "there is no Jackie Kennedy. That Jackie Kennedy, the perfect mother, the one who overcomes all tragedies and never fails, she doesn't exist. Even Jackie Kennedy isn't Jackie Kennedy."

"We know what you went through after Dad died," Patty said, "because you loved him so much. That's how I think of it. Your craziness was the result of your love, and that love has kept us together." She chuckled and added, "In spite of all of the shit we had to go through."

"And we went through a lot," Linda quipped.

A horn honked, and I started, and it honked again. I almost jumped up and headed for the door.

"God damn him," David hissed.

Barbara laid her hand on his fist.

Patty stared at me. "You're not going to go running out to him, just because he honks, are you? That's like a dog running to his master when he whistles."

I took a deep breath, sighed, and asked, "Can one of you give me a ride

189

home?"

All three of my kids said, "Yes."

Patty got up from the table. "I'll go tell him."

I wondered how Ken would respond, and what kind of reception I'd receive when I got home. And then I noticed David and Linda and Barbara staring at me.

Linda said, "You know, Mom, the operation gave you a second chance at life. You need to make the most of it."

I knew what she was thinking, but if I were to separate from Ken, there'd be attorney's fees, a fight over what was left of the estate and ownership of the trailer, and God knows what else. And there are feelings. Deep feelings. It's not simple.

Patty returned, and I asked, "How did he respond?"

"He said, 'Okay,' but looked angry. And drove off angry."

"We're talking about Mom having a second chance in life," Linda said.

"A second chance since the operation," David added.

"A second chance," Patty repeated. "I'd love to have one of those."

"Wouldn't we all," David said. "So, Mom, what will you do with yours?"

I smiled. "See all of you and my grandchildren more often."

"You think Ken's going to allow that to happen?" Linda asked.

"He will. I've told him what I want."

"Would you believe him if he said it was okay?" Patty asked.

"Why wouldn't I?"

"This is the man who told you he'd lost his wife," Linda said, "and then she showed up at your door."

"When I met Ken," I said, looking at each one of my kids, "I felt abandoned and alone, and he made me feel secure and loved. Grief sets you apart. It isolates you. You do crazy things, and you don't even know it. Family, friends, everyone was uncomfortable around me. They never knew what to say, or what I might do—stare at them, without saying a word, or say weird things, like, I visited John's grave yesterday. My place is ready, next to his. Sometimes, I'd hear the things I'd say, and they felt like a scream following me as I fell through the sky. I started falling the moment your dad died, but it wasn't until a year later I realized I was falling, falling like someone who'd opened the emergency door on a plane thirty thousand feet up and stepped out, and two years later, still falling, I realized where I was. You do things when you're grieving that make no sense in your right mind, if you could ever again be in your right mind. Mine died with your dad. Ken caught me, he broke my fall, he held me and kept me warm and alive. And something else." I looked each of my kids in the eye. "Sex. You have to be dead not to want it anymore. Sometimes you can't control what you want."

"Mom," Patty said, "you told me once Ken no longer had sex with you, because you made him quit drinking."

I bit my lip. I couldn't find the right words, so I just said, "Relationships change."

"Maybe you should think about changing relationships," David said. "You deserve—"

I silenced him with a glare, and then looked at Patty. "I think it's time for me to go. Are you ready?" Too upset to hug anyone, I just said goodbye, and Patty and I left.

As we drove down the street, I saw Alan and his cousins walking toward the house, carrying their baseball gloves. We pulled over, and I rolled down my window.

"Did you boys have a good time?"

"Yeah," Chris said, "but we got hungry and decided to go home."

"There's still plenty of food," I said. "Have a good night. I love you. Oh, and Alan, I'll be coming with your mom and dad when they take you to the airport."

They shouted, "Goodbye, Grandma!" as Patty and I pulled away. I closed my window, and my eyes, and felt depressed that a month had already passed since Alan's arrival, and I'd only gotten to see him a few times. I tried to make his departure bearable by reminding myself I'd be able to see him again at Christmas. I opened my eyes and stared at the houses as we drove down a thoroughfare on our way to the suburb. Patty turned into the court, stopped next to my trailer, and looked at me. I took a deep breath and sighed. "I'm sorry I got angry."

"That's okay, Mom. Don't worry about it." She leaned toward me, and we hugged. Before she let go, she looked me in the eye and said, "We love you.

191

You taught us to love. That's the best thing a mother can do for her kids."

I hung on to her, my eyes teared up, and I said, "Thanks, Patty." We hugged again, and I got out.

I found Ken in his chair, watching a game. I went over to the table, grabbed the remote, turned the TV off, and said, "Why did you go sit in the truck and sulk?"

"What makes you think I was sulking?"

"What else do you do when you sit outside?"

"There's usually a game."

"Patty said you were angry."

"I don't like waiting."

"Maybe you won't need to anymore."

"What does that mean?"

I stared at his eyes and dropped the remote on his lap. "I'm going to bed."

I heard the crowd on the TV scream as I entered the bathroom and closed the door. I washed my face and brushed my teeth, thinking of what my kids had said about a second chance, and walked back through the living room, passing between Ken and the TV, and slammed the bedroom door on him and his goddamn game. I undressed, got into bed, opened my novel, tried reading, set it on my lap, and wondered about separating from him. If he wasn't going to stop trying to put walls between me and my kids and grandkids, maybe I should. It's twenty years since I last had to pay an attorney, to get Ken off that bigamy charge. I thought of leaving him a few times over the years, but whenever I did, I'd remember the feeling of being alone, after John died, and that memory would strike such fear in me, I'd forget about divorcing. But now, I had all of my children nearby, and someday Alan's going to come here to live, and I'll have all my grandchildren, too. And so the day after tomorrow, when Ken's out on the road, I'd start looking for an attorney.

Ken opened the door, and I realized he'd turned the TV off. He stared at me, as if trying to read my mood, and I picked up the book and looked at it. He undressed down to his underwear, tossing his clothes across the back of a chair, and crawled into bed and tried to kiss me on the cheek, but I turned my face away. He said, "Okay," lay down, and in no time was snoring.

I set the book on my night table, turned off my light, and lay on my side, with my back to him. As I drifted off, I remembered a Shakespeare comedy that John and I had seen when David was a senior in high school. He had the role of a fairy king, who drips a love potion on the eyes of his sleeping fairy queen that makes her love the first creature she sees when she awakes, and that creature's a jackass, but she's blind to that and adores it. I woke one morning to the sound of Ken snoring like a barnyard animal, and with the sight of his face as he lay on his back, his short gray-brown hair and long nose, his lips almost rippling with each breath, it wasn't a stretch to think of him as a jackass, and of me as the fairy queen, who unlike the one in the play, gets to see what she's fallen in love with. Would I have fallen in love with Ken if I hadn't gotten hung up on the drugs and the alcohol? Over the years, I've often thought of the queen and the jackass, and sometimes in my mind I refer to Ken as *Bottom*, my bottom, my ass, and I laugh inside at my little joke. But other times, just like the queen in the play, I fawn all over him.

My "Bottom" was on the road when I went to David and Barbara's place to spend time with them and Alan, whom I wouldn't see again until Christmas. Barbara greeted me with a warm smile as always and told me David and Alan were in the backyard, kicking the soccer ball around with Alan's English friend and his dad. She led me past Alan's suitcase near the door, through the living room, and across the patio to the backyard, where we watched the two boys and their dads dribble the ball, trying to get it past their opponents and score a goal in the net they'd set up beneath the limbs of the oak tree. Alan amazed me with his ability to dribble and cut one way and the other so fast neither his friend nor the father could stop him. And David, when he got the ball, tried to kick it to Alan as quickly as possible.

"It's wonderful to see the two of them so happy," Barbara said. "After we take Alan to the airport, David's going to be down." She looked at me. "Thanks for coming along. I think it'll help to have you with us. He gets so emotional when Alan leaves. It's really hard for him." She paused. "When we were living in Iowa, there were no direct flights from Tulsa to Iowa City, so David would drive all the way to St. Louis to pick him up, and then turn around and drive back. I'd be waiting in the kitchen, and I'd hear the car pull into the driveway, and the two of them would be singing a Talking Heads song. They'd be so happy when they came in, it was like a tornado blew them into my arms. And for the entire time Alan was with us, David was happy. When it was time for Alan to return, David would take him back to St. Louis, and then turn around and drive home." She took a deep breath. "And I'd wait up for him at the kitchen table, smoking one cigarette after another. Late, usually after midnight, he'd pull into the driveway, and I'd feel so relieved—until he'd talk about the trip, about his mind wandering as he drove, and the car wandering, too, and the lights of an oncoming semi suddenly flashing in his eyes and the horn blasting him out of the state he was in, or the car throwing up gravel, and he'd suddenly realize he was falling asleep and manage to pull the car back on the road just in time." She sighed. "Now, it's a quick drive to the airport, and he won't be alone."

David and Alan and their two friends came toward us. David introduced me, and then the boy and his dad went around the corner of the building toward their townhouse, and David, Alan, Barbara, and I went into the living room, and Alan ran upstairs to put his ball away. David gestured toward the couch and invited me to sit down. Barbara sat next to me, and David in the armchair. He checked his watch and looked off. Alan came running down, David made room for him, put his arm around him and pulled him close, and Alan looked up at him with a grin.

I watched the two of them, and when my eyes snared Alan's, I asked, "What did you enjoy doing most since you've been here."

"Going to the island with Dad." He grinned and looked up at David again.

"What island?"

"Nicollet Island," Alan said.

"It's just a short hike from here," David said. "It's fun, because we get to walk on Minneapolis's original Main Street, a cobblestone road, with the Mississippi on one side and buildings over a hundred years old on the other. They contain restaurants and shops, and there are some empty old sawmills and flourmills. Walking around them and the houses on the island, built in the 1850s and 60s, it's like we're explorers entering the past."

"So," I asked Alan, "you like exploring the past?"

"It's okay. It's like when I'm in Paris with Mom, and we go look at old castles and churches."

"And what else do you like about the island?"

"Dad and I usually bring a soccer ball. And sometimes we fly a kite."

"Part of the island is just an open field," David said.

David's smile faded, and he looked down at his watch and off to the side.

It was so quiet, Barbara startled me when she said, "I need to show you a drawing Alan did a couple years ago." She went upstairs and returned with a black poster board and two pieces of paper attached to the board. On one piece was a drawing in red crayon of two figures running, the one in the foreground holding a black string tied to a black kite in the form of a large bird, flying high in the foreground. The figure in the background was tiny in comparison with the one in the foreground. On the other piece of paper, a hand-printed message read, "My kite was 1000 feet away from the ground I lost my kite."

"David," she said, "always assumed he was the bigger figure, the one running with the string attached to the kite, but the other day, Alan told him no, he was."

"Yeah," David said. "He's already grown up, and I'm the tiny little guy in the background." David smiled down at Alan. I hoped Alan would never leave him in the background.

We drove Alan to the airport, walked him to the boarding gate, and spoke with the flight attendant who'd be responsible for him until his arrival in Tulsa. While we sat and waited until it was time to board, he stood in front of the glass wall and watched the planes take off and land, and then came over and plopped down between David and me and leaned against his dad. We talked with Alan about what he was going to do in France, and how lucky he was to go there every year with his mother, and David told him to say hello for him to his grandpa and grandma. When it was time to board, the flight attendant approached us. David took Alan in his arms, asked him to call as soon as he arrived, and told him he loved him, and Alan said, "I love you, too, Dad." He hugged Barbara and me, and the three of us watched the attendant walk him toward the entrance of the boarding tunnel, where Alan looked back, waved, and disappeared. I started to turn and stopped at the sight of David staring at that empty space.

Driving us toward the airport exit, he said, "I can't stand the idea of returning to the house. It'll feel so empty. Do you mind if we go for a ride, listen to some music?"

"I'd like that," Barbara said, touching his shoulder and smiling at him.

We entered the freeway that circles the Twin Cities, listening to classical music that felt like long waves building upon one another and carrying me off.

Over an hour later, we arrived at the house and sat down in the living room. The sun shining through the glass door revealed the stillness and the silence in the room. I was trying to think of something to say to get us in a good mood, when David stood up and asked if anyone wanted a whiskey. Barbara said, "No," and I said, smiling, "You know I don't drink." He went over to a cabinet and took out a bottle and a glass.

"Would you like something?" Barbara asked.

"I'd love a cup of ginger tea, if you have any." While she went to put the water on to boil, I watched David set the glass on the table next to his chair, pour, sit down, and take a drink. I saw a vacant look in his eyes and felt his pain.

Barbara returned and sat down next to me. "Would you like to join us for dinner? David and Alan and I made chicken noodle soup yesterday, with carrots, celery, onions, and fresh sprigs of dill. Alan cut the celery. We cooked it for a long time, so it should be easy to digest. I just need to warm it up. But, if you can't eat that, I can boil an egg, or cook some ramen noodles, and, oh, what else—"

David smiled and shook his head. "Yeah, we had a great time making that soup. Listened to music and sang and told jokes and goofed around."

Barbara started at the whistle of the tea kettle, ran to the kitchen, returned and handed me my cup of tea, and sat down next to me.

"Didn't we, Barbara."

"What? I didn't hear what you said."

"It was fun, you and Alan and I making the soup together."

"A lot of fun." She smiled at me. "Alan had a really good time."

"It wasn't like when I worked with Dad in his bakeries." He shook his head and took a drink.

Worried about what was going on with David, I decided to stay for dinner and find out. "The soup sounds good," I said to Barbara. "If it's cooked for a long time, my stomach should be able to handle it."

"Good. I hope you like it. I've already put it on the stove to warm up."

I felt David staring and saw his eyes fixed on me, as if they could see through me.

"You remember that picture of Johnny Boy you and Dad used to have hanging in your bedroom?"

"Of course."

"You still have it?"

"What do you think?"

"Who's Johnny Boy?" Barbara asked, looking back and forth from David to me.

"My first child. He died when he was three months old."

"Oh, Virginia." Barbara's eyes looked as if she felt the pain I still remembered. "That must've been so hard."

"It was."

"My dad loved him so much, he named him Johnny Boy, when he was still just a bump in my mother's belly. Well, first he named him John Junior, and then he named him Johnny Boy, after he'd started fantasizing all the things he and his darling son would do together." David took a drink.

"David," I said, "do you want to talk about something?"

He fixed his eyes on me, snorted, "Huh," and took another drink.

"You know, Virginia, I was wondering yesterday what you do when Ken's on the road, and if . . . if you'd like to get together with someone, we'd love to have you over."

"That's really sweet of you. I'll keep that in mind. I usually have things to do, but I'd love to come over from time to time, when it's convenient for you."

"In the beginning," David said, "Johnny Boy was like a ghost living in our apartment. He had his picture in its own, special place on a shelf in the living room. Every August, when his birthday would come around, we'd visit his grave, and you'd hand me a bouquet of flowers that I'd lay on his tombstone, and Dad would stare at it, with a sad look in his eyes. It made me sad to see how much he missed Johnny Boy. I think we went there a few times after Patty was born, didn't we?"

"A few."

"David, are you okay?" Barbara asked.

"I'm fine."

She stared at him, until something sizzled. "The soup's boiling," she exclaimed, and rushed to the kitchen, and I followed her. We set the table in the dining area, putting the kettle of soup in the center. I sat down, and while Barbara ladled soup into our bowls, David put the bottle of whiskey back in the cabinet and returned to the table with a bottle of wine, two glasses, and a corkscrew. He set the glasses and the wine down, uncorked the bottle, poured for Barbara and himself, and sat down. During dinner, our conversation turned to Minneapolis as Barbara's new home. She liked what she'd seen of the city, the art museums, the lakes, and the parks, and being close to the river and the restaurants that look out on it.

And then David said, "It's strange. I spent so many years of my life trying to get away from here. And now, here I am, in a place that reminds me of everything I wanted to forget. I remember you saying, Mom, the first time you came over, that this neighborhood reminds you of the one I moved to after Dad told me to leave, for the obvious reason it is the same." He stared at the table, then looked at Barbara. "The argument happened a few weeks after my twentieth birthday. I finally told my dad how much I hated his guts for the things he'd done to me, all the ridicule and abuse. I recited a litany of memories, and when I finished, I looked him in the eye and said, 'If I wanted to be perfect, all I'd have to do is be the opposite of *you*.'" David's eyes glared.

"Did you really say that to him?" I asked.

"I did."

I shook my head. "He died four months later. Those were the last words he heard from you."

"And these are the last words he said to me. 'In the morning, I want you to pack your things, call a cab, and leave. And don't ever come back.' And that's what I did. I moved into a rooming house a few blocks from here and didn't see him again until the last hours of his life."

"I wanted the two of you to make peace with one another."

"I know, Mom." He shook his head. "But that wasn't possible. Not after all the things he'd done. I remember when I came home on the train, at Christmas, my first year of college, and I did something that pissed him off,

198

and he said, 'It cost me a twenty-dollar bill for you to come home. A twenty-dollar bill!'" David hissed the words, his eyes riveting me. He took a deep breath, and I saw the anger and hatred he was imitating mutate into pain and sadness. "I might be a long ways from perfect, but I'm not him. Every time I talk to Alan, every time we write to one another, I tell him I love him. My son will never wonder if he's worthy of being loved."

I laid my hand on his. "You're a good father."

"Alan will never be destroyed by the past he carries inside him."

I caught my breath.

"David," Barbara said, "are you all right?"

"I've been living with this shit forever." He snorted a laugh and looked back and forth from me to Barbara, as if he were coming out of a dream. "Of course I'm all right." His facial muscles relaxed, and his eyes softened and warmed as they fixed on hers. "I'm fine. Well, would anyone like some dessert? Mom, what'll it be? Applesauce or cognac?"

"Applesauce," I mumbled, as I studied his face, stunned by his sudden happiness.

"Applesauce it is." He stood up.

He and Barbara cleared the dishes, she brought a bowl of applesauce for me and a carton of yogurt for herself, and David returned the nearly empty wine bottle to the cabinet, brought back a bottle of cognac, and sat down and poured himself a drink.

"We're so looking forward to Alan coming back at Christmas," Barbara said.

"Yeah," David said, "we're gonna take him up to Itasca State Park, where the Mississippi is so small you can jump across it. The park has great cross-country ski paths. We'll go to bed early on New Year's Eve, get up when everyone's sleeping off their hangovers, drive up and spend the day just skiing through the woods. The silence, the stillness," he shook his head, "there's nothing more beautiful than a forest covered with snow, and once Alan hears that silence and feels that stillness and sees that beauty, he'll always want to be here." David's eyes glowed. He finished his cognac and poured himself another as he continued talking, and from the way he gripped his glass, I could see the alcohol was feeding the fire burning inside him, and he had a tenuous hold on the lid covering that fire.

I left about an hour after dinner, when I started feeling intense pain in my stomach. As soon as I arrived home, I took four pain killers, went to bed, and lay on my side, curling like a fetus, holding my stomach and gritting my teeth. I wondered if the pain was due solely to the difficulty my stomach—what was left of it and my other organs—had digesting the soup, or if I'd eaten too much, or if the tension I'd felt coming from David had caused it. The pain subsided, I changed into my pajamas, got under the covers, propped up the pillows against the headboard, opened my novel to where I'd left off, and after reading a few lines, lay the book down and thought about the evening with David and Barbara. Long after I'd turned off the light, I heard David talking in the dark about Johnny Boy, the ghost living in the house, and repeating what he'd said to his father. I wanted to see David again. I had to.

The next morning, I woke to a dull, vague pain in my stomach that radiated to my back. I took more pain killers and lay down, holding my belly, feeling bloated. When I felt better, I got up. While brushing my teeth, I noticed how thin my arms and neck appeared in the mirror, and how hollow my cheeks were. But I wasn't surprised, as my appetite had steadily decreased over the last few weeks.

I called David and told him we needed to talk. After a pause, he said, "Sure, come on over."

Less than an hour later, I was sitting at his kitchen table, sipping ginger tea, and staring at him as he leaned back in his chair, a look in his eyes that seemed to say, Well?

"What are you doing today?" I asked.

"Getting my course ready. I start teaching next week."

"You sure you've got time to talk?"

"I would've told you if I didn't."

"Okay." I took another sip, wondering how best to start. I smiled and said, "I'm really happy you moved back. But, after the way you talked last night, about the argument with your father, and you telling him you wanted to be the opposite of him—"

"And I am."

200

"Maybe not as much as you think."

"Oh, really? If ten years from now, Alan were to talk to me about a college with some creative writing program that turned him on and he wanted to go to school there, can you imagine me saying, 'Lots of luck finding a patron?' No, I'd do the opposite. I've always done the opposite with my son."

"Your father died a year after that conversation. Did you ever think about the possibility he might've known he was going to die, and his family would have to go on without him? Don't forget, doctors and hospitals cost a lot of money. He might've felt he couldn't afford to send you to a school on the East Coast. And what about your sisters? He felt responsible for all of us, even though he was going to die."

"You can't be sure he knew he was dying."

"No, I can't."

"And you can't deny the things he did to me. That time he pinned me by my neck against the wall and was going to smash my face in, and I was, what, twelve years old?"

"You can find things he did that I can't deny. But I ask you again, David, if you still feel so much hatred toward your father, if this city brings back such horrible memories, then why did you move back?"

"I wanted Alan to grow up close to you."

"Oh, it's nice of you to say that, but there's more to all of this than you wanting Alan to grow up close to me. This move seems to have been going on for years—from Austin, to Tulsa, to Iowa City, and finally Minneapolis. And so much destruction along the way. Chantal meant everything to you, you were so in love with her, and then you divorce and you're with another woman, and then you leave Alan behind in Tulsa when you move to Iowa City. And that job interview at Harvard, can you explain to me how you get that kind of opportunity and then, the night before your interviews, you go out and get drunk? What's going on?"

He put his elbows on the table, bowed his head in his hands, closed his eyes, and took a deep breath.

"David, when someone destroys so much in his own life, there's something wrong. What is it?"

He sighed and leaned back in his chair. "I realized after the divorce from

Chantal that she wasn't the problem. I was." He shook his head and took a deep breath. "And the job interview at Harvard—the night before, I just wanted to have a drink and relax. I needed that drink. I knew getting the job would make Chantal happy, and I'd be proud to be a Harvard professor—me, a kid who'd never even planned on going to college until my junior year in high school. But I had this obsession I'd be teaching a bunch of pampered, spoiled rich kids, with a huge sense of entitlement, who'd treat me like a servant. I remembered the way kids with money sometimes looked down on me when I was in college and when I was wandering around Europe, living however I could. I hated them. I never wanted to do anything for them. Once I started drinking that night, I couldn't stop. When I got back to the hotel, I passed out and woke up four hours later with the worst heart palpitations I've ever had. I thought I was going to die, until the palpitations went away, and then I went to the interviews. A whole day of them."

"What about the divorce from Chantal? If you loved her, why did you start seeing other women?"

"My dream was always to get away from here, and I did. But everything came with me. Everything. I hadn't thought about that. And when I was unhappy, when I'd get depressed, I'd . . . I'd blame her." He snorted a laugh. "If Dad wanted to cripple me for life, leave me with pain I'd never stop feeling, he succeeded. The psychiatrists and the psychoanalyst I saw, none of them could help me get over what he'd done. He was so good at making me feel worthless, utterly worthless. I always thought there was something wrong with me, and I'd wonder what it was. And then, a few years ago, a therapist said, 'Maybe there's nothing wrong with you. Maybe there was something wrong with him.' Wow." David snickered and repeated, "Maybe there was something wrong with him," nodding his head with each word. "What do you think that could've been?"

"Your father was a good man. What you—"

"He was a good man? I know he went to Mass every Sunday, but—"

"What you don't know is the life his parents handed him."

"If you're going to tell me whatever was wrong with him was because of the way his parents treated him, I'm not interested. Not interested in excuses."

"Your dad's father was a tyrant, who used his children. He made your

202

father start working when he was just a boy and took all the money he earned. Your dad was expected to help his younger siblings make the move to St. Paul. He was like a father to them. He lent them money, which they often didn't pay back. Same thing with his father. Once that old geezer borrowed money from my father, and told your dad if he wanted to protect the family honor, he'd have to pay off the debt. And to top it all, your dad's youngest brother, one of the kids who'd borrowed money from him and didn't pay it back, used to call him a rich bastard. And another thing, your dad cared about people. He really did. You were just a kid when your Uncle Bob was killed in that car accident, leaving your aunt Marlene a widow with four kids, so maybe you didn't know this, but your dad stepped in and for at least a year after Bobby died, he made sure Marlene and the kids had the money they needed. Your father was a good man." Tears had welled up, and I started sobbing in spite of myself. "He was a good man."

David's hand touched my arm. "Mom. Mom, I didn't mean to hurt you."

I leaned back and, breathing deeply, took a tissue out of my purse and wiped my eyes.

"This compassionate side of Dad you talk about, I got glimpses of it, but—
"

"I never knew how to deal with the problems between the two of you. If I tried to intervene, tried to defend you, help you in any way, it just made everything worse. Maybe not right away, but over time."

"So why didn't he love me?"

"It's not that simple." I took a deep breath and sighed. "I might be to blame. When you talked about being the opposite of your dad by always telling your son you love him, you made me think of your dad and Johnny Boy. Your dad never would've said he wanted to be the opposite of his father, but I could see that's what he was trying to do. And when your dad talked about Johnny, before he was even born, and all the things the two of them would do together, and how he would make sure Johnny got what he needed to have a good life, he was being the kind of father he would've liked to have had, a father who loved his son. And when Johnny died, your dad was devastated. After a year had gone by, he wanted to have another child. A son. He needed that boy as a way of getting past the pain he felt with his own father.

203

"It took years for me to want to have another baby. But when I did, I was determined my baby . . . I was determined *you* wouldn't die. Your dad had chosen the name for Johnny Boy. This time I chose the name. I wanted to name you David, because David killed Goliath, and I thought of Goliath as Death. When we brought you home from the hospital, your dad was working long hours every day, and I spent all my time with you. Your dad would come home from work, and since you weren't used to being with him, you'd cry until I'd take you. I hovered over you. I'd get up every night, tiptoe to your crib, bend over and listen for the sound of you breathing, and if I couldn't hear it right away, I'd panic. And then you'd take a breath, and I'd almost collapse with joy. I'd go back to bed, feeling you, my little David, had defeated Death once again."

"For you, Goliath might've been Death. For me, Goliath was Dad."

I shook my head. "He needed your love when you were a child. He needed it to heal, to feel he was being the father that he'd wanted, when he was growing up. And because of me, he didn't get it. I didn't realize it, but I was so anxious, so possessive of you, I took you away from him. If anything turned him into Goliath, it was the separation I created between him and you."

"Children aren't responsible for making their parents feel loved."

"When you tell Alan you love him, don't you hope he loves you back? Doesn't his love have a healing effect on you?"

David looked away.

"Think of how hard it is for you every time Alan leaves, and how you so want him to move here and live with you. And think of what it would be like if you had to give him up forever."

David shook his head, and then looked at me as if he were accusing me of something. "How did you fall in love with him?"

"Oh, David, how does anyone fall in love? The first few times I saw him was in high school. Some girls were looking at him in the hall, giggling and acting crazy, because he was so handsome. His good looks attracted me. But what made me fall in love with him might've been that he reminded me of my father."

"What?"

"Yeah. I don't know if I realized it right away, but that's what I came to

204

see. He might've had more in common with my father than with his. Your dad was on his own at an early age, was determined to succeed, be his own man, as he used to say, and worked, and struggled, and didn't give up, and at the same time he was kind, caring, and loving. It wasn't until the Christmas Eve following Johnny Boy's death that I saw the anger in him. Some man stared at me in a bar, and your dad got into a fight with him and nearly beat him to death. That scared the bejesus out of me. I realized the anger was always there, the trigger always cocked, and that made him different from my father. But no matter how scared I might've been, I never thought of leaving him. He gave me life."

David looked down at the table, then up at me. "Did you ever worry about the damage he was doing to your kids?"

"The tension was between you and him. I worried about the two of you."

"The night he died, and we came home from the hospital, I heard Patty crying in her room. I went in, took her in my arms, and held her. And she said, 'He was so mean.'"

"I don't believe that."

"I know what I heard."

"Your father behaved like most fathers back then. He disciplined his kids, gave them spankings sometimes. But he loved them, and they knew it."

"You make him sound normal. Our family sound normal. Like all kids hate their fathers and grow up wanting to run away, like all widows abandon their children and go off with some guy, like—"

"I've spent the past twenty years trying to make things right. I think the girls have recovered. They know they're loved. But with you," I shook my head, "with you, it was always you and your dad. I wanted the two of you to love one another, but by the time you were a teenager, things had gotten so bad, and the anger you both felt seemed to evolve into hatred, and the hatred . . ." I shook my head and started crying again.

"There's never an end to this, is there. Sometimes I wonder, why can't I just let myself be happy with my wife and my son? Why should what happened twenty or thirty years ago still make me feel like shit?"

I laid my hands on his and peered into his eyes, brimming with tears. "I don't know, David. I don't know. I love you. Your sisters love you. Alan and

Barbara love you. Maybe being back home will give you what you need."

I was sitting in my chair, knitting a stocking cap for Alan, listening to the conversation with David playing through my mind, seeing the look in his face when he said, "There's never an end to this, is there?" And the tears in his eyes. The last time I'd seen him weep, he was standing next to me, over John's body, and I'd turned toward him and found him shaking his head and crying. No, David, there's never an end to remembering. As that thought passed through my mind, I noticed my fingers holding the needles hovering above the cap. I set myself back to work, as I had repeatedly, after each time I'd noticed the needles poised in the air, and as I made another stitch and pulled the yarn through, I thought, Our memories will have their way with us. They can make us happy, help us survive, and they can destroy us.

When I finished knitting, I left home. I walked down the narrow road to the exit from the trailer park, turned, and continued on the dirt path that borders the busy street with no sidewalks, feeling the whoosh of speeding cars and trucks, and passed mailboxes on wood posts that stand next to long gravel driveways to houses that look like they could be farmhouses. I crossed one side street and another, and turned down the next, where the ramblers remind me of the home in which John and I raised our children, the house with the lawn that slopes down to a street that also has no sidewalks—a street where I'd see kids on bikes and tricycles, and boys dribbling a basketball in a driveway and tossing it at a net above a garage door, and girls heading for the shopping center across a field, and a mother walking out to her car in the driveway and waving at me, or another in her housedress, pulling clothes out of a basket and hanging them on a line in her backyard, back in the day when everyone had clothes poles and lines in their yard.

I returned to the trailer, feeling as if during my walk I'd stepped into another state of mind, a younger state, and was free to do whatever struck my fancy. I had a sudden craving for pickled herring, in a Scandinavian brine of wine vinegar, sugar, and onions—the kind of food I loved to eat before I started having problems with my belly. I drove to the supermarket, bought an eight-ounce jar, returned home, and sat down and ate the whole thing, it was so good, and wondered, Why stop now? I opened the refrigerator and saw the rhubarb pie, which Ken had bought for himself, and served myself a large piece, with a couple scoops of ice cream. After I finished spooning up the last of the melted ice cream and the crumbs and smears of rhubarb, my stomach was seized with the worst cramps I've ever experienced. I found the pain killers in my purse, gulped a few, curled up on my bed and gripped my stomach, until I fell asleep.

Early the next morning, I woke up scratching my arms and feeling sick. I made some ginger tea, but still felt sick after I'd finished it, and the itching continued. While brushing my teeth, I noticed a tinge of yellow in the whites of my eyes. I examined my skin and thought I saw a yellow tint, but I was so emotional, I thought, Am I imagining this? I returned to the bedroom, pulled up my blouse, and looked at my belly in the mirror, turning one way and the other, and thought I saw some swelling, but I wasn't sure. I called my oncologist, told the receptionist it was urgent, I had some of the symptoms the doctor had talked about, I needed to see him, and she found a way to get me on his schedule. I arrived early and sat in the waiting room, my head throbbing with worry. I picked up a newspaper, looked at an article about the Democratic national convention, and wondered if I'd be alive to vote, and told myself, Who knows, it might be nothing.

A nurse called me, led me into a room, took my vitals, handed me a hospital gown, and left. I took off my slacks and blouse, put on the gown, sat down, and looked around at the exam table, the picture on the wall of trees in their fall colors, the window that looked out on big, puffy clouds, and the little desk where the nurse had sat, next to my chair. I felt like getting up and leaving but didn't move. A gentle knock, the door opened, and the doctor entered. He smiled, closed the door, and came over and sat next to me, his eyes never leaving me, and asked how I felt. I told him about the pain in my belly, the itching, the yellow tint to my skin, and the swelling—all the signs he'd talked to me about. He had me lie down on the examination table and raised the gown so he could see my belly and pressed his fingers against every part of my stomach, and each time it hurt. And then he helped me off the table, and we sat facing one another.

"Is it what I was afraid it was?"

"Yes. I'm sorry, Virginia. We didn't get all of the cancer."

"I'm going to die."

"Yes."

I stared at his face, as if it were a wall, and heard the words in my mind, I'm going to die. Small, simple words . . . that mean the end of everything.

"How long do I have?"

"It's hard to say. Once the cancer has metastasized, things tend to go fast. It could be three or four weeks, or months."

He continued talking, mentioning the CAT scan we'd have to do, while I tried to understand what the words three or four weeks or months really meant, because they didn't mean what they'd meant before. And then I became aware of him looking at me.

"Virginia, what do you want to do with the time you have left?"

"I want to spend as much of it as I can with my children, my grandchildren, and my husband. I'm lucky. My kids all live close to me. But my youngest grandchild is with his mother in France, and they're not coming home until the end of August. They live in Tulsa."

"The end of August. That's very soon."

"I got to see him this summer. He came to visit his father for about a month. Maybe he can come and stay over Labor Day weekend."

I took a deep breath, felt the trembling in my body, and wiped away the tears trickling down my cheeks with the tissues the doctor handed me. His eyes looked into mine as he talked about medications that would address the pain and discomfort, so I could enjoy as much as possible the time I had left with my family, and as he wrote the prescriptions, with his head bent over the desk, I looked out the window at the beautiful clouds and felt more tears welling up.

That night for dinner, I had a hard-boiled egg, a banana, applesauce, water, and morphine. And when I went to bed, I took more morphine and curled into a sleep that felt like a deep, dark tunnel.

Late in the afternoon, as I sat on the couch, knitting Alan's hat, I remembered I'd planned on talking to an attorney, back when I still believed I had a second chance, and felt relieved I hadn't. Someone walked up the stairs, the door opened, and Ken entered. "Hi, sweetheart." He tossed his canvas bag on the floor and hung his green Mayflower jacket in the closet. "You still working on that hat? That red nose tells me you've added Rudolph." He chuckled, bent over, and gave me a kiss. "You're gonna spoil that grandson of yours. I can imagine how you're gonna treat him when he gets here at Christmas." He sank into his chair with a big sigh and laid his arms on the armrests. "God, I'm tired. Really wears me out, going on the road." He shook his head. "So, what've you been up to? Aside from making presents to get your grandson to come live here."

"I need to talk to you about something. Why don't you come and sit here." I patted the cushion next to me.

"What's up?" He looked puzzled.

I managed a smile and patted the cushion again. "Come here and I'll tell you."

He came over and sat down, resting his hands on his thighs. "I don't have a good feeling about this."

I took his hand and pulled it onto my lap. "You remember, before the operation, I told you the doctors might not be able to get all of the cancer."

His brow furrowed. "Yeah."

"Over the last couple weeks, I've noticed the symptoms the doctor warned me about—pain in my belly and back, loss of appetite, bloating, jaundice." I took a deep breath. "I saw him yesterday." I tightened my grip on his hand, so I could hold onto him. "They've done everything they can do."

"Maybe you should see another doctor."

I shook my head. "I don't want any more operations. I wanna spend the time I have left with you and my kids and grandkids."

He gazed at me, tears welling up in his eyes. He moved his lips, as if he were about to say something, but couldn't find the words. He put his arm around my shoulders, pulled me close, until our heads touched, and said, "I'll take good care of you."

That night, when we went to bed, I showed him the morphine tablets I was supposed to take.

I sat on my armchair, my feet propped up on an ottoman, and my kids sat on the couch and the other armchair, telling me how much they loved me, their voices breaking with emotion. They'd try to smile but ended up biting their lips. However, they seemed happy once they began talking about their memories, like our road trip out West, through the Badlands and the Rockies, when John was alive, and the frequent visits to Papa and Mama on the farm, where the kids would ride the old workhorses bareback and play hide and seek in the hay loft with their cousins, scooching down between the bales. And the girls remembered the day they got freaked out when Mama cut off a chicken's head, and the body went running in every direction, as if frantically seeking its head, splattering blood everywhere, until it flopped to the ground and with a few last twitches of its feet gave up the search. And then Grandma plucked its feathers, cooked it, and served it for dinner. And they brought up our two-week vacations every summer at the resort up north, on a lake outside a town where maybe a hundred people lived. And that family from across the street in our old neighborhood, with two girls about the same age as Patty and Linda, they would also rent a cabin, and the girls would spend their days on the beach or in the water, except when they'd walk up the gravel road to the grocery store in town and come back sucking on their popsicles. And when Barbara asked if David was there, too, the girls grinned as they talked about his girlfriend, the blonde who lived in some little town and who'd stay with her family in a cabin at the same resort. She started wearing sexy bikinis after the summer she met David, and they'd disappear on long walks. The girls teased David and tried to get him to say what he and his girlfriend would do when they were gone, and I remembered how I'd worried, and when he'd finally show up after leaving her at her cabin, I'd ask where they'd been and what they'd been doing, and he'd grin, and I'd wonder if he was telling me the truth when he'd say nothing had happened. The first few months every fall, I'd worry about getting a call from a parent, but all that came to an end when he met Sandy. One of the girls mentioned her name, and I opened my eyes and saw everyone looking at David, and then my eyes fluttered shut.

Someone knocked at the door, Ken opened, and a woman with gray hair entered, looked at me, and smiled as I looked back. Ken whispered something to her. She nodded, came over, and sat down on the armchair turned toward the couch on which I was lying, and on which I'd been lying every day for some time, propped up on pillows so I could feel I was still part of the world and could see family and friends. It took me a while to recognize Marlene, and it seemed to take her a while to recognize me.

"It's good to see you, after all these years." She paused and shook her head. "I was so sad when I got the news. You and John have always been the kindest people I've ever known. I'll always remember the way you helped me after Bobby died. I would've never made it without you."

We didn't dwell on the present, didn't talk about the daughter who'd died of breast cancer in her thirties, or the granddaughter hit and killed by a car.

"Do you remember when you and John and Bobby and I went to the Castle Royal to celebrate your birthday?" she asked.

"The Castle Royal! I wanted to go there from the first time I opened the *Pioneer Press* and saw the ads, with the drawings of women in those beautiful gowns and men in tuxedos. And John took me."

"He was always so sweet to you."

I nodded, closed my eyes, and remembered John putting his arms around me, pulling me close, and whispering, his breath tickling my ear, "I'm going to take you to the Castle Royal for your birthday." I could almost feel him holding me.

"We wore those beautiful dresses."

I opened my eyes and looked at her. "And our men wore their best suits."

"That was strange, walking toward those bluffs that must've been a hundred feet high, dressed up like we were in Hollywood. I felt like we were in a movie. There was that brick wall around the two big doors to the cave that made them look like the entrance to a castle, and we went in, and the ceiling was like a vault, covered with red stucco. You forgot right away you were in a cave, down by the Mississippi."

"I remember walking through a room full of tables, with white cloths and candles, and sitting down and looking around at the faces glowing in the candlelight . . . the beautiful dresses and necklaces . . . the white tuxedo jackets and bow ties."

"And Cab Calloway and his band."

I laughed. "Oh, my God. John and I were going to try to dance to that music."

"I remember Bobby and I got out on the floor, and the orchestra started playing. We bounced around, threw our arms in the air, and tried to do what everyone else was doing, and then we sat down, because we'd never danced to anything but polkas and waltzes."

"Yeah. We just watched Cab sing and lead his orchestra, and everyone sang the lines from that song. You remember? He and the orchestra would sing a line, and then the audience would sing it back. Everyone seemed to know it. It started out, 'hi-de-ho.'"

"No, it was, 'hi-ho-hi.'"

"No, no. 'Hi-de-hi-de-ho.'"

"That was it. And how did the other lines go?"

"I can't remember." I could see John's face, the love in his warm green eyes. "I was a lucky woman. John loved to do new things. That's something he and David have in common. They have a lot in common, even though they never got along."

"I didn't know that."

"It became clearer as they got older. David told me not long ago that from the time he was a teenager he wanted to leave home and explore the world. John wanted to travel, too. We went on road trips with the kids, probably visited half the states in the country. He liked to take me to ritzy places, like Hot Springs, Arkansas, where we'd stay at the Arlington Hotel. During the days we'd go to the races and bet on the horses, or he and his friend would go golfing. Then his friend's wife and I would go to the Woodland Gardens, or the Fordyce Bathhouse, for baths, massages, and manicures. And at night we'd all go to the Southern Club and watch Duke Ellington play." I looked over at her. "Can you imagine, a farm girl from Wisconsin, doing all that?" I shook my head. "John was so curious, nothing could hold him back. We went to Canada, and then to Cuba, back when it was still run by that dictator. If John hadn't died so young . . ."

"Bobby never even got a chance."

"I know."

As she continued talking, my eyes closed, and her voice faded. When I woke, she was gone. I had no idea what she'd talked about, after mentioning Bobby. Cuba entered my mind, maybe because talking about it revived my anger. I'll never forget the sight of all those Americans going there to have fun at the clubs and casinos, and Cuban women, wearing practically nothing, dancing and prancing for them. Slowly I came to realize that Cuban children were being used as prostitutes, and once I started noticing them, I saw them everywhere. And poverty, I'd never seen so many poor people, not even in the South. I talked to David about all that, and maybe that fed into his politics, which disgust Ken, and would have disgusted his father, too, if they'd ever had more than one conversation. I learned early on, if I wanted to keep peace in the family, better not talk about that sort of thing, or tell John or Ken how I voted.

I opened my eyes and saw Gerda sitting on a chair, next to my bed. I was too woozy to sit up, what with all the morphine I'd taken, and just looked at her. When she noticed I was awake, she started talking. Soon she was going on about old times, when she and Hans and John and I would go out for drinks and dinner and dancing at some tavern, and Hans would get drunk, and John might also have one too many, and the two of them would get into a scuffle with other fellows who'd had too much, and when the fists would fly, Gerda and I would swing our purses in defense of our boys, or against the girls who were with the other fellows. Gerda told some other stories, too, and shook her head and laughed at the crazy things we used to do.

But her voice saddened with regret when she said, "I should've paid more attention to Hans's drinking. After we got married and had our first baby, and I wasn't working anymore, he'd always hit the taverns on the way home from work, and on payday he'd announce drinks were on him. He'd come home totally pickled and fall into bed, and I'd go through his pockets and pull out whatever money was left and hide it, and try to figure out how we'd get through the rest of the month. That was back in the days when my belly always seemed to be bulging with a new baby. And then we moved down the hill to the flats below the bluffs, not far from the railroad tracks, where the immigrants lived, the Germans and then the Irish and then the Jews. Once you ended up there, you didn't know if you'd ever get out."

I remembered standing in front of my window in our apartment on Summit Lane, looking down past the edge of the bluff at the narrow apartment buildings and wood-frame houses below that looked like tinder, and wondering how she and her babies could have a good life if her fellow didn't quit drinking. Sundays, John and I would drive down the hill, with a week's supply of bread and a few Danish, and visit her and her family in one cramped apartment or another. And after David was born, and I'd stay home with him, and when John and I moved to our first house, Gerda would pack her kids up and take the streetcar up the hill to our place. And she and I would sit at the kitchen table and smoke and drink coffee and talk about our kids, who were playing upstairs or in the backyard, under the apple tree; and about Mama and Papa and the boys, and the things we did when we were growing up, like in the winters, when we'd ski from the slope behind the barn past the pond at the bottom of the hill and across the wood bridge over the creek, all the way to the woods, where we'd stop, and the crows would caw to warn the other animals that humans had arrived; and the times when we'd shovel off the pond and clamp skates onto the bottom of our boots and go skating; and the sunny days when we'd tie the bobsled to the harness on one of the work horses that would tow us down the gravel road covered with snow, and we'd hide beneath the blanket in the sled when gusts of wind would whip that snow up and blow it at us.

"I wish I could remember all the way back," I said.

"All the way back where?"

"To when our mother was alive."

"I don't remember her alive. I just remember pictures. And that town, Sleepy Eye, where her parents lived, and where they buried her. And living with her sister and her family, and riding through town in a horse-drawn wagon, all bundled up in the cold, and seeing other wagons carrying coffins. I didn't understand why I couldn't stay with you and Papa and our grandparents, until the day Auntie brought me to their house, and I saw Papa walking and pushing a chair, and I learned he'd nearly died of the flu. Our grandparents didn't expect him to live, and they didn't want me to see him until they knew he would. You were just a toddler." Gerda paused. "Did I ever tell you I found her grave? I visit it every once in a while. It's strange having a mother you know only from pictures. And from what Papa told us. She died so young. Sometimes I have a question about her that I wanna ask Papa, but he's gone. Gone, now, for twenty years."

"Yeah," I said, drifting off.

I opened my eyes a while later, not knowing if I'd been asleep, or in some kind of a daze, and saw Gerda sitting close by, looking at a newspaper, waiting for me to come back, and my eyes filled with tears. I didn't want to let her go. After Hans died from all the booze, Gerda remarried, and by the time David turned eleven, she'd moved with her four kids to Albert Lea, and I rarely saw her after that. I missed her. God, I missed her.

Mornings and evenings blur, and I never know what day it is, or if I'll be alone when I wake or with someone. I lie propped up on my pillows, so I can doze off and wake up and continue whatever I'm doing. Lately I've been going through my photographs and deciding which ones to give to each of my kids. I see the happiness of those I love, and my own as well, as I look at myself, with white curls and glasses, posing with my daughters, one on each side of me, both of them beautiful, or holding my grandchildren while I read to them. I gaze at pictures of John in a suit and tie crouching on the front walk of our first house with David, a two-year-old standing in front of him, and of me with David in the backyard, when he was a toddler, in nothing but a diaper, standing in front of me, while I sit on my folded legs, holding him with both hands beneath his armpits, a blank look on his face as he gazes at the camera, and a look of bliss on mine. The pictures draw me back to our first years in that house, to the wedding that made me so happy, and angry, and to the house and the farm where I grew up with Mama, Papa, Gerda, and the boys.

As I went through the albums and the piles of pictures, one that I expected to see was missing—the one of my mother holding me in her arm, sitting in a chair in an open field, and part of the wall of a sod hut in the background. I quickly looked through the photos I hadn't gone through yet, and back through the ones I'd already selected for my kids and panicked. It was gone. I looked until I despaired of finding it and let go, and the morphine carried me off. Later, I hear the wind blowing, howling like a mother who has lost her child, screeching like someone gone mad, hurtling sand and dirt that rasp across the side of the hut, rattling the wooden planks, like it's about to tear them away, and my eyes snap open, the wind dies, and I see my mother, I see Anna, with her dark hair and pale face, looking down at me and singing, *"Den lille Ole med paraplyen, ham kender alle småfolk i byen, hver lille pige, hver lille dreng, han lægger sødt i sin lille seng."* It's the Danish lullaby about little Ole, the Sandman, whom children love, and who comes unseen to put little girls and boys to sleep.

David

Mom was lying in the hospital bed, her breath rasping her throat, the monitors bleeping, voices talking behind me, talking as if she were no longer alive. I held her cold hand and gazed at her thin face, her closed eyes, her parted lips. It had been hours since she'd opened her eyes or spoke. A nurse stopped at the other side of the bed, looked down at Mom's face as she touched her forearm and then up at the plastic bag suspended in front of her, injected the morphine that would blend with the liquid in the bag and flow through a tube into the IV attached to the back of Mom's wrist, and left. The nurses came more frequently now to inject morphine, just as they had for Dad, over twenty years before, when I'd stood next to Mom, during his last hours.

I bent over, my lips nearly touching her ear, and whispered, "I love you, Mom."

"I love you, too," she whispered, her words immersed in the stream of her breath.

I gripped her hand and held on to her and continued gazing at her face, seeing no sign of life, but still hearing each breath.

Patty whispered, "I thought she was unconscious."

I nodded. "So did I." Noticing Linda on my other side, I let go of Mom's hand, put an arm around each of my sisters, and held them close as we gazed down at Mom. After a while, I stepped back, leaving them my space, and as I turned to head for the hallway, I saw Ken sitting in an armchair, staring straight ahead. I ignored him and left.

I walked down the corridor, in the opposite direction from the waiting room, still upset about what had happened two days before, when I was anxious about Mom, not having been able to contact her for several days. I phoned Patty and Linda, and when we discovered none of us had been able to talk with her, we decided to meet at the trailer house. It was early evening when Barbara and I pulled up and found my two sisters and Tom waiting for us. They'd arrived just a couple minutes before. The five of us walked up the steps, I rang the bell, rang it again and again, and then pounded on the door, the aluminum rattling against the frame. Ken opened and stood there, in undershirt and slacks, his face covered with grayish stubble, his eyes bloodshot.

I barged past him, almost throwing him out of the way, and with the others following me, rushed through the living room to the bedroom and stopped, seeing Mom's eyes fixed on me. I moved toward the bed, watching her brows furrow as her eyes closed and her lips spread, and she gritted her teeth and groaned and rolled over on her side, gripping her stomach with both hands. I sat on the edge of the bed and put my hand on her shoulder, and the upper part of her body rocked back and forth. Patty and Linda also sat down on the bed, touched her face and shoulder, and cried, "Mom, Mom." I looked up and saw Ken, standing a few feet away, watching us. I got up and stood in his face.

"Why isn't she in a hospital?"

"She wanted to stay here."

"She wanted to, or *you* wanted her to?"

"I'm going to call an ambulance," Linda said, as she hurried by.

Ken shook his head, lowered his eyes toward the floor, sighed, and looked up. "I haven't slept for days." His eyes gazed past me at Mom and then focused on me. "I thought she'd be better off here. She seemed to want to stay."

He turned and walked out, and I followed him into the living room, where he sat down on the couch, next to a bed pillow resting on cushions propped up against the armrest. A blanket lay flipped across the couch, as if he'd given up on sleeping and tossed it off in frustration. He leaned forward and stared in the direction of the coffee table, the crumpled packs of cigarettes, the overflowing ashtrays, the coffee mugs, and the newspapers strewn about. I probably should've gone over and sat down next to him and put my arm around him, but I felt like beating the shit out of him.

Patty came up to me and said the ambulance was on its way. She followed my eyes and stared at Ken.

He returned her stare, then looked down at the table, took out a cigarette, and lit up. He took a couple drags, got up, headed the other way around the table to the door, walked out and stood on the deck, smoking.

Linda and I went back into the bedroom and joined Patty, who was sitting on the bed, holding Mom's hand. Mom rolled onto her back, while gripping her belly, her eyes shut, her mouth open in a grimace of pain. I wondered why Ken hadn't taken her to the hospital. Maybe he wanted to have her entirely to himself during the last days of her life. Or he thought she would die if he took her there, but she might live if he kept her at home. Or maybe he was just falling apart, too afraid to do anything.

I heard the sirens, doors slamming, and the paramedics barged in, with Ken right behind, explaining the situation, talking about his wife's condition, acting as if he were in charge. While one of the men stayed in the bedroom, checking Mom's vitals, and talking to the rest of us about what they'd do, the other two went back to the ambulance, returned with a stretcher, put Mom on it, wheeled her to the front door, carried her onto the deck and down the stairs to the ambulance. Ken wanted to go with her, but one of the paramedics told him no. The ambulance pulled away, he turned, our eyes fixed on one another, and he saw my anger and probably knew I hated his guts for always putting possession of my mother ahead of what was best for her.

Two days later, standing in a hall, the anger still gripping me, I realized I was no longer on the floor where Mom's room was located. With everything seething inside me, the voices shouting in my head, I'd rushed down flights of stairs, and maybe back up, and down a hall or two, and here I was, lost in another part of the hospital. I asked directions to get back to where I'd come from, but forgot them, and had to ask for more help as I walked down halls and up stairways. I finally found Mom's room and went in and stood next to Linda and Patty, across the bed from Ken, and gazed at Mom's face, her parted lips, her eyes that would never open again, and listened to her breathe, a gap between each breath that would get longer until she breathed her last.

After Mom's death, my mind became numb to everything around me, and I collapsed inside myself, except for moments with Barbara, who enfolded me in her love. One day, while sitting in the armchair, I became aware of a ringing sound. It was the phone. It might've rung several times. When it rang again, I went into the kitchen and answered and heard Patty's voice.

"I haven't heard from you," she said. "I've been worried. Are you okay?"

"No." I sighed. "But I'm alive. How about you?"

"The same. I just talked with Ken. You know what he's going to do?"

"No."

"He's having Mom's body cremated, even though she told us she wanted to be buried next to Dad. I reminded him of that, and he said Mom had changed her mind and told him she wanted to be cremated. He also said that in the new will she'd had drawn up after the operation, she'd given him power of attorney and left all decisions to him. He has all the power, and we have nothing."

"I know." I heard her crying at the other end of the line. "Are you going to be okay?"

"Yeah." She sniffled. "I'll see you tomorrow at the funeral parlor."

She hung up, and I continued holding the phone, until I heard the busy signal that brought me back.

Barbara and I sat in one of the rows of chairs at the funeral parlor, where we had come to attend the celebration of Mom's life. People I didn't know, but assumed Ken did, led some prayers. I heard the sound of praying, but not the words. Gerda, and then Marlene, and then Ellen stood up and talked about Mom, but I didn't hear their words, either. I closed my eyes, and remembered her, remembered bending over and whispering in her ear, "I love you, Mom," and hearing her whisper back, "I love you, too." She was dying when she said those words. I whispered again, "I love you." Everyone stood, I became aware that the celebration was over, and Barbara and I left.

We returned home, and as I took off my suit coat, I felt in my shirt pocket the funeral card, a bookmark, with the word *God* in large red letters on the left side at the top, and, in a blue box on the right, a pair of hands held together in prayer, and below those two images, the prayer of Alcoholics Anonymous—"Grant me the Serenity to accept the things I cannot change, Courage to change the things I can, and Wisdom to know the difference." On the back were the words, IN LOVING MEMORY OF, and Mom's full name, dates of birth and death, and two more prayers. I was too much in shock to feel anger as I gazed at the card and remembered that Mom stopped attending church services within a year of Dad's death and never showed interest since then in being part of any religion. I put the card in the leather-bound edition of the first volume of Proust's *A la recherche du temps perdu*, where I knew I'd always be able to find it. Barbara and I changed clothes and went for a walk along the same route that Alan and I would take, going a few blocks west and then south down a hill and west again up old Main Street, along the river shimmering with sunlight, and the birds flocking and chirping and singing in the branches above our heads. I stopped, took Barbara in my arms, and kissed her, and held her for a long time, my tears flowing onto her hair.

I continued working, teaching the survey course on the French novel that I'd taught at the University of Iowa, asking the same questions of my students about the characters falling in love, wondering how Mom could've loved Dad, and then Ken, trying to get through each day. And Barbara and I continued our walks along the river, sometimes having dinner at one of the restaurants that bordered it. And then one evening, Patty called.

"I've been trying to reach Ken for days, but no one's answering. I want to find out if we can come and get some of Mom's things, something to remember her by. He finally answered. He said he'd gone up north. I was surprised and asked him why. Guess what he said."

"No idea."

"To pour Mom's ashes in a lake. I asked him which one, but he wouldn't say. Just that it was a special place."

I imagined Mom's ashes flowing onto the surface of a lake and slowly disappearing, a gray cloud blending with the dark water, until there was nothing left.

"Isn't that disgusting," she said, "that he wouldn't even say which lake?"

"What difference does it make? She's gone. We only have memories."

"I know." Patty remained silent for a while, and then said, "I just wish there was a place where we could go and be with her."

"I do, too."

"Well, one good thing. He said Mom had divided up her pictures for the three of us, and we can come and get them anytime. We just need to call first."

I had no interest in calling Ken. But one night, I was awakened by a dream in which I saw, from a low angle, as if a camera were underwater, ashes streaming onto the surface of a lake and sifting down through luminous dark green water lit by rays of the sun, and I woke up, trembling, my cheeks wet with tears. The image stayed with me, and I saw it as I walked to and from campus and moved around the house, and each time I felt the loss of Mom all over again.

I finally called Ken and arranged to go pick up my share of the photographs the next evening. He'd always liked Barbara, so she and I decided it would be best if she were to come with me and serve as a buffer. We arrived, Ken let us in, and we sat down on the couch, while he went into the bedroom. His mail lay on the coffee table, the envelopes looking as if he'd tossed them, and they'd fanned out when they'd landed. One envelope had been opened, and on it lay a sheet of paper, a financial statement that included the words *Northern States Power* at the top, and at the bottom a check with a perforated edge where it could be torn off. Dad had invested a lot of money in NSP, and I wanted to see how much Ken was getting. When I reached for the statement, Barbara laid her hand on my forearm and whispered, "What are you doing?"

I whispered back, "I need to see this," and pushed my hand forward and picked up the statement. The check was made out to Ken, in the amount of nineteen hundred and some dollars. Not a huge amount, but enough to infuriate me, because neither my sisters nor I would ever receive a dime from our father's estate. Ken had had twenty years to go through it, and I suspect there was little of it left, but still . . . I tossed the statement with the check back onto the envelope and clenched both hands into a fist.

Barbara put her arm around my back and whispered, "He has everything that belongs to your mother. He won't give you a thing if you fight with him."

I took some deep breaths and tried to control my anger.

He returned with a box that looked like it had once contained a new pair of boots and set it on the table, brushing the envelopes out of the way. He took the cover off, revealing a green mitten and a stocking cap, with Christmas figures and a white ball on top, both designed to be worn with the scarf Mom had knitted for Alan. I picked up the cap and the mitten, looked for the other mitten, but instead found a little blue and white rectangular cushion, with a hole toward the top center, so it could slide onto a door handle, and the word GRANDMA crocheted in white letters across the middle. It was a Christmas present Alan had picked out for Mom, when Chantal had taken him shopping. I held it, took a couple breaths. I'd give it to Alan the next time he came. I looked again for the missing mitten, even though I knew it wasn't in the box, I would've seen it. Tears welled up, I wiped them away, sighed, and gazed at the hat, the mitten, and the cushion.

"Before Ginny passed," Ken said, "she went through all her albums and pictures."

"She probably would've liked to have given these pictures to us herself," I said.

Barbara heard the anger in my voice and said, "Thank you, Ken. It's so nice of you to have us over and give us these."

"Yeah," I said, looking up at him as I leafed through the photos, "thank you."

I noticed some of the pictures were attached to one another by Scotch tape that had yellowed over the years and had shreds of black album paper on the adhesive side, and I imagined Mom pulling the photos, which the tape linked to one another, off the pages, instead of trying to separate the photos from one another, and I wondered if she did that because the pain was getting worse, and she felt the end coming near. I sensed what she must've felt—the fear, the panic, the longing for her family, and no one but Ken to help her. And I wondered if she'd felt abused by him.

When Barbara and I got home, I set the box on the coffee table, and we sat down on the couch and went through the pictures of me in grade school and high school, and of me as a toddler, with Mom or Dad or both, and of the entire family. And pictures taken years after Dad's death, shots of Mom and Ken with Alan and the other grandchildren, and of Chantal and me. But there were a few I'd never seen, like the one of Mom, sitting on her folded legs on the grass in the backyard, in front of the porch of our first house, holding me, when I was about a year old, a hand on each side of my bare chest as I stood in front of her and faced the camera. She wore a house dress, little if any make-up, and gazed directly at the camera, her lips parted, with the hint of a smile, as if she'd been talking to the person taking the photo, probably Dad, about something amusing. As I gazed at her, I felt that the ashes that had sifted through the water had come back to life. She was about twenty-five in that picture, and the same age or younger in several others. The way she peers directly at the camera, pretending to be serious, or laughing, or romantically gazes off, I can see from the warmth in her eyes the love that had bound them together. In the pictures of him, when he too was in his twenties, he usually wore a suit and tie, and sometimes an overcoat, as he posed in front of his car, a 1940s model of some kind, or the house he bought, or one of his bakeries. But he never has more than the hint of a smile.

I came across a few black-and-white photographs that must've been taken before they met one another—pictures of Mom with Grandma, Grandpa, Gerda and the brothers, and one in which Mom looked like a gangster's moll, resting her foot on the front bumper of an old car. And another picture, of five little kids, three older ones sitting on the top step of a broad stairway leading to an open-air porch, two younger ones two steps down, and carved-wood balustrades on both sides of the staircase. I stared at the kids, and not recognizing any of them, turned the picture over and found the names John, Mildred, and Bobby, and underneath them the names of two of Dad's younger sisters, and the year 1924. I turned the picture back and focused on Dad, about ten years old, with thick dark hair, some of it standing straight up on the back of his head, like one of the little rascals in the *Our Gang* films. He wore a light colored short-sleeve shirt buttoned up to his neck, and held his hands together, as if in prayer, only pointing downward. His head held high, he looked directly at the camera, with a confident air, like it was just a pause in the busy day of a ten-year-old who had things to do. Mildred, looking like a little-girl version of Olive Oyl, to whom Mom compared her, bent her head and glanced sideways at the camera, a sullen look on her face, as if she wasn't happy to pose for a photograph. And Bobby, in a long sleeve shirt and dark tie, his head cocked to the side, seemed ready to play.

My eyes returned to Dad, and I wondered, What were you thinking? Who were you? Were you already planning on getting out of that house, that town, and leaving your father and mother behind? Did your father love you? Were you happy with yourself? Or did you feel worthless? I stared at the inscrutable face, knowing I'd never get the answers to any of the questions, and when I couldn't bear the silence anymore, dropped the picture on the others and moved on.

At the bottom of the box, Barbara and I found the black and white picture of Mom and Dad's wedding, the one I'd seen so often. I pulled it out, and we sank back into the couch and leaned against one another and looked at Mom, in her white satin gown that fell to the floor like a fluted liquid column, a small crown on her head, a bouquet of flowers that concealed her body from her waist to her neck, and the veil that flowed down her back, around her feet, and splayed across the floor. A big smile and sparkling eyes, she looked so happy as she stood next to Dad, in his dark suit and white boutonnière, with the closest thing to a smile on his face I'd ever seen. Bobby and Mildred stood on either side, while little five-year-old Uncle Frank stood in front of Dad and Bobby, a bouquet in his hands and a blank stare coming from his eyes.

I'd always clung to the moments of happiness between Mom and Dad, like when I was about to walk into the kitchen and saw her sitting on her chair, leaning her head back to kiss him, while he bent over from behind her and slipped his hand beneath the cup of her bra, and their lips touched. That moment made me believe a deep, strong love formed the foundation of my parents' relationship, and because of that somehow everything would be okay. When I was a child, and I'd see the wedding picture in Mom and Dad's room, I'd have the same feeling. But as I looked at it, I thought of the tensions between Mom and her in-laws, of the resentment I knew she'd felt about Gerda not being her bridesmaid, about no one from her family being in the wedding, about having to convert for him, and about always having to do everything his way, and the photograph felt like a screen that concealed the fractures between the two families that would become apparent after Dad's death, when his family abandoned her, and she wanted nothing more to do with them.

Barbara and I framed some of the pictures and placed them around the house, and I set two on my desk, the one of Mom holding me in the backyard, when I was a year old, and the one of Dad, at ten, sitting on the steps with his siblings. As I prepared my classes and graded papers, I'd look up and see Mom, with her brown curls, her eyes looking at me, and her lips parted, as if she were about to begin talking, and I always had the feeling this was as close as I could get to her, except in my dreams. And I'd look at the picture of Dad, at his inscrutable face, and hear the questions that had always haunted me as I stared, mesmerized, sad, angry, and I'd remind myself I'd never know the answers, and take a deep breath and try to focus on my work and stay sane.

I got home from class one day, and instead of having a snack and a cup of coffee, got out the yellow pages of the phone directory and looked up Catholic cemeteries, and found there was one in St. Paul, Calvary Cemetery, and another, Resurrection Cemetery, in a suburb just across the Mississippi River from the city. I called Calvary and asked if my father was buried there, giving the man at the other end the dates of Dad's birth and death. After a pause, the man said there was a John Habermann, but he'd died in 1937. I thanked him, realizing I'd found Johnny Boy's grave. I then called the other cemetery, and yes, they had a John Habermann.

I got in my car and followed Mississippi River Boulevard to the Mendota Bridge, crossed the river, and found the cemetery. I stopped at the management building, got directions to the grave, and followed them down the main road to a smaller road, rounded a curve, stopped, and looked at the graves, the mausoleums, the statues and crucifixes, and the tall tree casting its shadow. I didn't recognize anything, and even if Dad had died at this time of year, and not in January, I knew I still wouldn't recognize this place. I got out of the car and passed between the rows of graves in the direction of a low stone wall with a wire mesh fence, the green of the grass making the cemetery feel peaceful, as if it were a park. At the fourth row, I turned and walked slowly past the headstones, over which the sod had grown, and long blades of grass lay flat, looking for the name HABERMANN, until I came to a purple stone on which it appeared, in large letters engraved across the top. I stared down at the cross carved into the stone underneath our family name and at the rectangles beneath the bars of the cross, the one on the right filled with the word *FATHER*, and beneath it, *JOHN A,* and the years of birth and death underneath the first name and middle initial. The rectangle on the left was empty. That's the side where Mom was to be buried—until Ken decided otherwise.

I found it strange that Dad's headstone was the only one that didn't have sod growing across it, or long stems of grass lying flat and concealing our family name, and the stone itself was clean, at least enough so I could see the color purple, and I realized someone had come here and pulled out the sod and grass and washed the stone, and that someone was most likely Mom. That day in April, when she disappeared, she became a missing person for my sisters, me, and Ken, but Dad had been a missing person for her for over twenty years. Her love for him, like some gravitational force that operates through time as well as space, drew her back here. And I realized, too, as I looked down at his name, that the absence of love also exerted a gravitational pull. Dad had always been the missing person in my life, and that absence had haunted me and never let me go. I returned to my car and sat gripping the steering wheel, staring straight ahead, tears flowing down my cheeks, wondering if I'd ever get past the feeling of being unworthy of love. The feeling that had made it possible for a twenty-two-year-old kid to dance, drunk, on the broad stone balustrade of a bridge across the Seine while chanting *"Le Bateau Ivre,"* knowing, with one false step, he'd fall and drown. And as I drove back to Barbara, I remembered the young graduate student who'd get drunk and stoned and drive along the river and come to a curve and decide at the last second to turn and follow the road instead of succumbing to the temptation of driving straight ahead and ending the pain forever.

Saturday morning, a few days later, after Barbara had left for Al's Breakfast in Dinkytown to meet up with one of her colleagues, I sat down at my desk in our bedroom to grade the final exams in a stack of blue books and started reading the first essay, but by the time I reached the end I realized my mind had wandered and I had to start over. The same thing happened again, and again. The silence in the townhouse seemed to open the doors of my mind to reflection, and the thoughts that wakened me about my dead father and the pull he exerted on my life returned, and I found myself staring at the picture of Dad, sitting on the steps with his siblings. I decided if I couldn't focus, I'd go to New Devon, where the picture was taken.

An hour later, I drove down the town's Main Street, looking out the side window at the post office, the saloon, the bakery, the Jewel Theater, McNally Drug Store, and around the corner, the McNally Hotel, where Mom said she'd worked and lived when she was in high school. I stopped at a gas station, filled up the tank, and went in and asked for directions to the Catholic cemetery. Five minutes later, I pulled into a parking lot, between a church and school on one side and the cemetery on the other, got out and walked among the rows of tombstones, until I found a lavender-gray stone standing erect, with a picture of Jesus, in a white circle at the top, his hand raised as if he were blessing those who lay below, and underneath the Christ figure, the name HABERMANN engraved in a rectangle, with the names of Dad's mother and father below it, and the years of birth and death. His mother had died more than a year before he did, and I wondered if she'd known he'd follow her soon. His father died a few years later, and I wondered how one goes on living after losing a son. As I looked down at the graves, I felt alienated from these grandparents. I'd never known them and couldn't remember a single instance of kindness or affection on their part toward anyone in my family.

I walked a short distance away and saw the name ROBERT HABERMANN and the years of his birth and death engraved on a headstone lying flat on the ground. I was seven when Uncle Bobby died in a car accident. Mom and Dad had brought me to her parents' farm, where family members stood in the house, talking in hushed voices with their heads bowed. And then most of the adults left for New Devon, leaving me and the other kids behind, with the feeling something horrible had happened, but we didn't know exactly what, it was too serious to talk about.

At home, during the months that followed, upon entering the living room or kitchen or walking past an open bedroom door, I'd sometimes overhear fragments of conversations between Mom and Dad about Aunt Marlene's struggle to continue alone with the kids and Dad's visits to their house a few blocks away, and I might get a glimpse of the sadness in his eyes and of Mom leaning close to him, trying to console him. I'd also listen in on Mom's conversations with Aunt Gerda on the phone, or at the kitchen table, when she'd bring her kids up from the flats, and she and Mom would drink coffee, smoke, and talk. I'd linger at the table while eating something, or at the sink while drinking a glass of water, or at the door on my way out to the backyard to play with my cousins, picking up bits of information about Dad providing Marlene with bread and money, his feelings that he couldn't express, and the rumors that Bobby had been drinking at the time of the accident. Mom and Gerda would also reminisce about the good ol' days, before they and Marlene had kids, and they'd go out to bars and restaurants with their men and drink, listen to music, and dance, and the fellows would get rowdy, and about that time Mom and Gerda would catch sight of me and fall silent, wait for me to leave, and then they'd start talking and laughing again.

Staring down at the headstone, I remembered Bobby's big grin and his loud, boisterous voice and his laugh that could rattle a house; and Hans's jokes that would make some people laugh and others smile politely, like the one about wanting to be a priest instead of a housepainter, so he could drink on the job. I could imagine Bobby and Hans young and wild and having fun, but not Dad. I shook my head. No, not Dad. I looked up and around at the tombstones, the Cypress trees, and the old wood-frame houses that bordered the cemetery, and walked back to the car, wondering why I'd bothered to come.

While returning to Main Street, I thought about Mom and Dad and Patty and me moving to a suburb a year after Bobby's death. Marlene remarried and disappeared from our lives, and a few years after Bobby's death, Hans died of cancer, or alcoholism, depending on who was doing the talking, and Gerda remarried and moved to Albert Lea, the little town in southern Minnesota from which my maternal grandfather had come. Marlene's and Gerda's kids, the cousins to whom I was closest, I rarely saw again. And by the time I was fifteen, I was dreaming of leaving home.

I reached Main Street, and after a few blocks, saw the words HABERMANN'S HARDWARE on a storefront, on the opposite side of the street from the shops at which I'd stared while driving through the first time. I pulled to a stop, went in, and looked around at the aisles of goods that extended toward the back of the store and at the check-out counter off to my side, where a woman was going through some papers in a binder. I walked over, said hello, and told her I was looking for Mr. Habermann. She nodded toward one of the aisles and said, "He's right there." I turned and saw a tall thin man, nearly bald, with glasses perched on a long nose, in slacks and a shirt and tie, walking toward the front of the store, and recognized Uncle Frank.

I approached him as he asked, "May I help you?"

"I'm David Habermann, John's son."

His eyes bulged. "What?

"I'm John's son, David."

His eyes sparkled, his mouth spread in a big toothy grin, and he shook my hand. "Well, who would've thought? John's son!"

"Yeah."

"After all these years!" He looked at his watch. "You wanna get a cup of coffee?"

"Sure."

He told the woman he'd be back in a little while, and we stepped outside and headed down the sidewalk.

"I haven't seen you since . . . since your dad's funeral." The excitement faded from his voice, but after a brief pause it returned. "Where do you live?"

"Minneapolis, over by the U. That's where I teach."

"You teach? Really?"

"I'm a French professor."

"Huh. A French professor." He smiled at me and nodded.

We entered a coffee shop, sat down in a booth, and ordered coffee.

"What brings you back to New Devon?"

"This might sound a little strange, but . . . I never really got to know my father. He was working all the time, and I was on my own, away at college, when he died. So, I'm trying to find out more about him. Who he was. I thought the best place to start would be his family."

"And you know I own the hardware store, so you drove out to see me."

"No, I came out to visit the cemetery."

"The cemetery?"

The waitress set our coffee on the table, and we thanked her. Frank leaned forward on his elbows, and I noticed his large hand, next to his cup, and the big knuckles, and remembered the size and strength of Dad's hands. And of his fist. Frank lowered his head a little to catch my eye, and I realized I'd been staring at his hand.

"The one where my parents and Bobby are buried?"

"Yeah. And when I was driving back through town, I saw your name on the store."

"Huh! Strange you'd go to the cemetery, if you want to learn about your pa."

"Yeah, maybe it is strange."

"I don't know if I'm the best person to talk to. John was eighteen years older than me, and by the time I could sit up and look around, he was gone."

I remembered Mom telling me stories about Dad's siblings being envious of his success in business, so I asked, "Did you like him?"

"Did I like him? Of course! He was my brother."

"You think he was a good guy?"

"You bet he was. He was always there if I needed help, above all help with money. But honestly, I didn't really know him. He worked his ass off, earned a good living, and provided for his family. My pa used to talk about John proving you could succeed with hard work. Other than that . . ." Frank shook his head. "The people who knew him best were Ma and Pa and Bobby, and they're gone. Now, your Aunt Mildred, she was a year older than John, she might be able to tell you some stuff. I've got four other sisters, too. I heard about John helping the ones who moved to St. Paul, but I don't think they knew him any better than I did. Got a brother out in North Dakota, about ten years younger than John, but the two weren't close the way your pa and Bobby were." Frank looked down at his coffee, then up at me with a grin on his face. "We used to call our old man Pa, and John, Papa, because he was kind of like a second pa to us. But I didn't know John as well as I knew Pa, and I didn't know Pa all that well, either. He was pushing fifty when I was born, so he'd already lived most of his life, and didn't talk much about it. Just told us what to do."

I nodded and took a sip of coffee, remembering visiting Grandpa and Grandma at their house when I was a kid, and all of us in the family bowing our heads at the table as he recited prayers, his loud voice booming in the narrow dining room. I could imagine what it would have been like to hear him tell you what to do.

"I wish I could be of more help. The best person to talk to is Mildred. Come to think of it, she was your mom's bridesmaid. I was in the wedding, too. Just a kid, about five. And Bobby was John's best man." Frank's gaze drifted past me. "That was a good fifty years ago." He shook his head, a sad look in his eyes. "John and Bobby died way too young. Way too young." He stared down at the table, then looked up at me. "I bet the town has changed a lot since you were here last."

"Yeah, it has. But the hotel's still here, and some of the shops. Like the bakery."

"That's where your dad started working as a baker, when he was in high school."

"How old was he when he started?"

"I don't know."

"Do you know how my parents met?"

"Nope. Mildred might." He paused. "By the way, how's your mother doing?"

"She died, a little over two weeks ago." I felt my voice tremble.

"Oh, I'm sorry." He shook his head. "Virginia was a good woman."

I felt a surge of anger. "You remember her name."

"Of course I do. And I remember her. She always stood by John."

"Your family seemed to have forgotten her, after my father died."

He shook his head. "John was the second son to die, and Ma died a year before. That was real hard on Pa. Hard for all of us. He kind of lost interest in life. Died a few years after John." He sighed. "That might not feel like a reason for losing sight of your mom, but everyone hurt." He gazed at me. "I'm sorry about Ginny's death."

I bit my lip and nodded.

The waitress stopped to refill his cup, but he covered it with his hand. She looked at me. I shook my head. He asked for the check and if she could also give him a piece of paper to write on. She set the coffee pot on the table, handed him the check, as well as a blank check from her pad, and he gave her a couple bucks and told her to keep the change. He took a pen out of his pocket, wrote on the paper, and handed it to me. The name Mildred was printed across the top and a phone number underneath, and Frank's name and home number and office number at the store beneath hers.

"Give her a call. She's the one who can help you, if anyone can."

We stepped outside and shook hands.

"I wish you good luck," he said. "And if you wanna come back, you're always welcome. You married?"

"Yeah."

"Bring your wife. Your aunt and I would love to meet her." He smiled and nodded. "Good talking to you, David."

He headed back to work, and I got in my car and stared at the hardware store, feeling Frank had opened a door for me.

I entered the apartment and heard Barbara shout from the living room, "David, is that you?"

Usually, I'd behave like a smart ass and say, "You'd better hope it is," but I just said, "Yeah," and found her in the living room, sitting in the armchair, reading. She studied my face and asked where I'd been. I bent over and kissed her, and she moved her feet on the ottoman so I could sit and be close to her. She looked worried as I told her about my inability to concentrate on the exams and the need I felt to drive to New Devon and visit the cemetery, but her eyes lightened when I talked about the encounter with Frank.

"He didn't know Mom had died."

"Well, that's not surprising, if he and his siblings didn't see her much after your father died."

I nodded. "I guess that's still an issue for me, the way my dad's family abandoned my mother. Frank tried to explain the neglect by saying his mother had died about a year before Dad, and Dad was the second son to die, and the family had gone through a lot, and . . . I don't know. He seemed sincere, but I didn't really believe what he said."

"Did you learn anything about your dad?"

"Only that some of his siblings called him papa, and their father, pa, because Dad was like a second father to them. Otherwise, all I learned is that no one knew Dad, except the dead—his brother, Bobby, and his parents. But Frank did give me the phone number of my Aunt Mildred, who was born a year before Dad. I'm gonna call her and see if I can stop by."

"You want me to come with you?"

I thought about my childhood experiences of visiting my aunt's home and said, "If I was certain we could have a good conversation with Mildred, I'd love for you to come. But I have no idea how this is gonna go. If it does go well, we'll visit her and my uncle together sometime. Okay?"

I phoned Mildred the next morning. She'd been expecting my call. She said she was sorry to learn my mother had died, but there was no sorrow in her voice. Then, without another word about Mom, she told me I could stop by the next afternoon and gave me her address in St. Paul. As I drove down her street, lined with modest houses, I recalled coming here as a kid on Christmas Eve, before I was old enough to stay home and play Santa for my sisters. I found her house, pulled over, walked up to the door, and rang. Mildred opened and stood in the entry, tall and thin, her big eyes peering down at me through the lenses of her wire rimmed glasses, her gray hair pulled back into a bun. I stepped back from the screen as she pushed it open and said, "You're David."

I said, "Yes." She invited me in, her lips spread in a tight smile, and while I shook her hand, I noticed she was only three or four inches shorter than me, and I was over six feet. I followed her into the living room, and Uncle Charlie, frail and thin, with long strands of gray hair combed over his bald head, folded the newspaper he'd been reading, got up from his armchair, and came over to shake my hand. I introduced myself, and Charlie nodded, smiled, and looked up at Mildred, as if seeking guidance. She pointed me toward a couch, with a crucifix on the wall behind it. I sat down and looked off to my side, toward the end of the room, where two more armchairs stood. That's where my grandparents would sit on Christmas Eve, during the latter years of their lives, when they'd stay here with their daughter and son-in-law, and my parents and sisters and I and some of my aunts and uncles and cousins would come by, and Grandpa and Grandma would look on in silence, Grandma sometimes smiling if anyone noticed her, and Grandpa never smiling, just poking the little ones with his cane if they got too close.

On the wall above and between the two chairs where Mildred and Charlie sat hung a reproduction of the popular *Head of Christ*, a painting of Jesus gazing upward with his luminous dark eyes, as if he could see God, and looking like a handsome white guy, with a nice tan, a well-trimmed beard, and lovely brown locks that fell to the white robe covering his shoulders. I'd seen the reproduction everywhere since I was a kid, so the original must've been painted before the sixties, but it looked like a romanticized representation of a hippie. I looked off in the other direction, toward the dining room, where a reproduction of *The Last Supper* hung, and then back at Mildred and Charlie.

"It's been about twenty-five years," she said.

"Actually, twenty-three, if you were at my father's funeral."

"I was." She pursed her lips and narrowed her eyes. "So, you just show up, out of nowhere." She shook her head, as if in disbelief.

Charlie's eyes darted back and forth, from Mildred to me.

"I recently moved back to Minneapolis."

"Where were you all those years?" she asked.

The hostile tone of her voice made me want to keep things simple, so I said, "I was teaching—in Texas, Oklahoma, Iowa, and now, here, at the U."

"Hmm. All that time, from when John died 'til now, you've been living in those places." Her eyes remained fixed on me. "You told Frank you didn't really know your father. How can a son not know his pa?"

"I know things about him, but there are a lot of things I don't know. I want to understand him better."

"And so, you come to us?"

I nodded. "I want to understand where I came from." And, I thought, I want to be able to sleep at night, live my life, be present to my wife and son.

"You waited all this time to learn about your pa, so you could find out where you came from?" She glared at me, her lips sealed tight, and then shook her head and snickered. "I think you're a little late."

I took a deep breath to loosen the grip of her eyes and said, "You're right. Maybe it was foolish of me to—"

"What memories I have of your pa are from when we were kids, over fifty years ago, and there aren't many of those left. What I do remember is that, after your parents got married, we saw them about once a year, usually at Christmas, even though we lived in the same city. John didn't have time for his family. He was always busy, making money. That's what counted for him."

"Yeah, I remember the kind of hours my dad worked." I paused, hesitated to say what was on my mind, and then said it. "I also remember hearing about him lending money to his siblings and his father, and not always getting it back.

Maybe there's a good reason he didn't have much time for his family."

"Like I said, you're a little late. And frankly, why should we care that you know where you came from? Why should that mean anything to us?"

"Obviously, it doesn't. My mother and sisters and I never meant anything to you. After my dad died, you and your father and siblings abandoned my mother. She never forgot, and I never did, either." I stood and was about to leave, and then stopped and said, "I remember hearing about you and a couple of your sisters showing up at my mother's door, just a few months after my father died, and insisting she turn over to you a set of china he'd inherited from his mother. How can anyone be so cruel?"

"Get out!" She leaped from her chair. "Get out!"

I headed for the entrance and stopped, turned, and glared at her. "How could you've been so heartless?" I slammed the door behind me.

I vented my rage in the car, cursing her, hitting the steering wheel. I took a few deep breaths, wiped the tears from my eyes, and drove home. I found Barbara standing in the kitchen, looking as if she'd been waiting for me. We hugged, and she leaned back to look up at me and said, "It didn't go well, did it."

I shook my head. We went into the living room, and I sank into the couch, and she sat down next to me. "What a heartless bitch," I vented, while repeating to her the stories Mom had told me about how Dad's family had treated him and her, and she'd never forgotten.

"And you haven't, either," Barbara said.

"Yeah. The rage that took hold of me is Mom's. It's been inside me for a long time. In some ways, she's very much alive."

Bam! The sound of something slamming against the glass door made Barbara and me jump. A kid on the patio, with blond bangs and thick glasses, the English boy, Alan's friend, scooped up a soccer ball, and I realized it had struck the door and he'd run onto the patio to retrieve it as it bounced back and forth. He saw Barbara and me on the couch, staring at him. He grinned, turned around, took a few steps, and tossed the ball back into play.

"Let's get out of here," I said. "I can't sit still. How about a walk around the lake?"

"What lake?"

"We can start with Lake Calhoun."

We stepped outside into the sunlight, and I stretched and felt the warmth of the sun relax my tense muscles. Driving to the lake, I continued to unwind by telling Barbara about Maria Mueller, my English teacher in high school. "She was beautiful, smart, compassionate, sexy. I had a huge crush on her. And that allowed her to have a huge influence on me. I probably wouldn't have gone to college if I hadn't met her, and maybe it's too bad I did, maybe I would've been better off a drifter, keeping a journal."

"I don't think so." Barbara grazed my hair with her fingertips. "I know you're not happy with where you are in your life, but it could be worse, and I doubt being a drifter and keeping a journal would've been as good a life as you might like to think. You'll find what you want to do."

"I know what I want to do."

She grabbed a lock of my hair and gave it a tug. "I hope you'll tell me."

I looked over and said, "Any more smart-ass stuff like that, and I won't."

"Oh-oh. I'd better be on my good behavior."

I pulled the car into a parking lot on the side of the lake, and we got out and walked on the lawn toward the water and then turned, and passing between the shoreline and the sidewalk, headed for a sandy beach a hundred yards ahead.

"One day, after school, when I was meeting with Maria, she told me she liked to come here on the weekends and sit in a lawn chair and read. So, every chance I got, I'd drive around the lake, looking for her, and one afternoon, I saw her. She was reclining on her chair, like a goddess on a throne, right about here, where we're walking."

"Don't tell me your dream came true. That would've been statutory rape."

"Being statutorily raped by Maria was my dream. Kind of sidetracks my thoughts, even today." I chuckled, and Barbara poked my ribs. "So, I'd better not think about it. That day, when I saw her here, she had company. Some guys had flocked around her and were sitting on the grass, lifting their heads, straining their necks, like seals, vying for her attention. I parked, walked toward her, and as I got closer, I could see her lips spread in a smile, under her sunglasses. Maybe she'd been expecting me all along. I stopped when I reached the ring of seals, and she welcomed me and introduced me to them. They were jazz musicians, going to perform that night at a club. I sat down on the grass outside the ring and watched the seals perform for Maria, trying to outdo one another with stories about the great musicians of the time, barking their exclamations and their laughter, while she reclined, looking down at them. I had nothing to say and felt outclassed, a little pup among the big guys. So, I came up with an excuse and left. I gave up on my fantasy of having a passionate relationship with the goddess. But the interest the goddess showed in me led me to go to college and made me feel more secure about who I was—a guy who loved to read and immerse himself in the world of fiction."

Barbara and I arrived at the beach, and I asked her if she wanted to walk straight ahead on the sand, or over on the sidewalk. She said, "On the sand." She stopped, held my arm, took off her shoes, and we continued, past kids filling plastic buckets with wet sand to build castles and others digging channels in the shore that allowed the water to flow into moats. A little boy ahead of us filled a pail with dry sand and walked across our path toward the lake, and my eyes followed him as I continued talking.

"Maria had the kind of effect on me that Mom had—she made me feel more self-confident. Mom and I loved to read, and she respected me for what I liked to do and what I did. She was so proud of me when I went off to France to do that doctorate at the University of Paris. One of my sisters told me Mom talked to everyone about it."

The little boy walked into the shallow water, stopped, and gradually tipped the pail until sand started flowing slowly into the lake. I froze, saw ashes streaming into the water, and felt once again Mom's disappearance from my life—nothing but ashes poured into one of the thousands of lakes in northern Minnesota.

"David, are you okay?"

The boy turned the pail upside down and watched the last of the sand disappear, while a puff of dust floated off.

"What's the matter?" Barbara asked.

"Nothing." And then I added, "No, that's not true. I can't go on anymore doing what I've been doing to earn a living. I've got to deal with what's going on inside me, what's been going on for a long time." I paused, felt her eyes looking up at me, and continued. "I've told you about the summer I spent in New York, writing a novel."

"You told me a little."

"I wrote one draft. I've tried working on it from time to time over the last few years, but every time I do, I become paralyzed by guilt, because I always feel I should be writing an article, or a book that will get me tenure. If I don't get tenure, I have nothing. No career, no income, no. . . ." I shook my head. "I don't want to do anything that might hurt us. And Alan." I thought of what I'd done to Chantal and Alan. I felt Barbara looking at me and looked back and saw the love in her eyes. "Writing the novel is a way of hanging on to my sanity. Not writing it is just a way to avoid thinking about this . . . this emptiness, this feeling of being worthless, this . . . whatever it is . . . that always comes back, because it never really leaves. I have to write this book. I'll go crazy if I don't. I might go crazy if I do, but I think it'll be easier to live with myself. And easier for you and Alan."

"What's the book about?"

"In that first draft I wrote in New York, the main character is Jason, a filmmaker, and his love, his muse, is Anna Céline, the lead actress in his films. Anna, by the way, is the name of my maternal grandmother. Of both my maternal grandmothers."

"Both?"

"Yeah. My mother's birth mother, who died a year after she was born, during the flu pandemic of 1918, and my mother's stepmother, both were named Anna. I remember Mom and Aunt Gerda joking that Grandpa might've been in the habit of making love with two Annas at once, because he loved them both. And my mother's middle name is Ann. As for Céline, that's the name of a French writer I've always liked. It's not his real name, it's a pen name, which is his maternal grandmother's name."

"Sounds like a lot of love for mothers and grandmothers."

"They deserve it. They nurture us."

Barbara leaned into me and looked up, and we stopped to kiss. And then, with the beach behind us, and the blacktop path ahead, she held onto my shoulder while she slid her shoes back on.

I looked ahead at the path and said, "We're just about to Lake Street, and

239

we can either continue around Lake Calhoun, or go under the bridge and follow the channel that flows into Lake of the Isles and walk around that lake."

"Let's go to Lake of the Isles. You've talked about how much you love that lake. I'd like to see it. So, you were telling me about Anna, the one in your novel."

"In the first draft, she's already left Jason, her loss devastates him, and perhaps in an effort to try not to think about her, or perhaps to understand, to confront what's going on inside him, he makes a coming-of-age film that brings him back into his childhood and his adolescence and twenties. But while watching the first fully mounted version of this new film, he can't stop thinking about Anna, and a close-up of the eyes of the actress playing his young mother, or of the expression on the face of the one playing the first love of his life, triggers his memory of a scene from one or another of the films he made with Anna, and from that scene his mind might wander to memories of their life together. The novel is made up of these scenes and memories braided together. It feels poetic, elegiac."

"It sounds beautiful. I'd love to read it."

The look in Barbara's eyes as she gazed up at me made me feel the power I had over her, the power that love gives to the beloved, and looking away from her, I stared at Lake of the Isles and the first of the two islands up ahead and thought of the pain I'd inflicted on Alan and Chantal.

"Oh, yeah," I said, "it's beautiful. Beautiful, but, dishonest. The scenes that deal with Jason's childhood and adolescence often evoke something sinister, something violent that seems to haunt him, but the reader never learns what that thing is, just as he, or she, doesn't learn what caused the separation between Jason and Anna, a separation that feels tragic. Well, the book I wrote is no longer the one I feel I have to write. In the new version, Anna is not an actress, Jason is not a filmmaker, and there is no film, no beautiful cinematographic scenes to weave together. This book begins with violence, a scene in which the main character is a boy about twelve. His father grabs him by the neck, pins him against a wall, has pulled back his fist and is about to pulverize his face, when his mother throws herself between them. The kid never knows what to expect from the father, what will set him off. He tries to keep a safe distance, but there is no such thing in that house, because at any minute the father might lose it and come looking for him and slap him or beat him with his belt. And from the time the kid's fifteen, he dreams of leaving home, and eventually does. But the father dies when the kid is only twenty, and from that time on the kid looks back and wonders, Who was that man? Why wasn't I worthy of being loved? And those questions transform his inner self into a black hole that sucks him in and makes him feel worthless. He drinks until he reels and recites lines of poetry about Huffy Henry sulking, and it was the thought that they thought they could *do* made Henry wicked and away, and he should've come out and talked, but instead he raged against the dying of the light and played with death as if it were a game, a game of chicken, and the loser wins."

"What . . . what are you talking about?"

"I'm trying to recreate the kind of mishmash of poetry and crazy thoughts that would go through my mind when I was young, and I'd get so drunk I couldn't walk straight." I took a deep breath and shook my head. "Lines by poets who were intent on drinking themselves to death." I remembered seeing John Berryman walking down the stairs in a classroom building, shaking so bad he collapsed, sat on a step, and stared at nothing, his mouth hanging open and his eyes bulging. "Well, Jason, the filmmaker in the first draft, doesn't seem to have any understanding of why his relationship with Anna Céline comes to an end. He just feels the tragedy of it. The loss. That draft was my way of making myself feel innocent. In the version I'm going to write, Jason is a professor, married to Anna, and they and their son live in Tulsa. He goes to New York for a summer, supposedly to write a book on French cinema, but instead writes a novel, because he feels he has to. And in that novel he describes his drinking, his infidelities, his destruction of his marriage. And later, after the divorce, he describes his remorse, when he realizes what he has done."

Barbara's eyes fixed on me. "Do you regret marrying me?"

"No. I regret hurting Chantal and Alan. They did nothing wrong." I shook my head. "I've destroyed so much."

After a pause she asked, "Do you love me?"

"I do. But, will you still love me, once you see how destructive I can be?"

"I know you, and I love you."

"Like Mom said, I'm very lucky."

"Let's sit down here." She gently pulled me by my hand toward a park bench. "Come on."

We sat down, facing the lake, and I wrapped my arm around her shoulders, she leaned into me, and we gazed at the two islands that lay before us, each covered with trees and bushes and tall grass, and at the tree limbs fallen into the water, their branches rising above the surface, and at the sun descending into the gap between the islands. The water was boiling with carp, their heavy bodies rolling onto the surface and sinking, and sometimes they'd leap into the air, lunging at something, and splash back into the lake. I felt the resemblance of the world in the novel I was creating to the world before us, a world that felt like home. I watched a man and a woman paddle a canoe from the shadows of one island into the shimmering coins of light on the surface to the shadows of the other island, and a flock of mallards swimming in front of us, their tail feathers sticking up as they plunged their heads under water looking for food, and geese waddling across the grass, stretching their necks, and pecking at things I couldn't see.

I'd grown up in a world of grassy banks, sandy beaches, and lakes and islands, streams and rivers, ponds and marshes—the stream that wove through my maternal grandparents' farm and passed beneath the wooden bridge and formed a pool where I'd swim in the nude on hot days with my cousins and other farm kids; the pond surrounded by cattails on which red-winged blackbirds would perch and pursue me if I walked too close to their nests and peck at the back of my head; the lakes near our house in Roseville, to which I'd ride on my bike with my buddies; and the resorts in northern Minnesota, where my family would go for vacations. And this lake, Lake of the Isles, around which I used to walk when I was an undergraduate, the lake on one side and the parkway lined with mansions from the early 1900s on the other, and sometimes I'd feel as if I were in a world of provincial affluence, like in the Chekhov play with the dead seagull and the young writer who kills himself. And as I walked, my mind might wander from that world to the places to which I wanted to travel—New York, Paris, London, Berlin. Lake of the Isles was a place to which I'd go to dream, and then to which I'd return, because somehow it retained those dreams, and even now I could feel them, enter them. As I gazed at the two islands and the dead limbs rising from beneath the water, something came back.

"A lot of things from my life will find their way into this book. When I was a kid, I used to have this dream, in which I'm maybe five years old. I'm sitting on the seat in the middle of a flat-bottom fishing boat, with one of my paternal grandparents sitting at one end, and the other at the opposite end. We're holding long cane poles that arch gracefully from the boat, the lines dangling lazily. Water spiders dart across the still surface of the lake that shines like the scales of an immense fish. I feel a sense of calm, of peace. I'm so happy. I look at my grandparents, but I can't see their faces, because they're wearing straw hats with large brims and are looking away. Somehow, I know it's them. I always loved that dream, and I'm sure I dreamt it often because it made me feel so good. I could see that scene as if it were a painting. I knew it wasn't just a dream, it was a memory, a memory that came back to me as a dream.

"One day, I told my mother about it, describing it in detail. She looked baffled and said, 'David, you never went fishing with those grandparents. They never would've taken you. And probably none of your cousins, either. And you've never gone fishing with my parents.' I was shocked. And then I thought, Well, maybe I'd gone fishing with Mom and Dad. And so, I asked her, and she said, 'You know I hate going out in boats. I never learned how to swim. And I don't remember your father ever taking you.' I found it hard to accept the idea it was just a dream, and not a memory. But I should've known that, because, aside from the dream, I didn't have a single positive memory of my paternal grandparents, nor did my sisters, who thought of our grandfather as mean. When I was a kid, Mom and Dad and my sisters and I would go to my aunt Mildred's house, and my grandfather would sit in an armchair, and if his grandchildren got too close to him, he'd hit them with his cane. Not so hard as to injure them, just hard enough to tell them to stay away. And, believe me, they stayed away. And so did I. Eventually I came to accept the dream as just a desire to belong, to be loved.

"I say *just*, but that dream was very powerful, and I never forgot it. At the end of my junior year in high school, I fell in love with a girl named Sandy. We were together for almost two years. One of the things I remember about her parents' house is a painting, a landscape entitled *Autumn Woods*, hanging in the living room. The foreground is a large inlet, and a channel bordered by trees connects it to a lake in the background. The evening sun shines over the top of trees in the background and lights up the sky and the leaves along the channel and just inside the inlet, and the different shades of red and gold of those leaves glow in the sunlight and on the mirror-like surface of the water, except in those areas where the sun can no longer reach. The colors reflect on the surface because there's nothing but darkness beneath, and those areas of the inlet where the sun can't reach are murky and evoke something menacing, a feeling that's reinforced by the branches of a fallen limb that rise from beneath the dark surface of the water, like the fingers of a dead hand.

"The first time I saw that painting, I froze. It reminded me of something, but I couldn't figure out what. And then later it came to me—the dream of fishing with my grandparents. The dream I came to interpret as a desire for love, for being part of a family united by love." I paused, and repeated the words, *united by love.* "When I think of the fear I grew up with, and the feeling of not being loved by this man whom my mother loved so much, this man who was at the center of our lives and had all the power and abused it whenever someone did something that pulled his trigger, I want to ask her, How could you love someone who treated your child that way? I look at Alan and think, How could anyone do to their son what my father did to me? How could you try to destroy what was inside your child and leave him feeling hollow? He never told me he loved me, never looked at me with love in his eyes, and yet, I've spent my life wondering if he did or didn't. Sometimes I'll remember something, like the way he almost smiled at me once, when I was very young, and I try to use that quasi-smile as an argument to convince myself he did love me. It never ends. Never. One of the times I stayed with Mom for a couple days after his death, she talked to me about the last time I'd moved home for a few months. She described how, at dinner, as she sat at Dad's side, with the two of us at either end of the table, she'd feel the tension, the hatred between us, and by the end of every meal, she'd feel sick to her stomach, and it was such a relief when I left home. I'll never forget that. And I'll always remember that she loved him so much she went mad with grief after he died. Not long before she died, I told her about the argument Dad and I had a few hours before I left home, when I told him, 'If I want to be perfect, all I have to do is be the opposite of *you.*' When she heard that, she wept.

244

"All of that love, that hatred, that confusion, the intensity of those emotions, the destruction and self-destruction, the drinking and the depression, and the attractiveness of suicide that feels like such an easy solution to depression, all of that was missing from the character of Jason, in the novel I wrote about the filmmaker and the actress. It's as if their relationship had just run its course, and nothing, no madness in either of the characters, had ended it." I fell silent, thinking of the anger and frustration raging inside me and that I hadn't understood when I was writing that novel, and that would cause me to destroy my marriage to Chantal. "There's always darkness on the other side of the screen, the other side of the mirror. And what I want to do in this book is accumulate all the emotion in that darkness, press it together into a block, sculpt my characters out of it, and tell the story of a mother, a father, and a son. Tell the story that has always haunted me."

I didn't want Barbara to see my tears, so with my hand lying on her hair, I held her head close to my chest. But after a short while, she pulled back, looked at me, and wiped the corners of my eyes with the edge of her finger.

"You want to remain married to me?" I asked.

Her smile radiated her response. "I've always known you were complicated."

"A complicated mess."

She shook her head. "Complicated," she said and kissed me. She nestled her face against my neck, and I gazed at the lake, feeling her breath on my skin, relieved at having revealed so much of myself and happy she still loved me.

The sound of people talking as they passed behind our bench drew us out of the state we were in. We got up and, with our arms around one another's backs, walked along the lake, under the bridge, and up the side of Lake Calhoun, glancing from time to time at the sun sinking into a warm red puddle of shimmering light that flooded the horizon on the opposite side of the lake.

We got in our car and drove to the Black Forest, where we ordered drinks and dinner. I looked down at the table, wondering one last time if this was the right thing to do, and then looked at her and said, "You remember me telling you about my friend, Serge, who has arranged for me to give a paper at Dartmouth in November, so I could be on the same stage as a bunch of big names from Paris?"

245

"Yeah."

"Well, I'm not going to give the paper. I'm all done with academic conferences, papers, articles, books, and the politics of academe. I have to write what's going on inside me, focus on the story that's been looming there for so many years, hear again the words that echo through time as if through a deep cave, feel the losses that send ripples through the chambers of my heart. I have to do this. I have to."

Barbara extended her hands across the table, laid them on mine, and looked into my eyes. "You might lose a friend."

"I can't go on like this. I'll explain, and hope he understands."

The next morning, after Barbara and I'd finished breakfast, and I'd stopped tracing lines in the egg yolk with my fork, I got up, took the phone off the wall, and dialed Serge's number in Hanover. After the fifth or sixth ring, when I was thinking of hanging up, he answered and upon hearing my voice, said, "*Salut mon pote*," and asked how Barbara and I were doing. I said fine and started pacing back and forth, while Barbara watched my face as I listened to him talk about the gorgeous weather and the beautiful campus, and he couldn't wait until we came to visit. When he asked me what we'd been doing lately, I told him about Mom. After a pause, he said, "*Désolé*, such a horrible loss, I feel for you." After another pause, he said he was looking forward to seeing us and talking about . . . everything.

He paused yet again. When the silence became unbearable, I said, "I've decided not to come."

"What do you mean?"

"I'm leaving the profession. I don't do papers anymore. Papers, conferences, articles, nothing."

"And now I learn this?"

"I'm sorry."

"I'm putting you on the same stage as some of the most prestigious people from Paris, and at the last minute you back out?"

"It's not the last minute. There are two months left. Look, I have something else I have to do. It's a book, a novel, and I have to write it."

"Why can't it wait a couple months?"

"It's already waited years."

After a long silence, he said, "*D'accord. Comme tu veux*, David." He hung up, and I wondered if we were still friends.

Barbara had left for work, and I was at my desk, with the intention of preparing my courses, but again found myself gazing at the picture of Dad. The people in the family who knew him best were dead, and as Mildred said, I was a little late. But the question still haunted me—Who were you? Wishing I could ask Bobby, knowing he could tell me, I remembered his face, the happiness he seemed to exude, and the hush in my maternal grandparents' house—the aunts and uncles standing in the kitchen and dining room, talking with their heads bowed, murmuring things I couldn't understand. I remembered hearing the same hush in another house, and seeing a woman, in profile, standing in a bedroom full of gray light and shadows, looking down toward an open drawer in a chest at a shirt that she was holding in her hands. She raised the shirt and crumpled it as she pulled it close to her chest, and bent her head and wept, her body trembling. She looked as if she might fall to the floor, when another woman came from the other side and put her arm around her and held her, and the weeping woman murmured, "No, no," while shaking her head. I was about twelve or thirteen when I'd stood in the open doorway, watching Aunt Evelyn, the mother of my nine-year-old cousin who'd drowned. His father was Joe, Dad's brother, the one who was ten years younger. I was there because Dad had brought me with him, when he'd driven to North Dakota to comfort his brother and family.

Dad and Mom had decided she should stay home with the girls, and he would take me with him. We set out in the morning, driving across the plains along two-lane highways bordered by barbed wire fences, fields, and an occasional farmhouse off in the distance. Dad remained quiet as he drove, a quiet that felt introspective, and safe for me, safe enough to relax and look over at him from time to time, at his face in profile, his eyes fixed on the road while his mind seemed far away. A few hours into the trip, we slowed down as we entered a small town and drove along the main street, with cars parked diagonally on either side in front of stores and taverns. He pulled over in front of a diner, and we went in and sat down in a booth across from one another.

The waitress set menus on the table, and he handed me one and almost smiled, some warmth in his eyes, and told me I could order whatever I wanted, so I ordered a chocolate malt with my lunch. We ate in silence, and from time to time I'd risk a direct glance at his green eyes staring at the back of the room. He left most of his sandwich and chips untouched, and when he noticed I'd finished my malt, hamburger, and fries, he asked for the check.

A few miles out of town, I was stunned when he asked me if I'd like to drive. I hesitated to answer because I had a hard time believing he'd really want me to. I'd driven tractors and pickups on the farm, but never a car on a highway. He looked at me and repeated, "Well, you wanna drive?"

I said, "Yeah." He pulled to the side of the road and got out. I slid over behind the steering wheel, and he got in on the passenger side. He showed me how to pull the seat forward and adjust the rearview and side view mirrors, and reminded me to set my foot on the brake before putting the car in drive, and look in both mirrors to make sure there was no one coming from behind. I followed his instructions, eager to please, and then stepped on the gas. The car shot forward, fishtailing as it hurled gravel that pinged against the inside of the rear fenders and bumper, and each rear tire squealed the second it hit blacktop. I expected Dad to scream at me, but he laughed and said, "Slow down, speedster. We got plenty o' time." I yanked my foot off the accelerator and then, as the car coasted, gently set it back on. I looked at him and again saw his lips spread almost in a smile—almost. I continued driving, while he watched the road, or stared for long periods of time out the side window, until we approached the town where Uncle Joe and his family lived, and then Dad took over.

We checked in at a motel, he changed into his suit and I into my dress shirt and slacks, and we arrived a little later at Uncle Joe's house, passing people sitting on the porch as we entered. I looked around the living room at the clusters of adults, all in a somber mood, and a few kids standing here and there, and felt the same hush that had unnerved me at my grandparents' house, the day of Uncle Bobby's funeral. Joe came over to greet us. Dad hugged him and whispered something, and Joe leaned back, looked up at Dad, and wiped away tears. He took a deep breath, looked at me, and tried to smile. He said it was good to see me, and if I was hungry, I could help myself to something in the dining room, his neighbors had brought over food. He pointed toward the table laden with platters and bowls and a stack of dishes. I started moving in that direction, when I noticed three girls, sitting like stone statues on a couch and staring straight ahead. I recognized my cousins, went over, and squatted next to a coffee table in front of the couch, where I could look at them at eye level. When they looked at me, I saw confusion and fear in their faces. I said, "Hi. I'm your cousin, David. I'm sorry about what happened to Willie." The oldest of the three nodded. I continued, "I miss him." That wasn't entirely true, because I'd rarely seen him, but I would've liked to have seen him more. I didn't know what else to say. I looked around and felt the gulf between the little girls, whose loss seemed to have left them speechless, and the adults who could talk. I looked back at the girls and all I could think of doing was repeating I was sorry. I stood up, went to the dining room, maneuvered among the adults standing around the table, and served myself a sandwich, potato salad, and Kool-Aid. When I finished eating, I weaved through the living room and mounted the carpeted stairs to the second floor. As I walked down the hall toward the bathroom, I passed an open bedroom door and glanced at the room, lit solely by the evening sun, and stopped when I saw Aunt Evelyn weeping over the crumpled shirt in her hands.

Aside from the grief that saturated the house like humidity on a hot day, what I would always remember from that trip, the only one that Dad and I ever made together, was the feeling that he approved of me. I saw nothing of his volatile temper, no criticism, derision, or contempt in his eyes, and never did he scream or ridicule me. Maybe that was because Willie's death had affected him so deeply. I felt sad every time I thought of my cousin drowning, of Uncle Joe with tears in his eyes looking up at Dad, of Aunt Evelyn clutching the shirt, of the three girls sitting lifeless on the couch. But I also felt happy, because of the feeling of Dad's approval, and that happiness made me want to play and have fun. Late in the afternoon of the next day, after the funeral and burial, I goofed around with some of the kids outside, mostly boys, but also two of Willie's sisters. A few of us told wild stories about things we claimed to have done, and I came out on top with mine, about always driving with my bare feet, my toes wrapped around the steering wheel. When the kids refused to believe me, I inveigled them into following me to Dad's car, got in, took off my shoes and socks, and showed them.

Sitting at my desk, imagining myself in the car with my toes wrapped around the wheel, I shook my head and laughed, while gazing at the photo of Dad in my hand. I recalled the respect and admiration for him I saw in Uncle Joe's eyes and wondered what he could tell me about Dad. Maybe I could drive to that town and spend an evening talking with him. I remembered again the trip across the plains and through the little towns, the cumulous clouds hovering ahead, and looking over and seeing Dad close to me and feeling almost close to him, like we were a father and son who loved one another. I took a few deep breaths, wiped my eyes, and set the picture back on the desk, next to the piece of paper Frank had given me with his and Mildred's phone numbers. I thought of calling Frank and wondered if he'd be willing to talk to me, because Mildred had certainly talked to him. I called his office number, he answered, and when I told him who it was, he said, "Mildred's already called everyone. Sounds like the shit hit the fan."

"It did."

"That's too bad. Just one thing—ah, you brought up with Mildred that incident about the china set. Well, the two sisters who went with her had no idea what they were getting into. That was all Mildred's doing."

"Thanks. My mother told me about it, and, ah . . . she and Mildred never got along. Mom never spoke to her again."

"Yeah, that's what I remember. Well, what's up?"

"I was contemplating giving Joe a call. What do you think?"

A pause. "Well, he'd be a lot easier to deal with than Mildred. You want his number?" He gave it to me, I thanked him, and he said, "You might wanna wait until after dinner. Joe still works six days a week, even though he's in his sixties."

When I called and told Joe who I was, he said, "Oh, my God. Evelyn got a call from Mildred this morning. I've heard the whole story. Huh! Well, David, what can I do for you?"

I hesitated, hoping he'd be open to talking with me, and then decided to just say what I had to say. "I'm calling because I remember you seemed to have a lot of respect for my dad."

"I do."

"Like I told Mildred, I've been gone from the Twin Cities for a long time, finally moved back, and, ah, my dad died when he was young, and I was, too, and in a lot of ways I didn't know him. I'd like to know him better."

"He was the kind of guy you could count on. Always there when I needed him. Helped me out with a loan when I wanted to start my business. He helped us all out."

"When Willie died, Dad and I drove out to be with you and Evelyn and the family."

"Yeah," Joe sighed. "I called John and told him what had happened. He said he'd be there. And he was. When he arrived, he looked me in the eye and said, 'You're never going to stop missing your boy. Never.' And he kept looking at me, like he wanted to make sure I understood." Joe paused. "He told me to let him know if there was anything he could do to help." Joe took a deep breath and sighed again. "He never said anything like that before. He was quiet, hard to get to know, and by the time I was ten, he'd left home."

"That's what I remember about Dad when I was growing up—quiet, and hard to get to know."

"Yeah. There's another thing I remember. A few months after Pearl Harbor, I'd finished high school and was working in the bakery in New Devon. I decided to quit my job and enlist, and Pa and I got into it on the back porch. God, he was furious. Shouted at me I had no right, no right to quit that job, because I had a responsibility to the family first. I hadn't yet outgrown the fear I'd always had of him and couldn't find the words to say what I was thinking. Then I noticed John next to me. He looked at Pa and said, 'It's his life. His decision.' It was the first time I'd ever seen anyone stand up to Pa. Oh, you should've seen the look he gave John, but he didn't say a word. Just glared, and then went back into the kitchen."

"Wow! That's amazing."

"Yeah. I can't think of anything else. Like I said, John was gone by the time I was ten. Before you came along, he'd come home once in a great while with Ginny for a Sunday dinner, and we'd talk a little. Not much. And then I left home for the war, met Evelyn in San Francisco a couple years later, and moved to North Dakota, where her family lives. So, we were brothers, but hardly knew one another."

I felt like a door had been opened onto something I wanted, and then slammed shut.

"You still there?" he asked.

"Yeah. That confrontation between my dad and his father, that's quite a story."

"Yes, it is."

I didn't know what else to say, he didn't seem to either, so I said, "Well, thanks, Joe, for taking the time to talk with me about my dad. I really appreciate it."

"I wish I could give you more. If you ever want to drive out to visit us, we'd love to have you. There's always a spare room."

I told him I might take him up on that, and we said goodbye and hung up.

I glanced at the books and notes on my desk and leaned back and stared at the wall in front of me, thinking about the phone call and what I'd learned about Dad. I decided the closest I could get to him might be through Joe, and maybe I should take him up on his offer to come and visit. I had warm memories of the trip with Dad, of feeling he approved of me, and maybe that approval was a sign of love. And then I remembered what Dad had told Joe—"You're never going to stop missing your boy. Never." And I wondered if Dad had ever missed me. By the time he and I had left to come home, he seemed to have forgotten about me. He sped down the highway, his eyes fixed on the road, his mind riveted to something, and he rarely spoke, or looked at me, and never smiled. I stopped looking at him and stared at the blacktop and the plains that seemed to extend forever, and felt so alone, until my mind wandered to *War and Peace*, and the story of Prince André and Natasha, and I couldn't wait to get home and begin reading where I'd left off. A few weeks or months later, Dad would pin me against the wall by my neck, and about five years after that he'd jut his face into mine and hiss, "It cost me a twenty-dollar bill for you to come home. A twenty-dollar bill." And I knew I wasn't worth it.

During the weeks that followed my call to Uncle Joe, I finished preparing my classes and began teaching, lecturing, and discussing novels and films with my students, and Barbara and I frequented the bookstores and restaurants and movie theaters in our new neighborhood. But when I'd wake in the morning, or walk home alone from campus, or lie in bed staring into the dark at night, after Barbara had fallen asleep, I felt my life had been hollowed by my loss of Mom and haunted by the father who'd never seemed to love me, and I wandered through the cavernous passages inside, drawn by the voices in the silence and the words they uttered. And then, in late September, I got a call from Chantal that made me ecstatic. Her school had scheduled parent-teacher meetings over a three-day period that coincided with the meetings at Alan's school, and she wanted to know if I could take him for those three days and part of the weekend. She thought it would be good for the two of us to spend time together, because ever since he'd learned of his grandma's death, he'd fall silent at times and seem so withdrawn, and Chantal knew how deeply Mom's death had affected me, too.

Alan exited the jet bridge at the airport a few weeks later, and the second our eyes met, he grinned and rushed toward me. I picked him up and hugged him, and when I pulled back, saw Chantal in his dark eyes and felt close to her as I hugged him again. Over the next three days, while I taught, he'd sit in the back of my classroom and do cartoonish drawings that he'd show me after class—drawings of Luke Skywalker and Han Solo and Chewbacca and other characters from the *Star Wars* films. And he'd grin like a little mischief maker on the way back to my office as he talked about the scenes he'd created. When I was done for the day, we'd go home, drop our things off, head for the island and throw a football around, maybe stop off at Pracna on Main and sit on the terrace in front of the cobblestone street and have something to drink, and talk about his stay in France, or the book he was reading, *The Count of Monte Cristo*, or what he was doing in school. At night, after dinner, he and Barbara and I would watch one of the *Star Wars* movies, and then he'd go to bed. I slept well every night.

Before Alan arrived, I'd called Linda and Patty to let them know I'd have him from Tuesday evening to Sunday morning. Patty decided to invite the whole family over for dinner Saturday. She told me to come midafternoon, when the weather would be sunny, in the seventies, and we could spend time together on the deck, and Alan could hang out with his cousins. Barbara and I prepared a salad large enough for the whole family and brought it and a couple bottles of wine and apple cider with us. We pulled up in front of Patty's house, where we saw Linda and Tom's car and Ken's pickup parked in the street. We entered the house and were approaching the dining room, when cheers erupted. We stopped and looked in the doorway of the little room off to the side, where I'd slept the night Patty, Linda, and I had waited up for Mom, and saw Ken, sitting in the rocking chair, and Tom on a dining-room chair, and Patty's sixteen-year-old son, Scott, and Linda's eleven-year-old boy, Chris, lounging on the bed, their backs resting against pillows propped up against the wall, the four of them watching a football game on TV. Ken glanced up at Barbara and me and down at Alan and said, "Hey, buster, how you doin'?"

Alan beamed, "Fine, Grandpa."

I asked who was playing, and Ken said the Gophers, they'd just pulled off a long run against the Buckeyes. Tom raised his beer toward us as a greeting and said we were welcome to join them. Scott and Chris grinned at Alan and made room so he could hop up on the bed and sit between them. I told Tom that Barbara and I needed to check in with my sisters out on the deck.

We set the things we brought on the kitchen table and went out the side door and around the back to the deck, where Julie and Patty sat facing us from the opposite side of the picnic table and Linda at the end. They jumped up to greet us, and then we sat down, Barbara and I facing Patty and Julie. When they found out we'd brought wine and cider, everyone wanted something to drink, so Patty and I went to the kitchen, got glasses and a bottle of wine and another of cider, and returned, and I poured, while Patty and Linda puffed on their cigarettes.

I sat down, took a sip of wine, looked around the table and said, "So, what were you talking about?"

"Oh," Patty said, "I was just telling Linda and Julie about hearing someone knocking at the front door, looking out the window, and seeing Ken, and expecting to see Mom, too. I still forget she's gone."

Julie, gazing at her mother, laid her hand on hers.

"I do, too," Linda said. "And there's no place we can go to feel close to her."

"No," I said. "He made sure of that."

"She asks us to look after him, after she's gone," Linda said, "and then he

254

does everything he can to take her away from us."

"So, we look after him," Patty said. "However we feel about him, she loved him, and he loves her."

"That's Mom's one wish I might not be able to honor," I said.

"I can understand that," Linda said.

"Well," Patty said, "he was really happy to come over and join us for dinner. I think he's having a hard time. And this might sound weird, but we are the only family he's got."

I shook my head at the idea of Mom's death motivating Ken to want to be with us.

"He did give us the pictures," Julie said. "And he let us take some of her things."

"He what?" Linda asked, surprised.

"Yeah," Julie said, "when we went to get the pictures, he told us we could go through her clothes and take whatever we wanted. I picked out a black, sleeveless dress, but when I got home and tried it on, it was so tight, I couldn't zip it up. How could Grandma have gotten into it?"

I remembered the photo of Mom, emaciated, in a black sleeveless dress, and wondered if it was the same one Julie had tried on.

"There was a time when she didn't weigh anything," Patty said.

"Well," said Linda, "he never said anything like that to me. Just handed me a box of pictures. I'm going to talk to him about letting me go through her things, too."

"I think it was just a spur of the moment decision," Patty said. "He didn't want us to leave. He invited us in for coffee, and while we were sitting at the table, he said, 'Oh, if you'd like to keep some of her things,' and that's how it happened. I'm sure he'll let you come back and go through her stuff."

"How did he seem when you saw him?" I asked, looking around at Linda and Patty and Julie.

Linda stubbed out her cigarette. "I asked him how he was doing, and he said okay. Nothing else. I felt awkward and left."

"Well," Julie said, "when Mom and I went, he was kind of friendly."

"He did offer us coffee." Patty smirked. "If Mom had been there—"

"Oh," Linda said, "he would've closed the door in your face."

Patty said, "Yup," and the rest of us nodded and stared at the table.

I asked my sisters and Julie about the pictures Mom had selected for them, and soon we were talking about the photographs of Mom and Dad and ourselves, our baby pictures, our first steps, our grade school and high school years, and then life starting all over again with our kids, and the photos of Mom reading to toddlers sitting on her lap. Recalling pictures of Alan and her, I used the phrase, "right up to the end," without thinking, and the smiles faded.

The screen door to the mudroom slammed shut, and Ken appeared a few seconds later, cup in hand, walked up the two steps of the deck and announced the game was over and the Gophers had lost. He remained standing, until Patty invited him to sit down. Tom appeared with the three boys behind him and asked if I wanted to play some catch, and I noticed Chris carrying a football. I gave my place up to Ken, and Tom and the boys and I went out to the dead-end street, where I played quarterback, lancing long arcing throws and side-arming quick flings to Alan, covered by Chris, and with less success, to Scott, covered by his uncle. Alan had the advantage as a receiver, because of the throws I'd made to him on the island. He seemed to have learned how to position himself to make a catch and focus on the ball, and I could see in his grins when he tossed the ball back how proud he was to impress his cousins. The receivers and cover guys switched roles, and I continued throwing, watching Alan struggle to cover Chris. Barbara came and announced dinner was ready, and I put my arm around Alan, feeling the dampness from the sweat in his T-shirt as we walked into the house.

At Patty's direction, I sat down at one end of the table, with Barbara and Alan on either side, and Ken at the other end, and I reflected with amusement that once again I was seated at the end opposite an antagonist. My thoughts continuing in the same vein, I considered toasts I might propose, such as, To Mom, if only you'd been able to live out that second chance. Or, To Mom, may you forever be near the spirit of the man you loved. But I remembered Alan saying, "Hi, Grandpa," and Patty remarking that Ken was suffering from Mom's loss, and weirdly, we were the only family he had, so I controlled my impulse to get revenge for the suffering he'd caused the rest of us, and instead, raised my glass and said, "I'd like to propose a toast." Everyone raised their glasses, and I said, "To Mom, whose love continues to bring us together." We underwater film shot. The camera is pointing up toward the barely rippling surface of the lake lit by the sun, shafts of light dimming as they descend. He sees the image so clearly, he wants to reach out and touch it. It feels like a memory, like when he was a boy and he'd swim from the bottom of a cold lake toward the warm light shimmering on the surface. And then someone pours ashes that cloud the image, and he stops. The cloud clears, and he watches the ashes filter down through the light and his outspread fingers and disappear in the dark below. He's starting to get lightheaded and panics, kicks and pulls with his arms, lunges upward and bursts through the surface and into the light and gasps the air. He sees the shore, the trees, a row of cabins, and in front of one of the cabins, his mother, young, sitting on her folded legs, her outstretched hands under the arms of a bare-chested toddler standing in front of her. Jason swims, reaches water shallow enough to touch bottom, stands up and begins walking toward her and the toddler that he knows is himself. He is close enough to see the light in her eyes, the smile on her parted lips, and she looks as if she's about to tell him something.

And then his father walks out on the beach, squats in front of the mother and toddler, points a camera at them and takes the picture. And Jason sees again that the memories of the love his mother gave him will bring back memories of his father, and of the absence of his father's love, and that the gravitational force of one memory is just as powerful as the other, and they're inseparable. Love was never simple in this family, Jason thinks. But he has hope, because he has a dream he is determined to realize—to write his story of a father, a mother, and their son, and telling that story will help him go on living and find happiness, or maybe just survive. Poor Jason, I think, considering the hell I'm going to put him through.

Thinking of the characters I want to create, the story I want to tell, the darkness beneath the screens I want to explore, and all the work I have to do, and my age, just six years younger than Dad when he died, I felt the urgency of writing my book and stepped on the accelerator, and we took off, until Barbara screamed, "What are you doing?" I pulled my foot off the gas and glanced at her and saw her bulging eyes looking at me as if I were nuts and said, "Sorry, I must've been dreaming," and we slowed down and coasted past some dormitories. My thoughts returned again to the book, and the lines went through my head— "We are such stuff as dreams are made on, and our little life is rounded with a sleep." I placed my hand on Barbara's thigh. She looked at me again, and I felt the love in her eyes and smiled at what lay ahead.

Acknowledgements

I am most fortunate to have been able over the years to become part of a community of gifted, insightful writers and passionate readers who have supported me in my artistic aspirations. I want to acknowledge the support of those members of the community who read drafts of *The Gravity of Love* and provided me with suggestions and encouragement: Peter Geye, Cary Griffith, Richard Lentz, Jeff Kellgren, Amy McCumber, and Victoria Tirrell.

This book would not exist without Between the Lines Publishing. I thank BLP's former acquisitions editor, Deb Alix, for recognizing and appreciating the quality of my work and offering me a contract; my editor, Misty Mount, for working collaboratively with me to improve my manuscript; Cherie Fox, for her lovely cover design; and Abby Macenka, co-founder of the press, for ensuring that my dream became real.

Above all, thank you to my loving family—Jane, Cathy, Neil, Michael, and Daniel.

Brian Duren was born and raised in Minnesota. A former French professor and university administrator, he holds doctorates from the University of Paris and the University of Minnesota. His first novel, *Whiteout*, described by the St. Paul Pioneer Press as a "stunning debut novel, worthy of national recognition," won the Independent Publisher Gold Medal for Midwestern Fiction. Duren is also the author of *Ivory Black*. He is working on his next novel, *Day Brings Back the Night*. www.brianduren.com

CPSIA information can be obtained
at www.ICGtesting.com
Printed in the USA
JSHW030900160723
44689JS00005B/220